Herbert Hochberg • Introducing Analytic Philosophy
Its Sense and its Nonsense

λ ο γ ο ς
Studien zur Logik, Sprachphilosophie und Metaphysik

Herausgegeben von / Edited by

Volker Halbach • Alexander Hieke
Hannes Leitgeb • Holger Sturm

Band 3 / Volume 3

Herbert Hochberg

Introducing Analytic Philosophy

Its Sense and its Nonsense
1879 - 2002

Bibliographic information published by Die Deutsche Bibliothek
Die Deutsche Bibliothek lists this publication in the Deutsche Nationalbibliographie;
detailed bibliographic data is available in the Internet at http://dnb.ddb.de

Paperback Edition

©2003 ontos verlag
Hanauer Landstr. 338, D-60314 Frankfurt a.M.
Tel. ++(49) 69 40 894 151 Fax ++(49) 69 40 894 194

ISBN 3-937202-21-8 (Germany)
ISBN 1-904632-10-6 (U.K.)

2003

Alle Texte, etwaige Grafiken, Layouts und alle sonstigen schöpferischen
Teile dieses Buches sind u.a. urheberrechtlich geschützt. Nachdruck, Speicherung,
Sendung und Vervielfältigung in jeder Form, insbesondere Kopieren, Digitalisieren, Smoothing,
Komprimierung, Konvertierung in andere Formate, Farbverfremdung sowie Bearbeitung
und Übertragung des Werkes oder von Teilen desselben in andere Medien und Speicher
sind ohne vorherige schriftliche Zustimmung des Verlages unzulässig
und werden verfolgt.

Gedruckt auf säurefreiem, alterungsbeständigem Papier,
hergestellt aus chlorfrei gebleichtem Zellstoff (TcF-Norm).

All rights reserved

Printed in Germany.

PREFACE

Absorption in language sometimes leads to a neglect of the connexion of language with non-linguistic facts, although it is this connexion that gives meaning to words and significance to sentences.
                                              Bertrand Russell, 1950

The book attempts to sketch, not work out in detail, an account of reference, meaning, truth and intentionality that stays within the "linguistic turn" characterizing twentieth century analytic philosophy. But it seeks to avoid following the contemporary variants of analytic philosophy that have turned from the analysis of things and facts to a preoccupation with and virtual worship of language and its use. The classical focus on ontology, combined with careful and precise formulations, that marked the writings of the early founders of the analytic tradition, has degenerated into the spinning of intricate verbal webs of analysis. The latter supposedly yield "theories of meaning" but more often signal the rebirth of idealism in the guises of "anti-realism" and "internal realism." The focus on the world, as what words are about, is often lost as "analytic philosophers" concentrate on language itself—the world being "well lost," in Nelson Goodman's honest words. Such trends, oddly enough, have come to typify both the analytic tradition and what some call "continental philosophy." We shall also note examples of a remarkable combination of arrogance towards and ignorance of the philosophical tradition that is displayed in some writings within the analytic tradition, including influential works. A number of the details supporting the themes that will be set out have been addressed in earlier essays and books that are cited at appropriate places. Others, as is invariably the case, remain to be spelled out.

I am indebted to discussions, as well as e-mail "dialogues," in recent years with Per Lindström and D. M. Armstrong. Ignacio Angelelli's knowledge of Frege and the history of logic and his forthcoming review "On neo-Fregeanism" have also been of help, as has R. Grossmann's familiarity with the intricacies of Meinong's thought.

Austin, Texas
November, 2002

CONTENTS

PREFACE

INTRODUCTION

CHAPTER 1: THE LINGUISTIC TURN

1a. Frege: Reference and Meaning	19
1b. Frege's Context Principle and Dummett's Linguistic Turn	39
1c. Frege's Objects and Quine's Criterion of Commitment	58
1d. Bradley and Bosanquet on Predication and Judgment	61
1e. Russell's Analysis of Definite Descriptions	70
1f. Meinong's Pure Objects of Thought: The Turn to Intentionality	72
1g. Predicates, Propositional Functions and Properties	78
1h. Reincarnating Meinong: Searle's Intentional Speech Acts	82

CHAPTER 2: DESCRIBING AND DENOTING

2a. Russell's Critique of Frege	89
2b. Facts and the Analysis of Judgment	99
2c. Referring to Facts	112
2d. Strawson's Critique of Russell	115
2e. On Distinguishing Descriptive from Referential Use	129
2f. Kripke's Causal Theory of Reference	131

CHAPTER 3: MEANING, TRUTH AND ANTI-REALISM

3a. Tarski's Conception of Truth: Twisting the Linguistic Turn	147
3b. Positivism and Pragmatism in Carnap and Sellars	156
3c. Truth: Davidson's Fast Track to the Meaning of "Meaning"	174
3d. Dummett's Anti-Realism: Meaning as Use and Truth as Proof	200
3e. Quine's Attack on Dogma: Analyticity and Meaning	215

CHAPTER 4: FACTS, INTENTIONS AND ABSTRACTION
    4a. Facts: Problems and Solutions   219
    4b. Truth and Modality   229
    4c. Meaning and Intending   245
    4d. Access to The Abstract   252

References   273
Index   279

INTRODUCTION

Philosophy in the twentieth-century took what Gustav Bergmann, once a member of the Vienna Circle, memorably characterized as a "linguistic turn." (The phrase was popularized by being used as the title of a collection of essays edited by R. Rorty and was possibly inspired by the title of Schlick's 1930-31 paper "The Turning Point in Philosophy.") Bergmann meant something, in the 1940s, far different than Michael Dummett did in his repeating the phrase in the 1990s, as we will note. One manifestation of that turn is seen in the preoccupation with theories of meaning and of reference, while another is seen in the phrase "philosophy of language" itself. While philosophy always involved a concern with language and the analysis of meaning, as is evident to even a casual reader of Plato's dialogues, there was a significant shift of focus in the late nineteenth and early twentieth century, particularly in Great Britain, in Germany and Austria and, as is less well known, in Sweden. One sign of the change was the shift of interest to the "analysis" of key terms and phrases, such as "some thing," "the," "there is," "number," "a," "good," "every thing," "exists" and so forth, in the writings of Frege in Germany, Moore and Russell in England, of C. von Ehrenfels, Husserl and Meinong in Austria, and of P. Wikner, A. Hägerström and A. Phalén in Sweden; while another was the focus on scientific concepts on the part of the positivists of the Vienna Circle and the Berlin Group and their resultant concern with "philosophy of science." One simple cause of this was the logical positivists assuming that, as traditional philosophical questions and statements were meaningless, the task of philosophy was shifted to the analysis of the concepts and language employed in the various sciences. Another was that many of the members of "the Circle" had themselves been trained as mathematicians and scientists, rather than as philosophers. As the sciences dealt with questions of fact and with theories about the world, philosophy was derivatively concerned with questions about the methods and statements of the empirical sciences (physics, psychology, etc.) and the formal sciences (mathematics, logic)—what is "a proof," "a theory," "induction," "confirmation"—what is "the logic" of measurement, the meaning of "probability"? Viewing the shocks produced by developments in physics as resulting, in part, from uncritical use of critical concepts was another influence, as was the impact on the positivists of Frege, Russell, Moore and Wittgenstein. Even the writings of Nietzsche and Freud were factors, as they suggested that traditional philosophical systems, like theological ones, were better understood as reflections of personality characteristics and unconscious drives, as rationalizations rather than as rational constructions. Hence philosophers were to be understood in psychological and causal terms, rather than judged by the merits of their arguments. Paradoxically, the psychoanalytic concepts themselves gave rise to further issues regarding their scientific status, empirical basis and meaning. It is often overlooked that the Circle's "membership" included psychoanalysts, while other members were well read in psychoanalytic literature.

According to Plato, Socrates was wise. Assume that Plato's judgment is true, and, hence, that the sentence "Socrates is (was) wise" is true. Suppose that the same judgment was made by both Wikner and Russell. Two questions that traditionally arise are: (1) What furnishes the basis or ground for a judgment being true? That is, in virtue of what is the judgment true? What is it to be true and just what is Truth? (2) What provides the basis or ground for truly asserting that different individuals have the same thoughts or make the same judgments—or that one person has the same thought at different times? In virtue of what is the content of the judgments, made by different people and expressed in different languages on different occasions, said to be the same? These are two classical questions that give rise, in the one case, to "theories of truth" and, in the other, to "theories of meaning." Thus one hears that true sentences like "Socrates is wise" and "Sokrates är vis" correspond to facts or have facts as their grounds of truth and that the different sentences express the same "proposition" that constitutes their meaning or provides the content of the judgments that they are used to express. In appealing to facts—existent states of affairs in Wittgenstein, facts that have "being" in Moore—to explain the notion of truth, each of the Cambridge trio proposed a version of what has come to be called a "correspondence theory of truth." They all, in one way or another, took a judgment expressed by a sentence like "Socrates is wise" to be true if a certain fact existed. This meant that in addition to taking Socrates as the object that the judgment was about (and thus, as such terms are used, the subject that wisdom was ascribed to), they acknowledged, in the early 1900s, something else in order to account for the truth of the judgment. Clearly Socrates could be the object of such a judgment even if he was not wise, and thus Socrates, as a particular object, did not suffice for the judgment being true. For the Cambridge philosophers more was required—the property that he exemplified and the fact that he did exemplify it. (I ignore the once popular view that properties are not recognized in the *Tractatus*.) Thus, consider another (presumed) truth about Socrates—that Socrates was bald. Since Socrates is the wise and bald individual that both judgments are about, it appears obvious, if not trivial, that what distinguishes the relevant facts is that one involves the attribute or property of being wise, while the other involves the attribute of being bald. The shifts from "is wise" to "being wise" or "having wisdom" and from "is bald" to "being bald," or to speak of his "baldness," signal shifts in what is being talked about—the subject of discussion. In speaking about attributes, and classifying them as attributes, one classifies them much as one classifies Socrates as a person or as the subject that is said to have various attributes—a subject that we would not classify as an attribute of anything, as it makes no sense to attribute Socrates to some subject. And, if one judges that "Socrates is wiser than Plato" one judges that a relation holds between them and not that an attribute holds of each one.

What all this suggests, as it did to Russell, Wittgenstein and Moore, is that the facts that are the "truth grounds" of the various judgments are of different kinds. One kind involves an object having an attribute (such as *wisdom*), while another kind involves two objects standing in a relation (such as *being wiser than*). Facts can then be thought of as relatively complex, since specifying the facts that we are talking about in terms of one or more objects *and* an attribute or relation suggests that the latter are components of facts, as the term "Socrates" and the predicate "is wise" are obvious linguistic components of the sentence "Socrates is wise." Taking facts to be required as truth grounds of simple judgments like those we have considered, Russell and Moore argued that attributes, in addition to "particulars" or "individual objects," were required as constituents of facts and as the basis for correctly classifying diverse particulars as wise or bald. Thus, in early papers and books both Russell and Moore tried to prove that universals—as common attributes of objects and as relations between objects—existed, as did the particulars that exemplified them. They also argued that the only viable account of truth was a correspondence theory, according to which existent facts grounded the truth of simple judgments expressed by sentences of forms like "Socrates is wise" and "Plato is wiser than Socrates."

This led to a number of further questions. Suppose, for example, that we recognize colors and shapes as such attributes: being red and being square, say. Is there also the compound attribute of being red and square? Is being red one attribute or is "red" a general term covering a number of more "determinate" attributes—the diverse shades of red? Are there contradictory attributes, like being both round-and-not-round? Are there other kinds of facts, such as negative facts that ground the truth of judgments expressed by sentences like "Socrates is not alive"? Are there general facts in virtue of which judgments like "All men are mortal" are true? What is the basis, if any, for the "rules" governing logical inferences and truths, such as: "If all men are mortal and Socrates is a man it follows that Socrates is mortal"? Is such a basis, if there is one, an *objective* ground for logical truth and valid inference, or are such matters based on conventions embedded in our linguistic habits and social customs or in "normative" features of social life, and, hence, like ethical norms? If attributes are common properties, what are the particulars or individuals that are instances of the attributes and what is the "connection" they have to the attributes that they are said to instantiate or exemplify? How do a particular and an attribute combine to form a fact? Is a particular object simply the *sum* of or *composed of* its attributes, or is it something quite distinct from them but which combines with them, and if so, what? Thus, one heard of "substrata" or "bare" or "thin" particulars that were simply "thises" without qualities.

It is sometimes difficult to see the point of such issues. Dummett has put the problem concisely: "The two most abstract of the intellectual disciplines, philosophy and mathematics, give rise to the same perplexity: what are they *about*?"(2002, 19) This perplexity has been particularly prominent in the twentieth century and, as one of the consequences of "the linguistic turn," has led to the idea that such questions are pointless or meaningless. A sensitivity to problems about "meaning" came to be seen as a guide for avoiding the pitfalls of philosophical perplexity that departures from ordinary usage give rise to. The problematic nature of the questions themselves seems especially noticeable when one asks about whether there are such *things* or *entities* as meanings, given that the words and sentences that we normally use clearly do *have* meaning. For asking a question about the meaning of a given word is usually understood as asking for a definition of the term or an explanation of how it is used in various contexts—the sort of explanation found in dictionaries, where the meaning is often clarified by providing examples of use in various sentences. Thus one may well be puzzled by what philosophers are getting at by proposing "theories" of meaning and debating the relative merits of alternative views, especially when one reads about propositions being entities that are expressed by sentences and about "concepts" being what words "mean."

Yet, it is not difficult to see how such notions arise. For, while sentences in different languages are literally different sentences containing different words, they are often said to state or express the same *thing*. A proposition, taken as what is expressed by a sentence, seems to be somewhat like a common property, such as a color or shape, of various particular things. Yet it is clear that a person can have a cold without there being some thing that is the cold had by the person, which is quite unlike there being a ticket when someone has a ticket in hand. And it would seem that to speak of a word having a meaning is not at all like having a ticket and somewhat more like someone having a cold. A meaningful expression has certain uses and not others; a person having a cold will do certain things, like sneeze, and, very likely, not others, like say "I hope it gets worse." Yet, we do speak of understanding the meaning of a word like "red" in terms of knowing what color red is—what color the word "red" refers to or represents—just as we speak of understanding which person is "meant" by understanding which person is referred to by the use of a name on some occasion. And, if one does not think of the meaning as the, or a, referent in such cases, what is a viable alternative account? In responding, one might naturally ask why one raises such questions? Why not simply explain the meaning of words in terms of other words we understand, as we do when we explain a term or phrase to a child or to someone who is not a native speaker of our language? This is what some philosophers have done, while others have looked to various sciences to avoid traditional philosophical perplexity.

Quine, in speaking of "epistemology naturalized," suggests the replacement of traditional epistemology or theory of knowledge by the psychology and social psychology of the learning process—thereby replacing philosophical questions by "scientific" questions. This is also reflected in his suggesting, in the style of classical logical positivism, that this will do "in so far as philosophy of science is philosophy enough"—which, being less extreme, allows him to address classical questions in the philosophy of logic and mathematics, as well as philosophical questions about the concepts of science. One need only recall that some of the positivists of the Vienna Circle rejected the classical philosophical questions and answers as "meaningless" and to be replaced, in a progressive and scientific age, by the logical analysis of the concepts, methodology and theories of the various sciences, including the formal sciences of logic and mathematics. In this spirit, Quine goes further and replaces epistemological questions by questions in behavior psychology and social psychology. This tendency to replace philosophical questions by other questions is also seen in philosophers who shift the focus from questions about what "concepts" are to questions about what it is to "possess a concept," and then take the latter as the ability to use language appropriately in various situations.

Yet the contrast between philosophical and non-philosophical questions is easily seen in the context of mathematics. Consider elementary arithmetic—the arithmetic of the natural numbers with the operations (functions) of addition and multiplication. We all know the basic truths and even immediately recognize as true some truths about the numbers that we might not have thought of before, such as that every collection of natural numbers contains a number less than all the other numbers in the collection. You just have to think about it a moment. But when we talk about numbers (let alone "collections"), recalling Dummett's question, what are we talking about? What is the subject matter of elementary arithmetic? It is very easy to reply: "numbers, of course!" But, then, are there really numbers? And do the numerals "mean" or refer to such "entities"? If they do not so refer, what are we talking about? And, if they do not mean what they refer to, what do the numerals and the function signs mean? It is helpful to keep arithmetic in mind when one thinks about questions of language, meaning and reference. For, it is obviously one thing to learn to add and multiply; it is quite another thing to ask, if one does, what one is talking or writing about when one "does" those operations and why the arithmetical truths are true. Some find the philosophical questions intriguing, if puzzling, while others find them to be a waste of time or even not to be sensible questions at all. But arithmetic is a helpful subject matter for seeing the difference between philosophical questions about arithmetical truths and "objects" and "ordinary" arithmetical questions—questions that lie *within* the subject itself.

This book will be, in part, a commentary on ideas of Russell, Moore and Wittgenstein, that remarkable Cambridge trio that not only contributed to the history of philosophy but greatly influenced its course in the last century. We will also consider a number of contemporary philosophers who have commented on and discussed themes found in the Cambridge trio, in some cases in significant works of their own, and are part of what has come to be called "the analytic tradition." But we begin with three earlier figures that provide a background for that tradition—Gottlob Frege, Francis Herbert Bradley and Alexius Meinong.

CHAPTER 1

THE LINGUISTIC TURN

1a. Frege: Reference and Meaning

Frege ingeniously used a few basic ideas to attempt to resolve a number of fundamental philosophical problems. Like Bradley, he saw a problem in the analysis of predicative judgments that led to holding that the existence of facts grounded their truth and falsity. Suppose we consider a tentative answer to the question raised earlier about the judgment that Socrates is wise to be the following. We distinguish the sentence "Socrates is wise" (a linguistic item) from the thought that the sentence *expresses* (is used to express)—as the "thought" expressed is not itself a linguistic item, whether or not someone's having such a thought is dependent on the person's ability to use language. And we make a further distinction. Let two people think that Socrates is wise. Consider each to have a particular state of mind, where we need not consider or be concerned with whether such a state of mind is taken as a mental state or a brain state (or some other neuro-physiological state) or a disposition to behave or what have you—matters that arise in the philosophy of mind. We merely distinguish the particular states of each person from the common thought that those states are cases or instances of. In a way it is much like the case of Plato and Socrates being wise. We have, as we are considering matters, the attribute of wisdom that characterizes the two distinct persons. Similarly we can distinguish the thought that Socrates is wise from the individual cases of thinking—the various cases of making such a judgment—that our hypothetical persons are presently engaged in. Thus the notion of a "thought" is used in two senses—in speaking of an occurrence particular to a given person and of something common to different occurrences in diverse people or in the same person at different times. If I think that Socrates is wise on Tuesday and, again, on Wednesday, the thought that I had on Tuesday differed, in one sense, from the one on Wednesday, which is why I can be said to have had the thought twice—on different occasions. In another sense, it was the "same" thought that occurred on both occasions. So, if we speak in terms of mental states, we can say that two mental states of the same kind are involved. They are of the same kind since they are both thoughts with the same content.

Frege spoke of the "kind" or content of the thoughts, somewhat unfortunately, as a "thought," while others have spoken of a "mental content" and still others of a "proposition," as distinct from a sentence or statement that is a linguistic correlate of or is used to "express" such a content. A proposition or Fregean thought or mental content is then what a sentence expresses and is not to be identified with a sentence, written or spoken, which is a linguistic item composed of other linguistic items, subject terms, predicates, verbs, etc. It is common to also distinguish "the sentence" in the sense of a series of words written on a blackboard from "the sentence" of which that particular series of meaningful chalk marks is an instance. Thus just imagine writing the "same" sentence one hundred times, as a philosophical exercise. In one sense there are one hundred sentences, taken as instances of "the sentence," taken in another sense. Typically one speaks of the many "tokens" of the same "type." The similarity to the distinction between a common attribute and the various particulars that are instances of it is obvious—and made even more so by recognizing that "type" and "kind" are sometimes used interchangeably.

Since the word "thought" easily lends itself to blending what we just separated, I will use the fairly standard term "proposition" for Frege's "thought." We then have a sentence, "Socrates is wise," a proposition expressed by that sentence, and, let us assume, the fact of Socrates being wise. The sentence expresses the proposition and the existence of the fact is the truth ground or basis for the sentence being true. Once propositions are introduced, along with facts, we face a question about their analysis. In the case of the fact that Socrates is wise we considered that fact to involve Socrates, the attribute wisdom and a connection between them—reflected by the use of the copula "is," or "has" as used in "Socrates has wisdom." In the case of the proposition, a similar question arises about its structure and components. It would seem that we cannot identify propositions with facts, since we can have the thought that Socrates is wise, and hence the proposition, even if he is not wise, and hence there is no fact of Socrates being wise. Again, for the time being, let us assume that this is so and take the proposition to be something else. But then, what is it? Frege took the name "Socrates" to not only have a referent or denotation, the person Plato immortalized in his dialogues, but to have what he called a "sense," a "way" or "manner" of denoting something. The sense was what we understood by the name, and some have taken that to amount to a sort of description of the object referred to, a description like "the teacher of Plato who was put to death in Athens." Though I just provided a linguistic phrase and spoke of a "sort of description," Frege did not take the sense of an expression to be another linguistic item. It was not something linguistic but, rather, what provided the conceptual content or meaning for a linguistic expression on a given occasion of its use. The phrase "the teacher of Plato who was put to death in Athens" might be taken to inform one of the "sense" of the name "Socrates," as I understand it, but on Frege's account such a descriptive expression itself *has* a sense, but *is not* a sense. The sense or meaning of a name or a descriptive expression is a constituent of the proposition expressed by the sentence "Socrates is wise," rather than the linguistic phrase that enters into a further sentence, such as "The teacher of Plato who was put to death in Athens was wise."

One constituent of the proposition expressed by the sentence "Socrates is wise" is then the sense of the name "Socrates." But clearly there must be something else involved in the analysis of a proposition. One might suggest that the other ingredient is the attribute wisdom or "concept" of wisdom, since we are talking about propositions or thoughts, and not facts, and about the sense of the word "Socrates," and not the philosopher the word is used to refer to. Frege spoke of a concept in this connection. Shortly, we shall see why, but for the moment we will simply adopt his usage. Predicate expressions then represent concepts, as names like "Socrates" denote objects. But Frege did not think that the proposition expressed by "Socrates is wise" could be understood as consisting of the sense of the word "Socrates" being connected to the concept of being wise. He believed that thinking so forced one to recognize an additional element of the proposition, a relation or connection between the sense of the subject term and the concept represented by the predicate term. And, once this was recognized, a problem resulted.

The sentence "Socrates is wise" has three items: the name "Socrates" that denotes a particular individual, the copula "is" and the concept word "wise." We are considering a view that takes the copula (along with the arrangement of the various signs) to represent a relation, which we can call "predication," that obtains between the sense of the name and the concept to form the proposition. We thus take three "things" to be involved in the proposition. But, the proposition is not just three such things, as it consists of the sense and the concept standing in the predication relation. To see the significance of that we must digress to consider one of Frege's and Russell's major innovations in modern philosophy of language and logic: their construal of relations and relational predicates that went along with Frege's great achievement, the development of predicate logic. But before doing so, we can note that if one considers a language which does not employ a copula like "is" but simply juxtaposes the subject and predicate terms, the predication "connection" would still be represented by the order and arrangement of words. In English, we have such natural forms, without an explicit copula, in sentences like "He lies" as opposed to "He is lying." The device of juxtaposition is typically used in modern predicate logic, where a symbol pattern like "Fa" is read as "a is F" or "a is an F." In this context I speak of "predication," rather than "exemplification" or "instantiation," since, on Frege's view, one deals with the connection between the sense of a term, "a," and a concept, F. But the sense of "a" is not an instance of F—it is not an F—and thus does not exemplify a property in a Fregean proposition, as it does in the atomic facts Russell acknowledged. But the role of a property in a fact and a concept in a proposition may both be said to be predicative, in a "neutral" sense, as they both play a predicative role and are connected to predicate terms.

If one thinks of the judgment that Socrates is wiser than Plato in the way that philosophers and logicians did for centuries, one thinks of Socrates as being what the judgment is about and "being wiser than Plato" as the predicate being ascribed to him. In other words one construes such a judgment along the lines of the judgment that Socrates is wise, except that a more complex predicate expression is involved. It is now a commonplace in elementary logic books to show that so understanding such judgments results in serious limitations imposed on the system of logic. Frege and Russell offered another analysis. The judgment in question is of a different logical structure than judgments of a subject-predicate kind. It is a judgment involving two subjects and a relational concept. Thus, we do not ascribe an attribute, the attribute of being wiser than Plato, to the subject, Socrates. In fact, there is no attribute involved, there is a relational concept or property—is wiser than—which is said to relate Socrates to Plato. Such a dyadic relation, like all dyadic or two-term relations, requires two subjects to form a judgment, a relational fact or an appropriate sentence—depending on whether we are speaking of a "subject" as a linguistic sign, as what such a sign expresses (means) or as what it refers to. Earlier philosophers and logicians thus misconstrued the structure of relational propositions by taking them to be of subject-predicate form. They thereby failed to recognize that a two-term relational judgment must involve a relational concept (a dyadic relational predicate, a relation) that is distinct from both subject terms (objects) and is of a different logical form. This points to a feature of the use of such expressions in context.

Suppose one says that Stockholm is far away, and someone else responds—"Tokyo is even farther away." In one clear sense, both statements implicitly speak of cities being "far from" here. Yet, "is far" seems to function like "is wise"—as a one-term or monadic predicate. But that is misleading, as the context supplies the relational setting for the apparent monadic predicate term. The example has some importance as the role played by the contextual setting gives rise to various philosophical problems and disagreements. For the present, having noted that a question of context arises, let us simply stick to the example and apply the pattern of the analysis of the proposition that Socrates is wise, construed in terms of a sense, a concept and a predication relation, to relational propositions.

In the case of the proposition (Fregean thought) that Plato is wiser than Socrates, we then have the relational concept *is wiser than* combining with the terms, the senses of the words "Plato" and "Socrates." Thus, assuming in the monadic case that we deal with a relation of predication, connecting the "subject" with the "attribute" that is predicated of that subject, one would appear to deal with two relations in a case involving a relation like wiser than. Suppose one now thinks that just as we made the relational predication more explicit, in the above example of the sentence "London is far," we should do so in the case of the predication relation. The problem this creates is simple, though somewhat tongue twisting. For, if one treats the proposition that Socrates is wise as a relational proposition, with the sense and the concept playing the role of the terms of a dyadic relation of predication, then the relation of predication is playing the role of a two-term relational concept. And, in the case of the judgment that Socrates is wiser than Plato, we would have the relational concept "being wiser than" standing in a predication relation to the pair of terms, the senses of the names "Socrates" and "Plato." Thus we would have "predication" as a triadic relation that relates a relational concept to two terms—the senses of the terms "Socrates" and "Plato." But if such predication relations are really relations, they, in turn, are predicated of their terms. Thus, the predication relation, as a two term relation, is a further term that stands in a three-term relation that connects it to the sense of "Socrates" and the concept wisdom, while the three term predication relation, connecting *wiser than* to its subject terms, must itself be a term, along with the latter terms, of a four-term predication relation, and so on *ad infinitum*.

Frege thought such a pattern continues indefinitely and generates a vicious regress in that one never arrives at the analysis of the original proposition. There had been earlier anticipations of the problem that go back to Plato and Aristotle. In the case of Plato the question concerned the role of "participation" that supposedly connected particular things to the forms they "participated" in (as well as a question about connections among the forms themselves). Aristotle noted the problem, and it was apparently one of the motives for his view that forms "inhered" in things—with inherence not being a relation but simply giving rise to a compound entity that was an informed substance (a familiar Aristotelian composite of form and matter). Thus one did not have the facts of Socrates being human and being wise, but, rather, a substance embodying an essence, humanity, and an accident, wisdom. One may speculate that, in a sense, the Aristotelian tradition blocked the consideration of facts, as well as of the different logical forms required for the development of modern logic, by employing just such a pattern. (Though there are suggestions of appealing to facts in the fourteenth century figures Adam Wodeham and Gregory of Rimini, as well as an awareness of issues that facts raise.) Of course this made it difficult, if not impossible, to deal with relational predication, as in "Socrates is wiser than Plato." For not thinking in terms of facts or states of affairs in such a case invites construing it in terms of one substance, Socrates, embodying the non-essential property (accident) of "being wiser than Plato." Thus a relation like "is wiser than" is treated in terms of a monadic property "is wiser than x."

To appreciate Frege's attempt to resolve the problem, it will help to return to the variant of it that arose in Plato's reasoning that led him to introduce Platonic forms early in the history of western philosophy. Plato took there to be a form, wisdom, which Socrates was said to participate in. He thus recognized two kinds of entities—objects and forms—and a connection between them, *participation*. Forms came to be called "universals," as they were common to the various particulars of the same form or kind. Participation then seemed to be a further common universal, yet it could not itself be a form, since it was what connected forms to their diverse instantiations. To place it "among the forms" would appear to require that it be connected by another relation (or perhaps itself) to the various instantiations of participation. So put, we have the problem Frege seeks to resolve. His solution is simple. The problem with classical realism about universals is that Platonic forms or universal attributes are treated as objects, admittedly of a different kind, but nevertheless as "complete" objects that can serve as terms of relations. For Frege, the Platonic pattern does not recognize the radical difference between concepts and objects. Concepts are "unsaturated" or "incomplete" and thus must function in a predicative role and not as terms of relations. Propositions do not result from the connection of a concept to a sense by a predication tie. They result from the completing of an incomplete concept, like *is wise*, by something, such as the sense of the term "Socrates." In short, the predicative connection becomes an aspect of the conceptual component of the proposition. The proposition that Socrates is wise has only two constituents: the sense of the term "Socrates" and the concept *is wise*. The copula "is" belongs essentially to the predicate term and does not, itself, represent a predicative connection. The same is true for relational concepts. The relational concept is *wiser than* is doubly incomplete, requiring two senses for its completion to form a proposition like that expressed by "Socrates is wiser than Plato."

Thus Frege's analysis is based on a fundamental division between complete objects and incomplete or unsaturated concepts. These are the two basic kinds of entities he is led to in his philosophy of language by his attempt to analyze propositions. Yet, in a way, Frege still recognized a predicative connection. While the proposition expressed by "Socrates is wise" was analyzed into only two constituents—a saturated sense and an unsaturated concept—the object, Socrates, was said to "fall under" the concept, given that the proposition was true. This appears to suggest a connection between the object and the concept, over and above the joining of the sense of the term "Socrates" and the concept in the proposition—especially as Frege appears to speak of something as "falling under a concept" as if that indicates it "has a property" and he recognizes "falling under" as a relational concept. But Frege does not recognize facts as truth grounds for propositions and rejects a correspondence theory of truth. Yet, if he takes *falling under* as a concept, to say that the object Socrates falls under the concept *is wise* introduces a further proposition, one in which the relational concept *falls under* combines with two terms, the sense of the word "Socrates" and the sense of the concept expression "is wise." This poses two problems. One concerns the question of the nature of senses of concept expressions; the other concerns what Frege takes to be an account of truth.

Consider Frege's distinction between sense and reference. The point of it becomes clearer if we consider the name "Socrates" and the descriptive phrase "the husband of Xantippe." Both may be said to be used to refer to or to denote a particular individual. Yet what we understand when we use the different expressions may also be said to be different in that different propositions are expressed by the sentences "Socrates is wise" and "The husband of Xantippe is wise." For Frege, "Socrates" and "the husband of Xantippe" have different "senses" but the same denotation. In fact Frege took the expressions to denote the same object since the different senses that they expressed denoted that object. Denotation was basically a relation between the sense of an expression and a referent, and only derivatively a relation between the expression and the referent. This allowed him to hold that "names" like "Pegasus," which did not refer to anything, were meaningful, in that they had a sense, but did not have a referent. This meant that the referent was not what gave sense or "meaning" to a name. In a way, Frege's distinction is reminiscent of an earlier and familiar distinction between the connotation and the denotation of a name.

A question that then arises is whether the sense-reference distinction applies to predicate expressions as well as expressions for objects. Though interpreters of Frege have disagreed about this, it seems clear that a predicate has both a sense and a reference, the latter being a concept—though Frege speaks of the concept both as what is expressed and what is meant (denoted) by a predicate term. But while it is the sense of a term like "Socrates" that enters into the proposition expressed by "Socrates is wise," it is not the sense of the predicate but the concept itself that is the other constituent of the proposition. (A question arises here about identifying the sense with the concept.

We will briefly return to that below.) The sense of the expression referring to the concept plays different roles. One that is relevant here is that the sense seems to be the relevant constituent of a proposition expressed by a sentence like (C) "Socrates falls under the concept is wise." A problem, once widely discussed by Frege scholars, was Frege's insisting that a phrase like "the concept is wise" cannot denote a concept since it must denote something that is an object—for the expression does not play a predicative role in (C), where the predicate is the relational predicate "falls under." He suggested simply avoiding such expressions as misleading and due to "...the awkward position in which language here finds itself..." (1967, 37). Moore would say something similar about his own talk of facts that did not exist.

The second question, concerning Frege's account of truth, can be given a more direct answer. Just as Frege took a name like "Socrates" to have both a sense and a reference, he took a sentence like "Socrates is wise" to have a sense, the proposition it expressed, and a referent. But its referent was specified as its truth value—the True, we assume in this case. Sentences with truth values denoted the True or the False, which were objects. The doctrine sounds strange. It is one thing to recognize "senses" in addition to "referents" to account for thoughts and judgments. It is another thing to recognize truth values as objects. To be sure, one who reads logic texts is familiar with the occurrences of the signs "F" and "T" and their being said to designate truth values, as one is familiar with the use of numerals to designate numbers. But in logic classes one no more stops to ask if there really exist truth values than one stops in mathematics classes to ask if numbers really exist. Frege explicitly took there to be such objects. This resulted in part from the application of his sense-denotation distinction to sentences as well as to names like "Socrates," in part from his division of terms into incomplete terms representing "functions" and complete terms representing objects and in part from his belief that attempts to define "truth" and purported theories of truth, such as the correspondence theory, were inadequate. Frege wrote:

> Can it not be laid down that truth exists when there is correspondence in a certain respect? But in which? For what would we then have to do to decide whether something were true? We should have to inquire whether it were true that an idea and a *Reality*, perhaps, corresponded in the laid-down respect. And then we should be confronted by a question

of the same kind and the game could begin again. So the attempt to explain truth as correspondence collapses. And every other attempt to define truth collapses too. For in a definition certain characteristics would have to be stated. And in application to any particular case the question would always arise whether it were true that the characteristics were present. So one goes round in a circle. Consequently, it is probable that the content of the word "true" is unique and indefinable. (1968, 510)

One can imagine him believing that we might as well take true propositions to denote the truth value the True, since it is hopeless to try to provide an account of truth. He may also be claiming that no definition of the predicate "is true" is feasible since such a definition will have to be of the form "x is true if and only if x is Φ," where Φ is some condition or "characteristic" had or fulfilled by whatever truth is ascribed to. But, then, one must hold that x is true if and only if it is true that x has or fulfills Φ. Thus, we would be involved in another vicious circle. Another claim that he could be making is that to offer such a purportedly explanatory definition (as opposed to a stipulation) is to assert that it itself is true. But then we must know what "truth" means in order to offer such an explanation, for we must know that it is true. Thus we cannot explain what it is to be true. Yet another way of construing his argument is to take him to claim that a theory like a correspondence theory proposes a definition of "is true" or claims to "analyze" the notion of truth along the following lines:

(1) Given any proposition p, p is true if and only if there is a fact that p corresponds to.

Frege could then argue that (1) is true if and only if there is a fact to which it corresponds. But then we have

(2) (1) is true if and only if there is a fact that (1) corresponds to.

Hence, by the correspondence theory that offers (1) as an analysis of truth, (2) must be true. But on the correspondence theory, (2) will be true if and only if a further statement holding that it corresponds to a fact is true and so on. Thus, a proposition will be true if and only if there are an infinite number of facts, and we cannot set down all the facts that its being true "presupposes." This argument assumes that the same ground of truth will not suffice as a truth ground for each element of the series of sentences containing "is true" that is thereby generated. That is, it is assumed that each sentence in the series corresponds to, or is "made true" by, a different fact. There is no need for a correspondence theory of truth to involve such a presupposition. For given the fact that Socrates is wise, there is no reason to hold that it does not suffice as a ground of truth for the entire series of trivial conjunctions "Socrates is wise and Socrates is wise," "Socrates is wise and (Socrates is wise and Socrates is wise)," etc., as well as for the series of sentences "'Socrates is wise' is true, " ""'Socrates is wise' is true" is true," etc. In both cases we have a series of different sentences, but we have no need to invoke a series of corresponding facts.

Dummett, in supporting Frege's attack on the correspondence theory, sees Frege as arguing, among other things, that one cannot derive what is known as the T-sentence for statements on a correspondence theory: "'Socrates is wise' is true if and only if Socrates is wise" (1973, Chapter 13, especially 444-52, 463-64). This, as we will see in later discussing Tarski's Convention-T, applies to only some forms of a correspondence theory. It is of historical interest that both Moore and Russell, impressed by the arguments of Bradley, Bosanquet and others against the correspondence theory rejected such a theory in the early part of the century. Thus Moore took true propositions to be true in virtue of their constituent concepts standing in a basic "true making" relation, as the constituent concepts of false propositions stood in another basic relation (Moore, 1899, 180-83; Hochberg, 1969, 107-109). In a letter to Russell he had written:

> Truth therefore does not depend on any relation between ideas and reality, nor even between concepts and reality, but is an inherent property of the whole formed by certain concepts and their relations; falsehood similarly. (1898)

This, perhaps, is where the identification of facts with true propositions, by some in the "analytic tradition," stems from. Russell, in a manuscript "The Nature of Truth" (1905), argued that the correspondence theory of truth was circular and involved a regress. He also objected to the theory's need to appeal to "objective falsehoods" (1906/7, 45-47). It is also of interest that Bradley had his own version of Frege's argument (1944, 110).

Frege's own discussion of truth, oddly, involves him in problems reminiscent of those he takes a correspondence theory to face. To say that the proposition that Socrates is wise denotes the True is to express a proposition that involves a sense that denotes the truth value, the relational concept "denotes" and the sense of the expression "the proposition that Socrates is wise" that denotes the proposition expressed by the sentence. At times, Frege suggested what is often referred to as the "redundancy theory of truth" by holding that the sentences "The proposition that Socrates is wise is true" and "Socrates is wise" were just different ways of saying the same thing, which amounts to denying that there is a concept of truth, in addition to the truth value, an object. At other times he appears to take there to be such a concept and that different propositions were expressed by the two sentences. In that vein, Frege suggested that all propositions can be taken to have the same predicate "is true," as well as holding that all true propositions denoted the same object, the True, while all false propositions denoted the False.

The distinctions between concept and object and sense and denotation enabled Frege to propose solutions to various philosophical problems. Consider the true identity statements "Scott=Scott" and "Scott = the author of Waverley." We may say that the first is trivial, the second significant. This raises a question about wherein lies the difference. For, if an identity is true, provided the terms flanking the identity sign denote the same thing, then the ground of truth is the same for both sentences. To Frege the difference lay in the fact that in the first case the senses of the signs flanking the identity sign were the same, while in the second case we have two different senses. Thus, in the first case we have one sense denoting an object while in the second case we have two senses denoting the same object. This is the characteristic difference between significant and trivial identities, and it depends on the distinction between sense and denotation.

Distinguishing between concepts and objects, Frege saw a connection between the use of predicates in language and the use of functional expressions in mathematics. As the function *square of* coordinated a number, say 9, to another number, 3, so the concept, *is wise*, could be seen to coordinate an object, say Socrates, to a truth value, the True. Thus he thought of concepts as functions whose values were truth values, and in fact offered that definition of what a concept is, with predicates being expressions for such functions. As there are also functions of two arguments, like +, so a concept like *is wiser than*, for the arguments Plato and Socrates, yields a truth value as value. Thus dyadic relational properties were construed as relational concepts of two arguments. In this way, Frege introduced a fundamental innovation in the treatment of relations as logically distinct from monadic concepts.

Frege was concerned with the perennial issues regarding the nature of mathematical truths and of mathematical "entities." What are numbers? What distinguishes arithmetical truths, such as "7 + 5 = 12," from factual claims such as "Seven people attended the lecture." Frege took a concept, e. g. is wise, to determine an extension, which he took to be what he called a "course of values" but which we can simply consider as the class of all objects falling under the concept. Thus every concept gave rise to another entity, a class, as every concept expression or predicate "Φ" gave rise to a class expression "the class of Φs." But classes, unlike concepts, were objects denoted by "complete" or "saturated" expressions that occupied the subject place in sentences. This fit with Frege's distinction between arguments and functions in mathematical contexts and with another fundamental set of ideas Frege had.

Consider two collections of three objects: three cups and three saucers. Having three elements can be seen as an attribute of both collections, for both have three elements, and thus share a property—as the three cups do since they are all cups. Take the collections to be classes, whatever it is that classes are understood to be. One can then think of the natural numbers or positive integers as concepts or attributes applicable to classes—of the number three as the concept "has three elements." But Frege's basic dichotomies of argument and function, in mathematics, and of object and concept, in more general contexts, require numbers to be objects (arguments) and not concepts (functions). A simple maneuver suggests itself. The concept of being a three-element class determines a class—the class of all three-element classes. Such a class, like all classes, is an object. This suggests taking the number three not to be a concept, such as having three elements, but as the corresponding class, the class of all three element classes. This is what Frege (1967, 99-100) and Russell later did. Frege's earlier version was somewhat different. (Again I ignore the difference between a "course of values" and a class taken as the extension of a concept.)

In his *Grundlagen*, Frege took the number three not as the class of all three-element classes, but as the class of all concepts that determined three-element classes. And so for all the natural numbers. The zero element class is determined by an empty concept. Thus the concept of not being self-identical, determines the empty or "null" class. One might find an apparent circularity in taking the natural number 3 to be a class of concepts (or of classes) applying to (containing) three-element classes. But it need not be. For one can consider the class of all concepts equinumerous with a given concept—equinumerous in the sense of there being a one-one function holding of them. This does not make use of the notion of a natural number as one is not speaking of any particular number of elements of a class. One simply takes a cardinal number to be a class of all concepts (or classes) equinumerous with some concept (class), as 0 is the class of all concepts equinumerous with the concept $x \neq x$. All one then need do is specify a way of getting the rest of the natural numbers from 0, without appealing to numbers in the process. We can indicate the idea guiding what Frege did. Having dealt with 0, we can consider the concept "being identical with 0." That concept has one object falling under it—the number 0. We can then consider the class of all concepts equinumerous with the concept being identical with 0. This gives us the class of all one-element concepts, which is then taken to be the number 1. Having 0 and 1 we can proceed to 2, via the concept—being identical with 0 or being identical with 1, which applies to two objects, 0 and 1. Of course one cannot proceed step by step in such a manner or simply say "and so on." But one can characterize the notions of successor and of natural number by means of "logical concepts" (such as "class" and the standard concepts of logic and set theory) in such a way that the class of natural numbers contains the infinitely many elements in the line of succession starting with 0, and only those elements.

Frege thus answers the traditional ontological questions about numbers—Do numbers exist? If so, what are they? The answer to the first is "Yes." His response to the second is, in effect: "A (cardinal) number is a class of concepts such that all concepts in the class are equinumerous and any concept equinumerous to a concept in the class is in the class." [What he actually does is closer to (i) defining "the number which belongs to the concept F" as "the extension of the concept 'equinumerous to the concept F'" and then (ii) define "n is a (cardinal) number" as "There exists a concept such that n is the number which belongs to it" (1953, 85).] The second part of his logistic construal of arithmetic was to find a way of showing that arithmetical truths could be logically derived from logical truths, having supposedly shown that arithmetical concepts could be construed in terms of logical concepts. Arithmetic could then be taken to be a matter of logic.

If every concept determines a class, consider the class of all classes that are members of themselves. The class of all classes would be an example of such a class, since it is obviously a class, and hence "falls under" the concept "is a class." But then, we can consider the class of all classes that do not belong to themselves—the class of wise men would belong to it since it is not itself a man, wise or unwise. Consider next whether the class of all classes that are not members of themselves is a member of itself, i. e. whether it belongs to itself. If it does then it does not; but if it does not then it does. Thus, if there is such a class, we face a paradox. We conclude that if there is the appropriate concept and if every concept determines a class, it follows (given standard logic) that there is such a paradoxical class. Something must be done to resolve the apparent difficulty. Russell, in a famous letter to Frege, called attention to the problem and sought to resolve it by means of his theory of types, which required properties (and propositional functions) and classes—and the signs for them—to be of a certain type for statements "about" them to be logically well-formed. Thus, where one can say "The apple is red" and "Red is a color," one cannot say "The apple is a color," as the property of being a color (as distinct from being colored) is a property that can only be sensibly attributed to properties of a certain "type" and not to particular objects.

Frege understood concepts to be functions that have truth values as values. But he also understood concepts in a second way. Consider the following table:

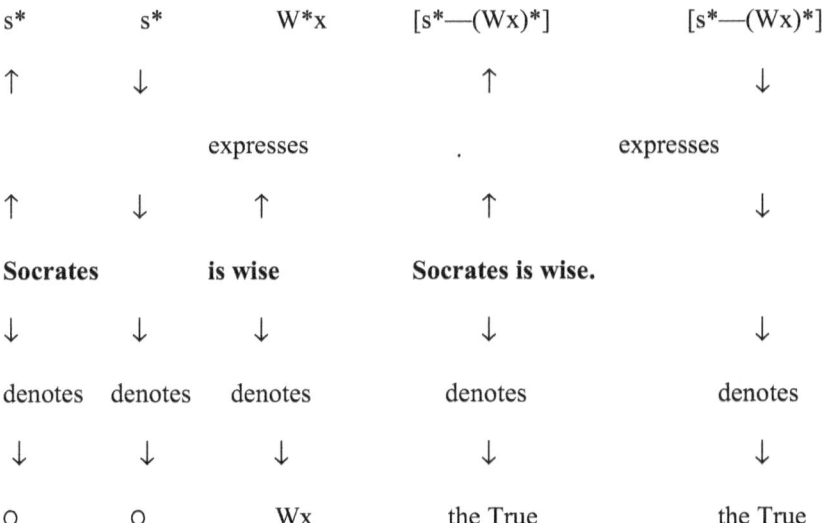

where the bold face expressions are taken to be the name, the predicate and the sentence in question, and where s* is the sense of the name "Socrates" and O is the denoted object, namely Socrates. Similarly, let [s*, (Wx)*] be the proposition expressed by the sentence, with (Wx)* being the unsaturated predicative element in the proposition. That is, the expression "[s*—(Wx)*]" is taken to represent (or denote) the proposition that the sentence expresses. The proposition [s*—(Wx)*], not the expression "[s*—(Wx)*]," denotes the truth value the True, as does the sentence that expresses the proposition, the sentence "Socrates is wise." The sense s* (not the sign "s*") denotes O, as does the name (the sign) "Socrates," while Wx is a function that takes the True as the value, for the object O as argument, and W*x is a function that takes the proposition [s*—(Wx)*] as value for the sense s* as argument. I omit using the word "expresses" to connect the predicate "is wise" to either the function sign "W*x," a sign for a sort of "sense" function, or the concept sign "(Wx)*," as I do not believe, as some do, that Frege takes the concept as the sense of the predicate sign —rather he fuses it with the function Wx, while W*x tends to be overlooked. When he talks about concepts as functions he tends to talk as if the predicate "is wise" denotes Wx. But he talks as if it denotes (Wx)* when he focuses on predication and propositions. Of course one can say that Wx is the same thing as (Wx)*, and that "it" operates as both the incomplete constituent of propositions and as a function coordinating objects to truth values. But then one makes use of two quite distinct senses of "incomplete" and "unsaturated." A concept is unsaturated, or incomplete, in that it plays the role of the predicative link combining the constituents of the proposition, including itself, into a unified whole. A function is unsaturated, or incomplete, in another sense in that it, as opposed to an object or argument, "maps" or "coordinates" one thing to another. The function Wx, for example, does not combine with the argument Socrates to form the object the True. Moreover, there is also W*x, which Frege does not, as far as I know, notice. It is no accident that Frege's heritage in modern logic involves the notions of "propositional function" and "truth function," and that sometimes, in discussions of propositional logic, these are not distinguished. Thus one finds "conjunction" and "negation" spoken of as propositional functions and as truth functions, while first order expressions with free variables, such as "Fx," are spoken of *as* (or as "indicating") sentential or propositional functions. Again, one can identify W*x with "both" Wx and (Wx)*, but the point is that quite distinct roles are involved in Frege's account of "concepts" as "functions" and as unsaturated entities. The matter becomes clearer when we consider another aspect of Frege's view, an aspect which shows the power of his attempt to resolve a number of fundamental issues in terms of very few basic concepts.

Negation, in one sense, is a function that, for a truth value as argument, yields the opposite truth value as value. In another sense negation is a propositional function that, for a proposition as argument, yields another proposition as value—the negative proposition that is the negation of the argument. Thus if the proposition expressed by "Socrates is wise" is the argument, the proposition expressed by "It is not the case that Socrates is wise" is the value. But then there is obviously a third role negation plays. In Frege's terms, the negative proposition is formed from the concept *not*, or *it is not the case that*, as concept, with the proposition, *Socrates is wise*, as argument. Thus a corresponding table would be:

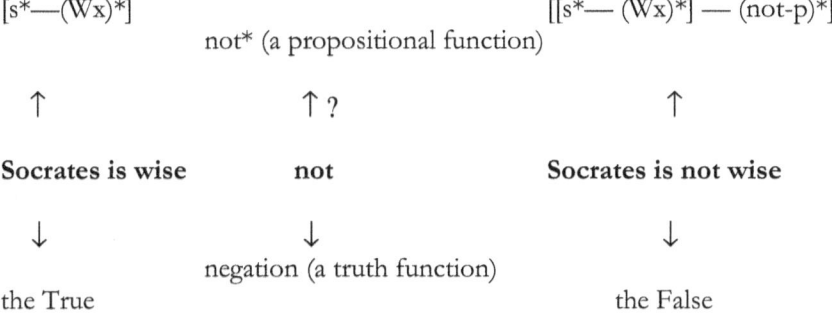

where (not-p)* is the unsaturated "predicative" component that combines with the proposition [s*—(Wx)*]—that Socrates is wise—as a saturated sense, hence an object—to form the proposition [[s*—(Wx)*]—(not-p)*]—that Socrates is not wise. The positive proposition saturates the predicative function (not-p)*. That predicative function is distinguished from the truth function, negation, and from not*, which is the function that takes one proposition, the positive proposition, as argument and yields another proposition (the negation) as value. It is thus no accident that we have come to speak of negation as a truth function and as a propositional function, just as we have come to speak of truth functional logic and of propositional logic. But, and it is a crucial "but," we, including Frege, also speak of negative propositions: "Consequently the thought that contradicts another thought appears as made up of that thought and negation." All "three things"—the two "functions" and the constituent negative "concept" in negative propositions—are involved in Frege's view, whether "they" are identified or not. There is also a question about the "sense" of the expression "not" or "not-p" (as there is about predicate expressions)—as to whether it is a further entity or to be identified with not* or (not -p)*, and as to whether it is, if different, itself a function or an object in the realm of senses. In any case, Frege's view is cumbersomely complex. Though questions in Frege scholarship need not concern us, it is worth noting that one of Frege's most well known commentators, Dummett, fails to appreciate the radical difference between the ways in which concepts and functions are incomplete.

> It is true that the notion of the incompleteness of a function is more readily intelligible than, and can be used to illuminate, that of the incompleteness of a concept or relation; but that does not require that concepts and relations be taken as actually special cases of functions, rather than merely analogues of them. (1978, 19)

The incompleteness of a function is not only not more intelligible, it can hardly "illuminate" the radically different kind of incompleteness of a predicative component of a proposition. Moreover, thinking along such lines can lead one to overlook the radical difference between a property and a propositional function, and consequent problems that we will focus on at a later point.[1]

Frege's pattern also enabled him to propose solutions to a set of problems involving intentional contexts. Consider the sentence "Plato thinks that Socrates is wise." As Frege considered such statements, which contain embedded sentences and intentional verbs (thinks, judges, believes, hopes, etc.), what was stated was that a person, an object, stood in a certain relation (thinking that, etc.) to a proposition, another object. Thus the relational concepts— thinks that, judges that, believes that—were dyadic functions that took a person and a proposition as arguments and a truth value as value. In the present case Plato is one argument for the function, while the proposition expressed by "Socrates is wise" is the other. The proposition expressed by the sentence "Plato thinks that Socrates is wise" also contains the concept, *thinks that*, and the senses of "Plato" and of "Socrates is wise." The latter expression denotes the proposition that Socrates is wise because the sense of the expression denotes that proposition. Thus, the proposition in question contains two senses—one that denotes Plato, the other a sense that denotes the proposition about Socrates. Since the proposition expressed by the sentence "Plato thinks that Socrates is wise" is then about Plato and the proposition that Soc-

---

[1]For a different, and in my view mistaken, analysis of Frege on senses and functions see Dummett (1973, 212-220, 268-69, 294).

rates is wise, it itself is not about Socrates. Hence, the name "Socrates," as it occurs in the sentence "Plato thinks that Socrates is wise," does not denote Socrates. The clause "that Socrates is wise," taken as a complete phrase, denotes a proposition about Socrates. The proposition denoted, that Socrates is wise, is itself composed of the sense s* and the concept (Wx)*. Thus, the sense that denotes the proposition must itself be complex, containing components that denote s* and (Wx)*, if the denotation of such a complex expression is to be determined by the denotations of its components, which Frege believed, and is sometimes called his "principle of compositionality." In order for it to be so determined, it must contain a sense that denotes the concept (Wx)*. Thus Frege must have senses that denote concepts. This suggests a reason for taking the predicate "is wise" to have a sense that denotes the concept being wise, and thus supports the interpretations of his view that take him to apply the sense-denotation distinction to predicates as well as to subject terms and sentences. There are numerous problems that beset such a view, but, as with various detailed questions concerning the interpretation of Frege, those are not our concern. We need merely note a reason for Frege's taking predicates to have a sense while denoting a concept.

Whatever problems Frege's view faces he saw it as resolving yet another logical puzzle. Suppose a present day student of philosophy believes that Socrates was wise but does not know that Socrates was the husband of Xantippe. Does the student believe that the husband of Xantippe was wise? As Frege considered the question, it is correct to deny that

> Jones believes that Socrates is wise
> Socrates=the husband of Xantippe
> therefore, Jones believes that the husband of Xantippe is wise

is a valid argument. But he did not wish to hold that it was invalid since the law allowing for the substitution of one term for another, where both terms represent the same individual, did not apply in such cases. Thus his task was to provide a reason for rejecting the argument while managing to preserve the "law" of the substitution of "identicals." For Frege, such a law was too crucial in logic and mathematics to be abandoned. His notion of the sense of an expression and his taking an expression to "shift" reference in certain contexts provided him with a proposed solution to the problem. He argued that in the sentence "Plato believes that Socrates is wise" the term "Socrates" does not denote Socrates. Rather, it denotes the sense that the term normally has, i. e. the sense it has in the sentence "Socrates is wise." Thus the term "Socrates" as it occurs in the first and second premises of the argument does not denote the same thing. Hence, the true identity—the second premise—is irrelevant to the substitution of "the husband of Xantippe" for the term "Socrates" in the first premise to obtain the conclusion. In short, an identity premise that would allow for the derivation of the conclusion would have to be something like:

the sense of "Socrates"= the sense of "the husband of Xantippe"

which is false. Thus one can reject the above argument as invalid without rejecting the principle of the substitution of "identicals." Frege's sense-reference distinction purportedly resolves the problem of how to reconcile the acceptance of substitution, based on identities, as an unrestricted logical principle that applies even in the case of intens(t)ional verbs and embedded sentences. That is, it applies even in cases where the truth value of the sentence that contains the embedded sentence is not a "function" of the truth value of the latter, as it is in the case of "Socrates is wise and Plato is wise."

The sense-reference distinction lies behind Frege's purported resolutions of three important puzzles. First, it allows him to provide a meaning for non-naming names and unfulfilled descriptions, such as "Pegasus" and "the king of France in 1905," without inventing fictional or "possible" objects for such expressions to denote. Second, it provides an account of the difference between significant and trivially true identity statements. Third, it furnishes a basis for purportedly resolving the problem about the rule of substitution in connection with non-extensional contexts like those considered above. But Frege's view can also be seen to become artificially *ad hoc*, if we probe into his idea that an expression shifts its denotation in certain contexts.

The proposition expressed by "Plato believes that Socrates is wise" contains the relational concept *believes that*, the sense of the name "Plato" and a sense denoting the proposition that Socrates is wise. But what can this latter sense be? As it denotes the proposition that Socrates is wise, and the latter is composed of the sense of the term "Socrates" and the concept is wise, it must consist of senses that denote that sense and that concept and which are somehow combined in a way that yields a sense denoting the proposition. Let us take s^{**} to be a sense that denotes the sense s^* and w^* to be a sense that denotes the concept is wise. There must then be some function, say one denoted by the expression "the proposition composed of --- and ....," where the first blank is an argument place for a sense expression like "s^{**}" and the second for a sense expression like "w^*." We then have a proposition composed of the sense of the name "Plato," say p^*, and the sense of the expression "the proposition composed of s^{**} and w^*." Let us represent that latter sense by the brief expression "prop (s**, w*)." Thus, with "believes (x, q)" denoting the dyadic concept x believes that q, we have the proposition [p*—believes (x, q)— prop(s**, w*)] as the proposition expressed by the sentence "Plato believes that Socrates is wise."

What if we then consider "Socrates thinks that Plato believes that Socrates is wise"? On Frege's view, the sentence "Plato believes that Socrates is wise," in such a doubly embedded context, denotes the proposition it normally expresses, [p*—believes(x, q)— prop(s**, w*)]. And, in such a complex context it expresses a sense that denotes that proposition. Moreover, on Frege's principles, the denotation of a complex expression is determined by the denotation roles of its components. One can see how cumbersome and apparently arbitrary, as well as *ad hoc*, the pattern becomes. It is also quite problematic. Just as one specifies a Fregean sense as the sense of an expression—as the sense of the name "Plato" for example, so one indicates a successive hierarchy of senses, and functions needed to form them, in terms of the expressions involved. For we end up using expressions like "the function that forms a sense that denotes the proposition consisting of the sense of the term 'Socrates' and the concept *is wise*," for example. But we need not pursue such complications.

D. Kaplan disagrees with the standard interpretation of Frege that takes him to adopt the above shift in sense and reference. He is led into an interpretation of Frege's use of quotation marks leading to his own device of "Frege quotes" and an account of quantifying into embedded contexts (1968-69). I find his interpretation unconvincing and pointless but note it as his account of "quantifying in," while being highly problematic and essentially duplicating Wilfrid Sellars's earlier pattern for doing the same sort of thing (Hochberg, 1978, 220-30, 369-79), is now widely known.

1b. Frege's Context Principle and Dummett's Linguistic Turn

One of the most widely discussed aspect's of Frege's philosophy of language has been the meaning and significance of his so-called "context principle." For Dummett that principle achieves the status of a philosophical dictum, along with the more familiar—to know the meaning is to know the use. In fact the two principles, for him, end up not being that different, thus reconciling Frege with the later Wittgenstein, and they allow him to recognize abstract objects as well as reject popular causal accounts of reference and meaning.

For such accounts question our being in "causal contact" with abstract objects and take that to be a ground for rejecting such entities in "nominalist" fashion. For Dummett, since we know when it is correct to say things like "We crossed the Equator" and know the connection of the Equator to certain truths about the Earth (its having poles, etc.), even though the Equator, unlike the Earth, is an abstract object, we can safely speak of the referent of the expression "the Equator":

> Grasping the reference of an expression just is grasping certain principles governing the determination of the truth-values of sentences of the language containing it. ... There is no further test it can be required to pass, such as providing us with a means of imagining its referent, or a possibility of encountering or contacting it: all nominalist objections on scores such as these spring from the vice of considering the meaning of the term in isolation. (1991, 156)

This points to the importance the context principle plays in Dummett's own thinking and its link to his focus on the "use" of language. But Dummett makes the solution to classical problems far too easy on his rendition of the "linguistic turn." For one can then solve classical ontological problems, like the problem about the existence of common properties that objects have—the problem of universals—quite simply. There obviously are common properties and referents of words like "red," "white" and "tan"—referents other than the red, white and tan things that "satisfy" predicates such as "red," "white" and "tan," as Quine and Davidson speak—since we determine the truth values of sentences like "Mondrian used the color red extensively, but not tan," "Red is darker than white" and "Red is a primary color but tan is not" quite readily. In fact just about everyone who knows English and has some knowledge of Mondrian's work, along with an elementary knowledge of colors, knows whether they are true or false. This will hardly do to solve the problem of universals, let alone any philosophical problem—but it illustrates Dummett's variant of what many associate with the later Wittgenstein's version of the linguistic turn. One can speak about the problems being simply resolved or of there being no real problem, as in the case of "the Equator." Answers that come so free and easy suggest that the questions and issues are pointless. Dummett's polemic against "nominalists" can just as easily be taken as a dispute with the raising of the question nominalists purport to answer. This point is both emphasized and illustrated by Dummett's view that Frege was the first to take "the linguistic turn" by turning "an ontological question into a linguistic one."

Dummett sees Frege's early attempts to define "cardinal number" as taking that turn for the first time. By considering defining cardinal number the way he did, Frege set down how one can decide questions about the truth or falsity of sentences attributing numbers, such as "The number of people in the room is the same as the number of chairs in the room," "There are three chairs here" and "7 + 3 = 10." But any elementary schoolchild could decide those questions without Frege's definitions, while having a difficult time understanding the definitions. What Dummett implicitly suggests is that the ontological or philosophical questions are to be rejected by being turned into what Carnap characterized as trivial (in the sense of the answers being "analytic") *internal* questions, as opposed to meaningless *external* pseudo-questions. "Do numbers really exist?" is such a pseudo-question, while "Is there an odd number between 6 and 8?" receives a trivial answer "within" the context supplied by a system of arithmetic.

The context principle may be stated as: Only in the context of a statement does a term (phrase) have a reference and sense. (Those who participate in the debates about it tend to distinguish taking it with respect to referents and truth values and taking it in terms of senses and propositions, as well as arguing about how it should be taken.) Whereas Russell would take the meaning of a genuine or logically proper name to be the object it is taken (used) to refer to—that it is interpreted into or correlated with—Frege supposedly holds that such a term would neither have sense nor reference outside a context supplied by a statement. Ironically, given Frege's later distinction between sense and reference, there is a way in which the context principle can be seen to be both true and trivial. Recall the earlier discussion of the role of the term "Socrates" in the sentences "Socrates is wise" and "Plato believes that Socrates is wise." On the view Frege developed after his *Grundlagen* statement of the context principle, the name "Socrates" does not have either the same sense or the same referent in both sentences, since it "shifts" its sense and reference as it occurs in the embedded sentence. Other complications to Frege's view are posed by the way in which a sentence may be "deconstructed," to use a fashionable but loose term in a somewhat precise way. Put simply, the sentence "aRb" can be "decomposed" in terms of the names "a" and "b" and the dyadic predicate "xRy," or of "b" and the monadic predicate "aRy" or of "a" and "xRb." Just how "b" functions in "xRb" is not as clear-cut as is its role as a subject term in the other two cases.

The context principle is generally defended on grounds that connect with the so-called verification criterion or theory of meaning and the familiar issue (or at least once familiar issue) raised by various interpretations of Wittgenstein's "private language" argument (purportedly showing that the notion of a private language is incoherent since there are no criteria for determining correct use). To see the point, imagine someone uttering a token, as one says, of the word "Socrates" and suddenly dropping dead before being able to say anything else. We might never be able to figure out what she was going to say. Whether she was referring to the historical figure or her neighbor's dog, named after him. Surely it doesn't follow that she wasn't referring to something on the grounds that she didn't finish the statement or since we cannot determine who or what was referred to. We would simply never know whether she was referring to some person, or other object for that matter. (Consider her having uttered "this" or "that" instead of a proper name.) But to even suggest that certainly suggests, by ordinary usage, that she could have referred to something or someone. There is no argument for the view that using the term on the occasion described above was a "non-referential" use. Was it a referential use when Xantippe called out "Socrates"? Or must she have said "Socrates, come here!" Or used "Socrates" in a declarative sentence with a truth value? Need we go into lengthy discourses about various kinds of "speech acts" here? Or is it not simply obvious that, for whatever purpose one uses the term on such, fortunately rare, occasions, one sometimes has referred (and intended to refer) to someone or something?

Whether Frege did or did not adhere to the context principle after his statement of it in 1884, prior to his explicitly distinguishing sense from referent, need not concern us.[2] What one should keep in mind is that Frege was really concerned with terms that occur in statements that have truth values,

---

[2]Angelelli (1993, part 4) argues that Frege later ignores his 1884 *Grundlagen* principle and that the context principle was simply a temporary feature of his view, associated with the early attempt to use contextual definitions. But we have noted there is a trivial sense in which it holds given his later taking expressions to "shift" their referent by denoting their normal senses in embedded contexts.

which meant he focused on terms that have a denotation as well as a sense. It is worth noting that the German term *"Bedeutung,"* now generally rendered in terms of "denotation" or "referent," as opposed to *"Sinn"* (sense), in translations and discussions of Frege, not only means "means," but also means "important."[3] It is also worth noting that Frege seems to explicitly reject the context principle in a December, 1899 letter to Hilbert:

> It is *absolutely* essential for the rigor of mathematical investigations that the distinction between definitions and all other statements be respected most thoroughly. The other statements (axioms, basic laws, theorems) cannot contain any word and any symbol whose sense and reference or whose contribution to the expression of the thought did not fully exist beforehand, so that there is no doubt with regard to the sense of the sentence, the thought expressed by the sentence. (1975, 62)

Moreover, little is to be gained, even in questions of Frege scholarship, if, like Dummett, one both preserves the context principle for the later Frege (for senses) and advocates it by taking it to state that "... the sense of an expression relates exclusively to its role in sentences, and consists in its contribution to the thought expressed by any sentence in which it occurs. So understood, it is indisputable that Frege continued to maintain it in *Grundgesetze*...." (1991, 184) That not only fits with the letter to Hilbert but seems to turn the principle upside down, depending on which words you stress, and into a way of supporting a principle of compositionality. Dummett, in fact, entitles a section of his book "A compositional interpretation of the context principle" (1991, 202) and is clearly aware of the obvious issues that arise. But his response is rather lame. What it comes down to is his repeating a theme from his earlier book (1973) that a mastery of basic "characteristic sentences" or "recognition statements" is required for our understanding of a term. And what are these? Well they are "... statements of the form 'This is T', where T is the term in question, or 'This S is T' where S is a sortal such as 'person',

---

[3]Angelelli (1982) has noted this ambiguity in linking Frege's taking sentences to denote truth values to his stressing that sentences that have the same truth value are of the same or identical "importance" for substitution, *salvae veritatae*. Frege writes: "Now Leibniz's definition is as follows: 'Things are the same as each other, of which one can be substituted for the other without loss of truth'. This I propose to adopt as my own definition of identity" (1953, 76).

'street'…" (1991, 204). This is most innocuous. Russell, who took the meaning of a logically proper name to be given by its referent and that of a primitive predicate to be the property or relation it represented, views Dummett rejects, could easily accept a context principle in such a form, even without accepting propositional entities. In fact his saying in the logical atomism essays that predicates and names referred in different ways just about amounts to that. Nor is any more said by Dummett's explication that "The context principle … amounts to the conceptual priority of thoughts over their constituents: the constituents can be grasped only as potential constituents of complete thoughts" (1991, 184). For this can be quite innocent, as well as simply a repetition of what Wittgenstein expresses in his version of the context principle in the *Tractatus*. All Dummett seems to be doing is making the familiar weak claim that to know the "meaning" (in one sense) of a term is to know its "logical grammar"—what kind of term it is. (As we will see in discussing Strawson's neo-Wittgensteinian critique of Russell's theories of reference and description, diverse senses of "meaning" are clearly involved in such disputes.) So, in knowing the referent of a logically proper name one not only knows its meaning, in the sense of reference, but that it can combine with predicates of a certain kind to form a sentence, that it cannot function as a predicate, etc. One can even stretch this into holding that one knows its "role" in "the language" as "a whole." (Perhaps that is why sentences like "Verbs play tennis better than adjectives" amuse students in introductory courses.) This is of no philosophical import but is merely a kind of logical "holism" or contextualism that need not be disputed by those who espouse a reference theory of meaning and seek to avoid the recognition of senses and propositions as entities, while rejecting the replacement of classical philosophical issues by a focus on the "use" or "role" of words and sentences in ordinary language, including ordinary mathematical usage. It is odd how such trivial notions, derived from the logical holism of Wittgenstein's *Tractatus*, have been transformed into extensively elaborated and endlessly discussed philosophical proclamations within the analytic tradition. Thus one finds G. Evans announcing a "Generality Constraint" whereby one can be said to comprehend a thought only if one can be said to also comprehend every thought of a certain kind. Such a network of connected thoughts form a kind of limited holistic context. Thus I can be said to understand "6 is even" only if I also understand "7 is odd" (1982, 100 ff.).

Some of the recent debate about the context principle centers on its connection to Frege's consideration of a definition of "the number of Fs" by giving a purported "contextual definition," in the *Grundlagen*. At first he considers defining "0" implicitly as "the number of the concept x≠x," along with specifying an inductive procedure for arriving at successive numbers of concepts. A few pages later he considers an implicit definition in the context of an identity statement: "the number of Fs = the number of Gs." But he briefly discusses a problem that supposedly arises in the first case since one has not determined the truth value of statements of identity involving an expression like "the number of Fs" and a name like "Julius Caesar," as in the sentence "The number of Fs = Julius Caesar." In the second case he raises the problem in terms of "England is the same as the direction of the earth's axis"— after having introduced the problem about what the *direction* of a line is in order to clarify the issue about numbers (1953, 78). For the discussion of parallel lines and directions can be put "less clumsily" and "can readily be transferred in essentials to apply to the case of numerical identity" (1953, 76). His point is that while one has specified when the number of Fs is the same number as the number of Gs, or when the direction of line A is the same as the direction of line B, by means of "F is equinumerous to G" and "A is parallel to B," and has thus specified the condition for statements of identity, like "the number of Fs = the number of Gs" and "the direction of A = the direction of B," to be true, one has not determined what a cardinal number is. Hence we cannot determine that England is not a direction of a line or a cardinal number. We supposedly have no way of determining the truth value of the sentences "The direction of the earth's axis=England" or "The number of planets=England." This has become known as the "Julius Caesar problem." The problem, as Frege indicates, "looks nonsensical" since, of course, "no one is going to confuse England with the direction of the Earth's axis; but that is no thanks to our definition..." (78). But it is a symptom of a real problem raised by the attempt to use an "implicit definition," not a "contextual definition," on the part of self-proclaimed "neo-Fregeans" like C. Wright and B. Hale who discuss the purported problem at extravagant length.

A significant portion of Dummett's book (1991) on Frege's philosophy of mathematics is devoted to the context principle and this problem, and to a critical discussion of Wright's 1983 *Frege's Conception of Numbers as Objects*. Dummett disputes Wright's claim that Frege can succeed in his program of arriving at a satisfactory account of arithmetical entities, truths and concepts. Wright's view, elaborated by himself and Hale in *The Reason's Proper Study* (2001), makes crucial use of what is known as Hume's Principle: the number of Fs = the number of Gs if and only if F is in one-one correspondence with G. That principle is essentially what Frege discussed, citing Hume, on the way to providing an explicit definition of "cardinal number" (1953, 73-74). He briefly considered it since it satisfies the requirement that one state a condition for when objects of a certain kind are identical. But the real issue that is raised is not about contextual definitions, for such definitions, as we will see in considering Russell's contextual definitions for definite descriptions, may be eliminable explicit definitions. Rather, the issue raised concerns the ineptness of appealing to so-called "implicit definitions" as providing philosophical analyses. Taking implicit definitions to be a species of "definition," and hence of "analytic truth," Hale and Wright devote a sixty-two page article, "To Bury Caesar," to the Caesar problem (2001, 335-96). [Actually they devote many more pages to it since other articles are devoted to Hume's principle, implicit definitions, Frege's related discussion of the identity of the direction of lines, Dummett's criticism of Wright, etc.] There we read about there having to be "facts of the matter" regarding what sorts of objects numbers are—showing, for example, that they are "not trees, tigers, persons or countries." Just what such "facts" turn out to be is, as we will shortly see, interesting, if somewhat puzzling. We are also told that "Hume's Principle could serve as a partial explanation whose epistemological status ... might rub off on the Dedekind-Peano axioms."

The Dedekind-Peano (hereafter, Peano axioms) axioms can be taken, simply put, as:

1) 0 is a number.
2) The successor of a number is a number.
3) If the successor of n=the successor of m, then n=m.
4) 0 is not the successor of any number.
5) If 0 is Φ and for any n if n is Φ then the successor of n is Φ, then all numbers are Φ.

[If the induction axiom (5) is taken as an "axiom schema" with "Φ" as a free variable, one speaks of a "first-order" version of the axioms; if one prefixes "for any Φ" to the statement, thus binding the predicate variable by a universal quantifier, one commonly speaks of a "second-order" version.] Some then hold that the axioms provide implicit definitions for the terms "0," "number" and "successor" since they are taken as primitive and are the only terms occurring in (1)-(5) that are not logical terms ("=", "if...then...," "and," "for any," "the..."). But the notion of an implicit definition is problematic. All that is said by its use is that we limit an "interpretation" of the postulates to terms that will render them "true." Thus we can interpret the term "number" in the familiar way in terms of—0, 1, 2...—or we can take it in terms of any other "progression"—0, 2, 4...—will do with "successor" then taken as "+2." To speak of an "implicit definition" as if it were a definition that gives an analysis of the concept expressed by the "defined" term is thus not only highly misleading, but incoherent, though there is a purely "verbal" link to the notion of a "contextual definition." For those who speak of implicit definitions, as in this case, think of the axioms providing a "context" that gives "meaning" to the terms. But, as mentioned, Russell's contextual definitions for definite descriptions (see 1e below) provide a way of eliminating the contextually defined expression in diverse contexts. Implicit definitions, as Hale and Wright note, do not do that. Thus they do not furnish an analysis of the concepts involved or a resolution of any philosophical problems those concepts pose. In fact Hale and Wright seem to have done nothing more than offer a problematic stipulation as a philosophical solution.

They argue that Hume's Principle suffices to "set up number as a sortal concept" (2001, 15), which is all that is needed. Why does it suffice? It suffices because that is what it is to be a sortal concept—i. e. to be a concept that is partially explicated in terms of having a "criterion of identity" (14, 15) for its application. [The book contains a lengthy, and overly repetitious, discussion of "sortal concepts," which includes a defense of Wright's earlier 1983 characterization of such concepts responding to various, equally verbose, criticisms of it.] Thus the "implicit," not "contextual," definition establishes "number" as a sortal concept (actually, if one is careful, what is implicitly defined is "(the) number-of-Φs") on a par with other sortal concepts. As one can then decide that Hale's horse is not identical with Wright's horse and the cabbage in Hale's kitchen is not the same cabbage as the one in Wright's kitchen, one does not have a problem posed by mixing sortal categories and asking if one of the horses is a cabbage. To think there is a problem about numbers would apparently "rub off" in that one would supposedly have to then think that there is a problem about cabbages and horses. This is what takes them sixty-two pages to articulate (more pages, actually, as the preparatory discussion dominates the twenty-seven page introduction to the book). The preoccupation with sortal concepts reflects a notion Strawson popularized in the 1950s during the heyday of manifest ordinary language philosophy—manifest as in Dummett's writings as opposed to its latent presence in the apparent consideration of metaphysical issues in the writings of Wright and Hale and, as we will see, of Kripke.

The specific problem with being content with implicit definitions in this context—with leaving any of the key terms as "uninterpreted" signs—is, as Russell observed long ago:

> ...it fails to give an adequate basis for arithmetic. In the first place, it does not enable us to know whether there are any sets of terms verifying Peano's axioms; it does not even give the faintest suggestion of any way of discovering whether there are such sets. In the second place, as already observed, we want our numbers to be such as can be used for counting common objects, and this requires that our numbers should have a *definite* meaning, not merely that they should have certain formal properties. This definite meaning is defined by the logical theory of arithmetic. (1953, 10)[4]

To deal with this long standing problem Hale and Wright take Hume's Principle to offer an implicit definition of an expression for a numerical operator, "the-number-of-Φs" and purport to then derive the Peano postulates in a "suitable system" of second-order logic allowing for predicate quantifiers. [I insert the hyphens in the expression to emphasize that we do not deal with

---

[4]At other places Russell took a less definite position with respect to his variant of "logicism" and held that "...any indubitable set of objects" that "satisfy the formulae of arithmetic" may be taken as numbers. It was simply that the variant of logicism in *Principia Mathematica* provided the "simplest set of objects" known to fulfill the requirement (1952, 209-10). One must keep in mind that, via the no class theory of the first edition, number expressions were defined in terms of class expressions which, in turn, were eliminated by contextual definition and thus did not represent anything—i. e. there were no classes and hence no objects that were numbers. Thus Russell's logicism was quite different from Frege's (1952, 212).

the term "number" but the entire expression. What is "implicitly defined" is not the sortal term "number."] Thus they cannot escape the problems posed by implicit definitions—the problems Russell cited. Hence, forgetting the absurdity of the "Caesar" problem, in their own terms they have not offered a resolution of the problem involved since they have not given an analysis that tells us what numbers are. What they have done, after wandering thru many pages discussing the Caesar problem, is arrive at an obvious conclusion, on the last page of the essay—people and numbers are different sorts of things, just as Frege had noted, in a sentence, that of course England was not the direction of the Earth's axis. But, recall, Frege had also noted that that was no thanks to the implicit definition he was considering—just as it is no thanks to Hale and Wright's use of Hume's Principle as an axiom.

Human beings cannot be numbers because the criteria for "personal identity" are not the criteria for the identity of numbers as stated in Hume's Principle! (2001, 396) What it all amounts to is that we rule out certain things from being numbers by being of the wrong "category." In effect we add postulates, covertly, to Hume's Principle by imposing restrictions on what we can take to be the number of something—separating "sortals" or categories. And, of course, as one would expect, the only criteria we have for doing so is found in how we talk about A and B being the same people, same numbers, same trees, same tigers, etc.—how we "sort" them. Such talk supplies the requisite facts and categorial differences. However, if we are not willing to accept that the purported problem is resolved by imposing such facts, in the form of establishing categorial restraints that forbid "cross-categorial identifications," there is no problem in any case. For we deal with a problem that "afflicts all sortal concepts" (2001, 396). Thus there is no special problem with appealing to Hume's Principle as giving us the understanding of numerical terms (since it "rubs off," recall, "epistemologically" on the Peano postulates)—"And that is good enough." (2001, 396) They seem to believe that if you reject Hume's Principle as being sufficient to provide a philosophical analysis of the problems posed by arithmetical "objects" you are faced with the insoluble problem of saying why a cabbage is not a human being. One cannot really take this seriously and, as already indicated, no real argument is presented for the claim, which overlooks an elementary fact.

Tigers, people, cabbages and trees are familiar objects with familiar properties. Numbers pose the problems of (i) whether there are such objects at all; (ii) specifying what they are, if we hold that there are numbers; (iii) explaining what kinds of truths arithmetical truths are (or why "true" arithmetical statements are not "really true"). What logicism purports to do is tell us what a number can be taken to be, in Frege's case, and how to avoid taking numbers to be anything at all, in Russell's case, while, for both Frege and Russell, specifying how the truths of arithmetic are to be construed. In the case of trees, cabbages and tigers there are neither corresponding questions about whether there are such objects nor about what sorts of objects they are. Of course one can raise classical problems about physical objects and our knowledge of them. But one who seriously doubts the existence of physical objects is mad, while one who raises a corresponding question about mathematical "objects" can reasonably be taken to have an "inquiring mind." That is why, typically, one who argues that numbers exist, and are to be taken in a specific way, tends to argue that attempts to avoid acknowledging such objects fail. Thus one is forced to accept numbers, in some fashion, in order to account for certain truths—that there are more people than chairs at a dinner party, laws of physics, that the number of natural numbers is not a natural number, etc. Alternatively, those who deny the existence of numbers tend to attempt to show how to accommodate or dismiss such truths without recognizing numbers as entities. Finally, one must keep in mind the general question of the viability of "implicit" definition as a method or tool of philosophical "analysis."

Since the statement of Hume's Principle is taken as an axiom embodying an unexplicated (undefined) use of "number of" that expression is open to various interpretations—and each "unwanted" interpretation must be ruled out—as one rules out "human beings." One has a general way of ruling out unwanted interpretations, in either Russell's or Frege's fashion, by offering explicit definitions of the key arithmetical terms. This is what will ground Frege's dismissal of the "Caesar-England problem" as nonsensical. But even with purported explicit definitions, there are further problems that all forms of logicism face. Russell and Frege each provided a specific interpretation of the three primitive terms in the Peano postulates. Such an interpretation is only one of many possible interpretations, since what it amounts to is a "model" of the postulates (Hochberg, 1956). One who offers such an "explicit" interpretation thus faces the problem of arguing why a specific interpretation is suitable to resolve the philosophical problems posed by arithmetic—What are numbers? What kinds of truths are arithmetical truths? (Hochberg, 1970) Hale and Wright do not get to the point of answering such questions since they do not offer a specific interpretation in that (a) "number" remains a primitive term in the form of —the-number-of-Φs—what they call the "numerical operator," and (b) they add an axiom, Hume's Principle, to a system of logic—an axiom that is not, as it stands, a statement of logic. They, somewhat misleadingly, suggest that it is a matter of "logic" by taking it to be "...analytic by virtue of being determinative of the concept it thereby seeks to explain" (2001, 14). In short, Hume's Principle, being taken as an implicit definition is analytic, and hence a matter of logic, since implicit definitions, being a form of definition, are declared to be analytic. This provides a sample of analytic philosophy at the dawn of a new century—almost a full century after Russell's "On Denoting."

Implicit definitions are supposedly viable (being "determinative of" concepts) since they provide a way to "fix the meaning of an expression by imposing some form of constraint" (2001, 117). But it would seem that if one can specify constraints so that only one interpretation is not eliminated, one has, in effect, offered an explicit definition. Wright and Hale believe they have a way around this. "Number" is the only sortal concept for which a one-one correlation supplies the criterion for determining identity. They declare that in dealing with numbers we deal with a sortal concept that has a unique method for determining the truth of statements of identity—establishing a one-one correlation between appropriate terms. Caesar and England, on the other hand, are not "objects" where statements of identity concerning "them" are typically explicated in terms of establishing such a correlation. But all this does, at best, is furnish a description of a characteristic of numbers and, in a way I will make clear just below, merely does, in a circuitous way, what Frege does. But there are two more serious objections.

One is simply that they do not employ a sortal concept, *number*, in Hume's Principle. They make use of a function expression, "the-number-of-Φs," in that principle in order to introduce the term "number" via that functional expression. Aside from the problematic baggage and arbitrary stipulations carried along with their notion of a sortal concept, the problem they face arises prior to their having such a purported concept. If one takes the time to think about what they do, one realizes, as Frege did, that all one does with Hume's Principle is introduce a condition (criterion), not for the identity of numbers, but for when two concepts, say F and G, are equinumerous. One simply then says that the *same number* "applies" to both concepts. All one has actually said, then, is "F is equinumerous to G if and only if F and G are in one-one correspondence." Once we realize that we see that the introduction of the purported sortal concept *is a number* depends on appealing to Hume's Principle—but the appeal to Hume's Principle as a basis for the analysis of the concept is justified by claiming that *being a number* is a sortal concept with a unique criterion of identity, that furnished by Hume's Principle. So, round and round we go generating words, not analyses.

What Wright and Hale do not seem to realize, and what Frege did realize, as becomes clear from the development of the *Grundlagen*, is that Hume's Principle sets out an *explicit definition* of the relational predicate "is equinumerous to," which is a "higher order (level)" predicate that takes predicates, like "F" and "G," as subject terms. Having defined such a relational predicate, Frege was in a position, as Russell would later be, to explicitly define signs that could be used to interpret the primitive non-logical signs of the Peano postulates—the number sign "0," the monadic predicate "is a cardinal number" and the relational predicate or function sign "successor of."

There is a second problem with not really using the term "number" in Hume's Principle (taken as an axiom added to the system of logic Wright and Hale employ), but, instead, actually employing the form of expression "the-number-of-Φs" (with "Φ" as an appropriate predicate variable). What they do is introduce a function expression that combines with predicate expressions and is, implicitly, taken to represent a function that takes concepts as arguments. For example, take the concept word "F." They form the expression "the-number-of-F's" from "F" and the "numerical operator" expression that represents a function. But now they face a fundamental problem about "identity." Just what is the function that is represented? Well, it is the function that for every concept, taken as argument, maps that argument onto a (cardinal) number as value. But what is a number—i. e. what is the "concept" that gives the elements of the class of values for the "range" of the function? The only answer they have is that a number is what is a value of the function. As Frege once put it, a number is what is a number-of-some-concept. Thus to specify (identify) the function we must have determined what a number is. But Wright and Hale seek to specify their "sortal concept" of *being a number* in terms of what *the function the-number-of-Φs* is. Thus, again, they spin in circles.

We can also note that, if they were to work things out, philosophically or ontologically, and not merely focus on the use of "sortal concepts," they would face the problem posed by construing the function *the-number-of-Φs* in the two-fold manner of Frege's construal of the concept of negation—as what maps a proposition onto its negation, and as a "component" of the negative proposition that "forms" a negative proposition from a proposition. In this case we have a function coordinating concepts to numbers, while numbers are implicitly construed (constructed) from a concept and an "operator" combining with it—a number forming operator, one might say. Such an operator would be in the style of Carnap's ambiguous employment of apparent "truth functional" connectives to form predicates representing complex properties, like "F&G" (Hochberg, 2001a, 349-51, 359-65). That is a problematic pattern that has been resurrected in recent years by Armstrong and others.

In the above discussion I have not employed a variant of the type of argument that Frege used in rejecting definitions of "truth"—that to offer such a definition you have to know what the concept is to start with, thus implicitly making use of it, and hence cannot be said to define it. That is another general issue that raises what is known as the "paradox of analysis." The point here is that Hale and Wright take Hume's Principle as a biconditional statement employing the primitive expression "the-number-of-Φs" as an "operator expression" that is added to the axioms of a system. The axiom(s) then supposedly supply the meaning for the expression, though we still do not know what sorts of things numbers are except that they are the sorts of things that satisfy the axiom(s). The sort of thing Hale and Wright do is aided by the fact that the standard construals of elementary arithmetic by logicists in the twentieth century have been in terms of set theory—with numbers taken as sets (0 as the empty set, for example). Set theory, as it is normally construed, makes use of two primitive notions—that of "set" and that of "membership"—and specifies axioms involving those notions.

> As a consequence of our decision we shall have, in principle, just one kind of variable, lower case letters, which will vary over sets....
>
> Our basic language consists now of all the expressions obtained from x=y and x ∈ y, where x and y are any variables, by the sentential connectives ¬ (not) ....(Levy, 1979, 4)

> In the present book we shall present set theory as an axiomatic system. In geometry we do not examine directly the meaning of the terms "point", "line", "plane" or other "primitive terms", but from a well-defined system of axioms we deduce all the theorems of geometry without resorting to the intuitive meaning of the primitive terms. ....
>
> The primitive terms of set theory are "set" and the relation "to be an element of". (Kuratowski and Mostowski, 1976, 5)

Since "set" and "∈" are generally taken as primitive, one might think that there is little point in offering explicit definitions of the primitive terms of the Peano postulates in terms of the concepts of set theory since set theorists, in effect, treat the axioms of (a version of) set theory as implicit definitions of the terms for those concepts. There is a "yes" and a "no" to this. However one treats the primitive concepts of set theory, one has still, by interpreting the primitive terms in the Peano postulates and deriving the interpreted postulates as theorems, offered an explicit interpretation of "arithmetic" relative to set theory. On the other hand, there are philosophical problems raised by the concepts of "set," "class" and "membership." Are there sets? And, if so, what are they? Does "∈" represent a relation? What sorts of truths are the truths of set theory? But the fact that such questions remain does not mean that one has not proposed viable answers to questions about arithmetic in terms of set theory. Thus, as noted, Frege's dismissal of the "Caesar-England problem" can be seen as ultimately grounded on such things not being classes (the extensions of concepts) given his explicit definition of a cardinal number as a class of concepts fulfilling certain conditions. That is why I said that Frege can be seen to do, in a short space, what Wright and Hale devote pages, articles and books to doing, while subjecting their readers to their concern with the appropriate way to talk about "sortal" concepts. Forgetting that, we should keep in mind that we have to face the questions raised about set theory in any case, given the mathematical strength of set theory and its implict and explicit use in much "ordinary" mathematics. In that sense Frege does not merely do, simply and far more neatly, what the neo-Fregeans do. We shall return to some aspects of such issues in Chapter 4. (On implicit definitions see Hochberg, 2001a, 289-96; on the existence of classes (sets), 236-74.)

In Dummett's view the belief that Frege should and could have stayed with the building up of a system of concepts employing the pattern of contextual definitions he used early in his *Grundlagen* and developed the pattern to achieve his goals is mistaken. For Dummett, Frege's logicism is inherently flawed as it involves the incompatible goals of recognizing a domain of abstract mathematical objects while supposedly deriving the truths about the natural and real numbers from logical principles alone (2002, 21). The term "logicism" is generally used to apply to both Frege's view in the *Grundlagen* as well as to Russell's early form of logicism in the first edition of *Principia Mathematica*. As both of those views are often taken to involve an appeal to a domain of abstract objects that numbers are identified with—classes (or extensions of concepts) of a certain kind, it is worth reiterating that Russell's logicism, employing his "no class" theory, clearly involved avoiding what Quine calls "ontological commitments" to such objects. In effect, Russell eliminated class abstract expressions by contextual definitions along the lines of the elimination of definite descriptive expressions (which we shall soon consider). Thus no "ontological commitments" to classes were involved. That aside, the question remains whether there is any real incompatibility between construing numbers as abstract objects in logistic terms, as sets say, and taking arithmetical truths to be logical truths. We shall consider aspects of this question in Chapters 3 and 4 in taking up Dummett's views about "proof" and "truth" and the so-called problem of "access" to abstract entities. In any case, Dummett provides no argument for such a purported incompatibility but simply seems to assume that logic does not involve ontological issues or "commitments," aside from his either ignoring Russell's variant of logicism, that rejects both classes and numbers as entities, or lumping it together with Frege's version.

As the issue between Dummett and Wright revolves around Frege's contextual definitions it revives disputes about the proper interpretation of the context principle and its application (to senses, to denotations, to both). Dummett, discussing Wright's interpretation, suggests that the principle, as stated in the *Grundlagen*, can be interpreted as saying:

>...that questions about the meaning (*Bedeutung*) of a term or class of terms are, when legitimate, internal to the language. We know the meaning of a term, say 'the Equator', when we know the conditions for

the truth of any sentence containing it; that is all we need to know, and all we can know. (1991, 192)

He takes that to be "... in large degree a faithful exegesis of Frege's use of the context principle in *Grundlagen*." But Dummett's statement is both unclear and, yet, clearly mistaken. It is unclear because of the use of the phrase "conditions for the truth of." He seems to be talking about a condition of truth as a "way of verifying" a sentence as true—in much the manner of the verification criterion of meaning of the logical positivists. But if he is talking about knowing what it would be to verify it, then he runs into the familiar problems of the classic criterion. Is he really serious that in order to know the meaning (referent) of the words in his statement of the context principle we have to know how to verify it? What is it to know how to verify the truth, or what the truth condition is, in any reasonable sense, for a philosophical claim of that kind? Does that mean we don't know what the word "sentence" means? Aside from some classic philosophical claims, and questions, which were declared meaningless pseudo-questions by the positivists, consider some of the typical objections that arose, such as the purported problem of "the inverted spectrum." Assume it is possible that someone's visual spectrum is "reversed." And, in spite of recent exotic arguments to the contrary—involving fancifully imagining replacing neurons one by one, focusing on an unclear notion of "metaphysical" necessity in place of logical necessity, etc.—it clearly is "logically possible." Assume also there is no way of telling that via neurophysiology, etc. Yet, the person uses the same word we all use in such circumstances, so there is never any odd disagreement about the color of an object. One cannot tell, under any circumstances, if the sentences "Dummett has a reversed spectrum" and "Dummett would be seeing color x when I see color y because his spectrum is reversed" are true. Does this mean I don't know what words like "Dummett," "I" and "color" mean (or are here used to refer to)? Or do we simply talk about "characteristic sentences" like "I am here" and "This is Professor Dummett"?

The context principle, as stated in *Grundlagen* (1953, 71-72) is not as clear-cut as one might think, if it is taken in the context of the presentation of it. First, Frege is focused on distinguishing between the "content" of a word and our having an "idea" of it to deny the view that "... any word for which we can find no corresponding mental picture appears to have no content"(71). The way to do this is to avoid taking words in isolation and to focus on propositions, for this will block our thinking in terms of an image or mental picture of some kind. Second, he is concerned with sentences like "The number 0 belongs to the concept F" being taken to indicate that "0" is functioning as a predicate representing a concept instead of being "only an element in the predicate" (68). Thus it can still be seen as a "self-subsistent [independent] object" (68). Third, he consistently violates the principle in (a) his discussion of words like "the," as "the definite article claims to refer to a definite object" (87), (b) his noting that the expression "the largest proper fraction" is senseless and "has no content" since no object falls under the concept represented (88) and (c) his saying things like "In this definition the sense of the expression 'extension of a concept' is assumed to be known" (117). Moreover, in speaking of concepts he constantly seems to presume we understand the meaning of concept expressions, like "is F," and not merely expressions like the one I just used to refer to an expression—the entire expression including the quotation marks. Thus, for example, he speaks of a concept being contradictory, though the concept expressions are only mentioned, and not used, in the statements about the concepts. Fourth, he emphasizes the incompleteness of concepts as opposed to the completeness of propositions. This he does by noting that concepts cannot be asserted, only judgment contents can. Thus, in the case of a relational proposition, if you withdraw both terms you are left with a concept that has no more "sense" than a simple concept has. [Austin, interestingly, interjects "assertible" to form "assertible sense" in the translated text (82).] There is a further point worth noting about Frege's context principle that is related to this focus on concepts as incomplete and his contrasting them with judgment contents. In his 1879 *Begriffsschrift* Frege had already indicated a quite interesting form of the context principle. There he contrasts concepts like "the number 20" and "every positive integer" as not being of the same rank, as what can be asserted about the number 20 cannot be asserted, in the same sense, about "every positive integer" [quotes included in the translated text]. And he goes on to write:

The expression "every positive integer" by itself, unlike "the number 20", yields no independent {selbstandige} idea; it acquires a sense only in the context of a sentence. (1972, 128)[5]

This early contrast between expressions that will be characterized as saturated or complete (expressions for objects) and those considered incomplete, unsaturated expressions, is worth keeping in mind when one considers the debates over the significance of the context principle and its role in Frege's analysis of meaning.

1c. Frege's Objects and Quine's Criterion of Commitment

In a way Quine refocused the attention of philosophers on "ontology" after the linguistic turn by the use of the memorable phrase "to be is to be the value of a variable." That can be seen as taking Frege's criterion for distinguishing objects from concepts and turning it into a criterion of ontological commitment. One was committed to objects of a certain kind if one quantified over a domain of objects of that kind. Thus if one employed only the quantifiers of first-order logic, one was ontologically committed only to "individuals"— whatever one took such individuals to be. This amounted to recognizing the objects that were represented by signs (if one had such constant signs in addition to the logical signs in a schema), and over which variables ranged, that could stand, like the bound variables, in the subject place in sentential formulae. Thus, in employing a standard schema for first-order logic, supplemented by proper names and primitive first-level predicates, one was not committed to anything the predicates "represented"—such as properties or concepts—only to the individuals in the domain that was quantified over and which were referred to by proper names. Primitive predicates were part of an ontological "free lunch," as Armstrong speaks. Thus Quine and his followers were free to use primitive predicates, and treat them on a par with defined predicates, without being "committed" to abstract entities like universal properties. The criterion of ontological commitment was only the first

---

[5]I am advised by German colleagues that the expression "a sense" should literally be "its sense."

step in Quine's ontological campaign, for it simply gave a criterion for determining what ontological commitments one made. The second step was Quine's suggesting that the ontological commitments made by the most parsimonious schema that would accommodate "science" gave the answer to the ontological question "What is there?" To keep the ontology minimal, one thus had to accommodate the statements of science within a first-order language. While this would avoid properties, as abstract entities, it would not avoid all abstract entities, as not only did empirical science require mathematics, but mathematics itself was a "formal" science. Yet set theory within a first order schema would do for accommodating mathematics. This had an important influence in the development of the linguistic turn. For philosophers became used to thinking of sets, or classes, as the prototype "abstract" objects. Given the history of the problem of universals, this is odd, as sets, if they are anything at all, are objects or particulars, as Frege well knew— for they are not predicable of anything. So one dealt with two types of "individuals"— concrete and abstract individuals (particulars). Thus philosophers became accustomed to thinking of classes (we need not distinguish sets from classes in this context) in place of properties. The use of a primitive membership relation (dyadic "predicate") in set theory was of no consequence, for in a first-order schema there are no predicate quantifiers. So even that "predicate" did not involve an ontological commitment in addition to the commitment to its "subjects"— sets. This contributed to a further twist. One could then think of Platonists as advocating unrestricted recognition of sets, including "impredicative" ones (sets whose membership condition was specified by a quantifier ranging over sets, including the one "defined"), while a conscientious "conceptualist," though recognizing sets, as required for the logistic construction of "mathematics" along the lines of Frege and Russell, would seek to restrict the commitment to the "constructive" sets, in so far as possible. The issues involved need not concern us. What is of interest is how the classical problem of universals was twisted beyond recognition.

There was a second twist Quine provided. The idea behind the criterion of ontological commitment, aside from having a criterion that simply and quite arbitrarily rules out properties by stipulation, is to hold that one takes something to exist if and only if one can state that it does exist. To take ontological commitments to be made by the primitive signs one employs—as their referents—does not involve being able to state, in the language in virtue of which the commitments are made, that what is taken to exist does so. But, then, take a proper name in a first-order language, say "Zeus." How does one say "Zeus exists," given that the rejection of a predicate of "existence" was a common theme held by philosophers of the period? To use "There is something identical with Zeus" is awkward, for a variety of reasons, not the least of which is that in a standard schema it follows from "Zeus=Zeus," which is entailed by "Everything is identical with itself, " a logical truth in standard systems. In this respect "Quine" is no different from "Zeus." Quine's solution was simple. One would not only avoid names that did not name, as we will see Russell did, but use Russell's theory of definite descriptions to replace every proper name by a definite description. If a normal description was not at hand one could always use a description like "The object that is-Zeus (=Zeus)." The obvious objection to the latter is that one makes use of the name one is eliminating in order to eliminate it. Quine saw no problem with this, since once it was used, one had a predicate, "being identical with Zeus" or "Zeus-izes" that could then be used in a description, while the name was dropped from the schema. A sub-schema, of the original language schema was employed, where the latter, but not the former, contained the name and the needed formula to warrant replacing the name by the appropriate description. Quine would go on to use this technique to remove psychological terms from a perspicuous linguistic sub-schema as part of his behaviorist-physicalist reduction of the mental to the physical. There he used a most astounding argument. Where we have a mental state μ and where M represents any "mentalistic predicate" that we "might want to apply to" μ, we can introduce a physicalistic predicate, P, characterizing a particular physical state, π, of an individual. We can then take whatever is evidence for attributing M to μ to be evidence for attributing P to π. Thus we achieve the identification of μ with π, given the "extensionality of scientific language," and can simply drop the "old" mentalistic idiom from our "theory" (sub-schema) and "get along" with P and π "rechristened as" M and μ (1957, 15). One is left somewhat speechless by such a line of thought. Though, as we will later note, it re-emerges in a way in Davidson's "anomalous monism."

In the simple case of removing proper names where there is an object named, one eliminates the purely labeling or indicative role of proper names as well as atomic sentences, such as "Fa," from a schema. Moreover, the "program" for eliminating names can only be coherently employed by one who presupposed that primitive predicates did not directly refer, as names purportedly do. In short, one must be a nominalist of Quine's kind. For if primitive predicates are directly referring signs, then the program for eliminating all directly referring signs by means of definite descriptions hopelessly spins in circles.

1d. Bradley and Bosanquet on Predication and Judgment

Bradley and Bernard Bosanquet were major figures in British philosophy at the end of the nineteenth century and into the early part of the twentieth. Influenced by German Idealism, especially Hegel, they espoused doctrines that were commonly held when Russell and Moore were students at Cambridge. [The simplest way to become acquainted with their doctrines is by reading Bosanquet's concise and fairly clear little book *Essentials of Logic*, given the tendency of idealists to write in what Broad characterized as a kind of "Hegelianised English" (Broad, 1953, viii). The fact that the book was designed as a course of lectures for "the University Extension system" possibly explains its accessibility.] One of their key themes was that the apparent predicative relation, holding between the subject and predicate of a judgment, was paradoxical. It was taken to be so since, as Frege had thought, if such a relation were to be a further constituent of a judgment, it seemed to be related, in turn, to the other constituents. This was one reason that led Bradley to deny that an apparent subject-predicate judgment, like that expressed by "Socrates is wise," could be viably analyzed in terms of a subject, whether Socrates himself or a concept or meaning that was expressed by the term "Socrates," standing in a predicative relation to a concept or attribute expressed by "is wise." A second reason such an analysis was rejected was based on the view that one had no idea or concept of a subject, such as Socrates, apart from its qualities, including relational qualities. One's ideas were only of universal concepts—wisdom, being human, being different from Plato, etc. This avoided what Bradley took to be pure subjects of judgments—"bare" particulars or pure "thises"—the underlying substrata ("matter") supporting qualities that Berkeley had earlier condemned as being based on a meaningless metaphysical notion—Locke's notorious "I know not what." Such a substratum supposedly required us to have an idea of an unqualitied subject of qualities to which the qualities adhered or in which they inhered. For Bradley and Bosanquet, to think that Socrates was wise was not to think of a subject, Socrates, but, rather, of various attributes, such as being a philosopher, being snub-nosed, etc. and to judge that such attributes coexisted with wisdom or were joined together with wisdom in Reality.

Subject-predicate judgments were construed as existential judgments—judgments that certain combinations of attributes existed together in Reality or were accepted by Reality. This led Bradley to the conclusion that the real subject of every judgment was Reality, for in judgment we ascribe a combination of attributes or concepts to that "ultimate" subject (1958, 33-34, 50). Thus one judged, of Reality, that it was such that the combination of attributes, wisdom + being a philosopher + being snub nosed + being ugly +...., was a part of it. Moreover, as the various components of the judgment were attributes or concepts, Bradley took the content of the judgment to be a property—a complex property—and not something "propositional" like a Fregean thought. In judging, one asserted that a complex attribute belonged to Reality, in the sense of being a part of *It* and not in the sense of being exemplified by Reality. "In their ordinary acceptation the traditional subject, predicate, and copula are mere superstitions." (1958, 21; a qualifying footnote added later does not effect the basic view.) In so putting matters Bradley thought he escaped from his paradox of predication, since he replaced a supposed predicative connection in the content of a judgment by an activity, ascribing to Reality or judging that Reality was such that a certain complex concept was a part of it. Complex concepts became the contents of judgments. In the activity of judging we took what was in a particular thought, a complex concept, to be a part of what was not in that thought, the "real" subject of all judgments, Reality. By so doing one avoided not only a problematic predicative connection, but the absurdity of holding that we had, in thought, ideas of pure subjects, or bare particulars, as subjects of predicative ascriptions. The act of judging or ascribing a complex content to Reality was not itself part of the content. It is interesting that in his rejecting the traditional subject-predicate form of judgment, Bradley makes a claim that will be repeated years later by Ramsey and is often associated with Ramsey's name, though for a different purpose. Simply put, one cannot take "Socrates is wise" to indicate a difference between what is the subject and what is attributed, as we can, supposedly, just as easily construe wisdom as the judgment's subject, as in "Wisdom characterizes Socrates"(Ramsey, 1931). Bradley is concerned to exhibit the difference between "the ultimate subject to which the whole ideal content is referred" and "the grammatical subject" (1958, 22), as part of his dismissal of the standard subject-predicate analysis of judgment. Ramsey was concerned to deny the Frege-Russell analysis in terms of "things" of logically different "types" leading to the recognition of universals (Russell) or Fregean concepts.

Bradley's claim that Reality is the ultimate subject of all judgments—"In every judgment the genuine subject is reality ...." (1897, 148)—has a correlate in Frege's view. As Frege held that propositions denoted one of two truth values, Bradley took Reality, or the Absolute, to either reject or accept complex concepts. Thus, where Frege took there to be one relation between propositions and truth values, denotation, with two truth values as denoted objects, Bradley took one ultimate entity, Reality, to be related in one of two ways to a judgment content. It accepts the latter—"connects the ideal suggestion with itself"—or rejects it—"expels it" (1958, 33). Thus both Bradley and Frege recognized, in their ways, the same kind of duality that would appear later in Russell's and Wittgenstein's talk of positive and negative facts and of facts being related in two ways to atomic statements—as propositions would be "made true" or "made false" by facts.

Taking subject-predicate judgments as ascriptions of a complex concept to Reality, and thereby rejecting individual concepts in thought, is related to the classical metaphysical view that particulars are really complexes of properties. As one does not have, even cannot have, an "idea" of a basic particular, a unique subject of properties, to claim that there are basic particulars is unintelligible. Particulars are really composites or bundles of properties. In implicitly advocating both themes, Bradley does not clearly distinguish between a particular object being a complex of properties and it being a complex property. This aids his argument that there is really only one subject of all judgments, since ordinary particular objects, really understood as complex concepts, are attributes of it. To avoid the obvious objection that he himself recognizes an ultimate substratum of such attributes, a kind of Absolute particular—Reality or the Absolute, Bradley held that it too was a complex of all concepts coherently attributable to it. Reality was a complex of all (coherently connected) concepts, not a substratum exemplifying attributes—that is why they are "parts" of it, not attributes exemplified by it. It is then the ultimate or Absolute complex concept or Idea, and Bradley's view was fittingly called Absolute Idealism (1897, Chaps. xiii-xv).

Reality, being composed of all concepts coherently attributable to it, could not be something that a judgment corresponded to or failed to correspond to. For Bradley, Reality is not something that is independent of the concepts attributed to it and which compose it. Rejecting any notion of a correspondence theory of truth, he adopted a coherence account of truth—"Truth is the predication of such content as, when predicated, is harmonious, and removes inconsistency and with it unrest." (1897, 145)—along with the idea that truth and falsity were matters of degree (1897, Chap. xxiv). In short, the more extensive the fit of the content of a judgment with the complex of concepts that it supposedly fit with, the greater was its degree of truth. Bradley seemed to envision the accumulation of concepts of judgment into an ever-growing coherent complex which, as the conceptual system expanded, approximated ever more closely to being Absolute Reality. Reality was simply the completed system of coherent concepts, each of which was contained in it. Thus the real subject of all judgments, Reality itself, and the ultimate predicate, the complete complex concept consisting of all concepts belonging to Reality, were one and the same. Bradley summed this up in his formula that the Absolute judgment was a judgment of identity: Reality is Reality. This supposedly allowed him to finally escape any connection with the problematic subject-predicate dichotomy, for the only truly unproblematic judgment was an identity, which was not a relation, since a relation required diverse terms, and thus did not involve a relational "predication." Moreover, in overcoming the dichotomy between subject and predicate one thus also overcame the dichotomies between Reality and Appearance and Truth and Reality, for Reality was composed of Appearances (experience) and judgments were complex concepts composing Reality. The accumulating of coherent concepts was thus seen as a road to the Absolute. The pattern, derived from Hegel, led Bradley to end *Appearance and Reality* by saying:

> And Reality is one Experience, self-pervading and superior to mere relations...in the end, the sole perfect realisation of spirit. ...But I will end with something not very different, something perhaps more exactly the essential message of Hegel. Outside of spirit there is not, and there

cannot be, any reality, and the more that anything is spiritual, so much the more is it veritably real. (1897, 489)

The same pattern would later be found in the American pragmatist (instrumentalist) John Dewey. In effect what he did was simply remove the Absolute as an ultimate goal and take the ever expanding, and progressive, "process of inquiry" itself to replace the Absolute. The process became the goal, as Inquiry, and the expanding coherent system of propositions that we were "warranted" to assert, replaced both Bradley's Absolute and the notion of "absolute truth." Dewey thus rejected the notion of a ground of truth that was independent of the procedures and hypotheses involved in the process of inquiry. The idea would eventually be expressed by later pragmatists in terms of the world not being separable from our "conceptual structures," "webs of belief," "ways of world making" and Wilfrid Sellars's "Peircean ideal" conceptual scheme. Given the linguistic turn, it is not surprising to find this put in terms of "linguistic frameworks" and our having to consider "what there is" in terms of and even as determined by such linguistic frameworks. Nelson Goodman puts the view in a dramatic way by using phrases like "ways of world making" and claiming that "The world indeed is the one most often taken as real; for reality in a world, like realism in a picture, is largely a matter of habit" (1978, 20). Goodman replies to objections concisely, while incidentally taking Dummett to have a similar view:

> To the ready protest that we might have total and permanent belief in a falsehood—that what is totally and permanently credible might not be true—perhaps the answer is that so long as the belief or credibility is indeed total and permanent, any divergence from the truth could never matter to us at all. ... if there is such divergence, so much the worse for truth: scrap it in favor of total and permanent credibility.... (1978, 124)

Bradley's Absolute could no more contain "negations" than Plato's realm of Forms could encompass a form of Non-Being. And, as in Plato, we did not have any real idea of "negation"—or not-being. Thus there was no correlate of Frege's logical function of negation or object denoted by false judgments—the False. The Absolute rejected concepts that did not sufficiently cohere with what It contained—and which, in that sense, were false.

(But that was a matter of "degree," as "truth" and "falsity" were always matters of "degree.") Moreover, in place of judging that Socrates was not wise, what one did was judge that Socrates had some attribute that was incompatible with wisdom. Bradley and Bosanquet thus sought to analyze negation in terms of incompatibility, as Plato has been taken to have attempted to analyze "Theaetetus is not flying" in terms of "Every attribute of Theaetetus is different from flying." Plato clearly recognized the forms of difference and sameness required in his purported analysis, but Bradley was not that clear about incompatibility. As Russell would later argue in the logical atomism lectures, in attacking a similar pattern advocated by R. Demos, "Φ is incompatible with F" is really understood in terms of "Nothing can be both Φ and F." Hence, incompatibility itself involved a "negative" concept. In Bradley's terms it was understood as the contradictory of coheres with, for as Plato had the two basic forms of difference and sameness, Bradley and Bosanquet took *coheres with* and *incompatible with* as basic and The Absolute's "rejection" or "acceptance" of a concept (judgment) to depend on such coherence or incompatibility.

One can of course construct standard logic using the truth function joint denial that Wittgenstein employs in the *Tractatus*. If one thinks in such terms, or in terms of alternate denial, then, of course, one does not need a sign for negation in the system. But Russell's argument would be that such truth functions are really negation functions. If one were to express Bradley's view in terms of something like joint denial, Russell's point would have to be that by employing the truth tables we appeal to both truth values with certain understood rules. It is common nowadays to read in logic books that the traditional laws of non-contradiction and excluded middle, as represented by "¬ (p & ¬ p)" and "p ∨ ¬ p," are merely tautologies among tautologies. In one sense this is true—all truth functional tautologies are tautologies in the same sense of "tautology"—but in another, fundamental, sense, it is not. For we specify such functions in terms of standard truth tables and employ two fundamental rules in doing so: (1) every line of a table lists one truth value under a sentential letter and (2) no line lists more than one truth value. (1) reflects the law of excluded middle and (2) the law of non-contradiction. Thus, the very truth tables used to specify the function of joint denial can be said to embody a concept of negation. If this is the way we understand Russell's point, it is clearly correct. Thus one need not argue that joint denial involves negation in that "neither p nor q" is simply another way of stating "not p and not q."

In their early realistic revolt against idealism, Russell and Moore had attacked Bradley's analysis of particulars as bundles of universal concepts. They saw this analysis as a cornerstone of idealism; a cornerstone laid by Berkeley, though Berkeley and Hume were nominalists who rejected both universal properties (concepts) and "abstract" ideas. What they saw was a simple line of development. If particulars were complexes of (universal) concepts and concepts were constituents of judgments, the road to idealism was open via the identification of concepts with "ideas." In early papers Moore and Russell argued that basic particulars must be acknowledged in an adequate metaphysics and that numerical diversity could not be reduced to conceptual difference. The latter theme reinforced the former. For, if a particular was a bundle of concepts, then two particulars, to differ or be two, must differ in a constituent concept. Thus they must differ conceptually. If, however, particulars could be conceptually the same, yet numerically diverse, they could not be construed as complexes of concepts. Hence, particulars could not be analyzed, in keeping with Bradley's idealistic analysis of judgment, as such complexes—and therefore not as complex concepts, characterizing Reality.

They also argued that concepts were not mind dependent "ideas" but "external" existents. This led them to hold that propositions, composed of concepts, were involved in judgments. Hence they recognized propositional entities, containing constituent concepts, as existing whether or not they were apprehended in judgment or thought. In this sense, they advocated a theme much like Frege's acceptance of objective propositions. In fact Russell clearly held, at times, to the existence of a self or mind as a constituent of the fact that Plato judges that Socrates is wise. And, though he questioned the existence of such a self in *The Problems of Philosophy*, it was not until 1918-19 that he clearly rejected the self as an object. His earlier view regarding a self was one of the targets of Wittgenstein's criticisms in the *Tractatus*, where Wittgenstein, in the manner of Hume, rejected a "substantial" self as an illusion. Russell would later follow Wittgenstein and adopt such a view, and, ultimately and ironically, he would reject basic particulars altogether in 1940 in *An Inquiry into Meaning and Truth* and again in 1948 in *Human Knowledge: Its Scope and Limits* (Hochberg, 2001b, 97-124). In his later books he would propose to analyze particulars in a way reminiscent of Bradley's analysis—as complexes of qualities that were themselves qualities (though they would not include relational properties linking them to all other such entities).

Bradley had argued that relations were incomprehensible (1897, Chapter iii). For, as in the case of Frege's worries about predication, a relation could neither be taken as being another term, since it would then require a further relation to connect it to its terms, nor taken as not being another term, for then it would not be recognized as something real. To recognize a relation as an entity required taking it, in Frege's terms, as an object, but then it would need to be related to its own terms by another relation. While Frege held that concepts were not objects, they could join with, and "saturate," so-called second level concepts. An example of a proposition involving second and first level concepts is that expressed by "There are lions." Here Frege took the second level concept to be "There is an x such that Φx" (there are Φs) and the completing first level concept to be *being a lion*. He took this to cause no problems since, in the resulting proposition, *being a lion* functioned as a concept occupying predicate place. This reflected another of Frege's important logical innovations. He took propositions like "Some lions are fierce" and "All lions are fierce" not to be adequately construed, in Aristotelian fashion, in terms of the concept lion being the subject and the concept fierce the predicate. Rather, the first proposition was taken to be an existentially quantified conjunction with being a lion as the concept in the antecedent conjunct and being fierce as the concept in the second conjunct. This sharply differentiated such a proposition from the universal proposition, which was construed as a universally quantified conditional statement. (Alternatively, the point can be put in terms of the distinction between statements of class membership and class inclusion—the existential statement taken in terms of two classes having a common member; the universal one in terms of one class being included in another. That distinction was clearly set out and emphasized by Frege.) First level concepts, in both cases, completed or saturated the second level concepts, "Some Φs are Ψs" and "All Φs are Ψs," while retaining their role as concepts.

Taking "predication" and all relations as incoherent, Bradley and Bosanquet construed relations in a traditional manner as monadic concepts. To take Socrates to be wiser than Plato was to take the concept of being wiser than Plato as one of Socrates' constituent concepts (Bosanquet, 1948, 105). This move was a key one in aiding their linking of "everything" to everything "else" in that relations are "internal." Since Socrates was diverse from every other "thing," for every such thing, x, there would be the concept, *diverse from* x, which was a constituent concept of Socrates. This meant that everything was, in some sense, a constituent of Socrates. To put it another way, if one had a complete representation of all the concepts that composed Socrates one would have a representation of the Absolute itself—a representation of all of Reality. Treating relations as monadic concepts that were constituents of terms was thus a crucial move of the Absolute idealists. Russell's account of relational predication, in the manner of Frege, as involving a logically different form from monadic predication, thus became another part of his attack on Absolute Idealism. But this required his giving an adequate account of the predication relation.

Suppose, analogous to Frege's treatment of propositions, one takes the object and the attribute in a fact to be "joined," not by an exemplification relation, but by the attribute's being unsaturated or incomplete. To Bradley that would merely be a metaphorical attempt to dodge the problem and its being so is revealed by giving the attribute a two-fold role to play "in" the fact. For Bradley no resolution of the problem is possible. Bradley took the regress that Frege noted and sought to avoid to be inescapable and to show the incoherence of the appeal to subject-predicate "facts." Russell responded with a reply that has become classic and repeated in different words by diverse philosophers throughout the twentieth century. At places he acknowledged that the first step of the purported regress was viable in that a monadic property can be construed in terms of a connecting relation linking it to an object. But such a relation did not require a further relation, in turn, to relate it to its terms, since no relation required such a further relation (1956, 100). The regress stopped with the introduction of the first exemplification relation. This meant that relations not only differed from monadic properties in that they required more than one subject, but also in that relational facts did not involve an instantiation relation—a further connecting relation. Russell's basic theme was adopted by W. E. Johnson in the 1920s, Strawson, Bergmann and others, in the 1950s, in a slight variant that held that only "ordinary" relations, like *wiser than*, require an instantiation connection, or tie, or nexus, etc. But such "ties" do not, in turn, require to be tied to what they tie together. To Bradley this would merely stop the regress by fiat, without making comprehensible how a fact is composed. And on this matter Bradley appears to be right, for it is not an answer to say that Bradley has shown us that we must assume that the instantiation connection(s) are of a different logical kind from ordinary relations and require no further tie. One can just as easily say, with Frege, that concepts provide their own connection or, with Russell, that all relations do so. [In *Principles of Mathematics* Russell held that the sentence "Socrates is human" could be interpreted in two ways. One, in Fregean fashion, involved only Socrates and the concept *is human*; the other involved Socrates and *humanity* connected by a predicative relation (1956, 77-78).] But to say that Bradley is not answered by introducing a "tie" does not mean that Bradley's purported "paradox" is genuinely paradoxical.

1e. Russell's Analysis of Definite Descriptions

Russell's "theory of descriptions" has been one of the most well known and widely discussed topics in analytic philosophy since it was set forth in 1905. Russell's analysis was, in part, directed at Meinong, as well as at Frege, and possibly, even likely, influenced by Bradley's construal of purported subject-predicate judgments as existential judgments. Russell took statements like "The author of *Waverley* is a Scot" not to be simple subject-predicate statements but as existential conjunctions used to assert that someone authored *Waverley*; only one individual authored *Waverley*; and that individual is a Scot. He held that what is, in ordinary language, a "grammatically" subject-predicate sentence, with a descriptive phrase as the subject expression, should be construed, in a logically proper language—one that revealed the "logical form" of statements, as opposed to relying on their grammatical form—as a complex existential statement. In first-order logic we can represent Russell's analysis by an existentially quantified statement with three conjunctive components, employing "Ax" to transcribe "x authored *Waverley*" and "Sx" for "x is a Scot" as follows:

$(\exists x)[Ax \ \& \ (y)(A y \equiv y = x) \ \& \ Sx]$.

[Russell actually employed the logically equivalent formulation "$(\exists x)(y)((Ay \equiv y = x)$ & $Sx)$."] He used the so-called "iota operator" to transcribe definite descriptive phrases such as "the Φ" as "$(\iota x)(\Phi x)$" and took the latter to be contextually defined in two contexts:

(a) $\Psi(\iota x)(\Phi x) =_{df} (\exists x)[\Phi x$ & $(y)(\Phi y \equiv y = x)$ & $\Psi x]$

(b) E! $(\iota x)(\Phi x) =_{df} (\exists x)[\Phi x$ & $(y)(\Phi y \equiv y = x)]$,

using the three part conjunctive transcription in (a), rather than Russell's own formulation. In (b) the sign "E!" does not occur as a predicate, and where "s" is a proper name (constant), the formulation "E!s" is not a well-formed formula, but a meaningless string of signs. "E!" occurs only with contextually defined signs, like "$(\iota x)(\Phi x)$" and class expressions in *Principia Mathematica*, to express an existential quantification in a briefer form. The simple point is that ordinary English definite descriptive phrases, perspicuously construed in a logically correct schema, will be coordinated to contextually defined expressions that occur in contexts that, when expanded, are existential quantifications. The important point is that such definite descriptive phrases "disappear" upon "analysis." Hence, one need not raise questions about what they "mean" or what they "denote" in order to employ them, whether there is or is not anything that is described (denoted). This avoids Fregean senses and Meinong's non-existent objects, while speaking "about" what "is not"—what does not exist.

One consequence of Russell's analysis is that given a negated sentence like "The king of France in 1905 is not bald," there is an ambiguity in its rendering. For one can construe "$\neg \Psi (\iota x)(\Phi x)$" either as "$(\exists x)[\Phi x$ & $(y)(\Phi y \equiv y = x)$ & $\neg \Psi x]$" or as "$\neg (\exists x)[\Phi x$ & $(y)(\Phi y \equiv y = x)$ & $\Psi x]$," where, in the present example, the first rendition yields a false statement and the second a true one. This led to Russell's distinguishing between the "primary scope" of a description, as exhibited in the first rendition, and the use of "secondary scope," as in the second, and employing a special device to indicate the intended scope. It is simply a matter of the scope of the existential quantifier, and, in the extensional contexts of *Principia Mathematica*, where the description is fulfilled the two renditions turn out to be equivalent, unlike in the present case, where we have an unfulfilled description.

1f. Meinong's Pure Objects of Thought: The Turn to Intentionality

Meinong's views have become widely known in the last decade of the twentieth century, and the Russell-Meinong "controversy" widely discussed. His analyses of thought and judgment, purportedly involving the recognition of non-existent objects (both possible and impossible objects), such as the notorious Golden Mountain and the even more odd, to some, round square, have become the butt of dismissive comments by many. Meinong's philosophy is complex, especially given his parallel work in act-psychology (he founded the second psychological laboratory on the European continent at the University of Graz in Austria). Here I will confine the discussion by briefly stating two basic themes of Meinong's accounts of reference and intentionality (1907, 1960, 1983) that are especially relevant to the development of the linguistic turn.

There is, we all know, no golden mountain, to use the example Meinong borrowed from Hume. Yet one can judge or consider the proposition expressed by the sentence "The golden mountain is golden." On the surface it appears to be trivially true, just as the judgment that the golden mountain is silver would be trivially false. To Meinong this meant that even though the golden mountain did not exist, there was an object "of thought," an intentional object, the golden mountain. There was also an intentional objective, the golden mountain being golden, of the thought, just as there is an assumed objective for the thought that Socrates is wiser than Plato, whether he is or is not. He thus recognized, in some sense, a *non-existent* object that was intended as well as a *non-subsistent objective*, a kind of entity, that judgments were directed at or intended as opposed to objects that denoting phrases represented. Denoted objects existed or did not; objectives of judgments subsisted or did not. What Meinong stressed was the independence of the object of thought, what was "assumed" in thought, from the psychological act of thought. In this vein he saw Frege as initiating the "theory of assumptions."

If there should ever be a history of the theory of assumptions ... then a sentence from Frege's paper on function and concept ... will probably deserve to stand at the head of it. Let us reproduce the sentence word for word here:

"This separation of the judging from that concerning which one judges appears indispensable; for otherwise we could not express a mere assumption—the putting of a case without any simultaneous judgment as to its arisal." (1983, 284)

The objects to which one attributed or denied existence, the golden mountain, Pegasus and Socrates, whether existent or not, were subjects of such judgments of existence and, as such, independent of such "ways of being." This he spoke of them as—*Aussersein*—pure objects of judgment. His notion of *Aussersein* applied not only to possible, but non-existent objects, but also to impossible objects, like the round square. As the golden mountain can truly be judged to be golden, the round square can truly be judged to be round and to be square.

In early papers (1973a, 1973b, 1973c) Russell argued that Meinong's theory was inconsistent in that the analysis offered entailed contradictions: both obvious and trivial contradictions, like "The round square is round and the round square is square," and more fundamental contradictions involving concepts like *existence*: "The existent golden mountain is non-existent & the existent golden mountain is existent." Defenders of Meinong have since rejected Russell's claims of inconsistency as involving too simple a view of Meinong's theory. One attempt to rebut Russell's attack focuses on the distinction between "narrow" and "wide" negation— and judgments involving negative concepts, like not-round, as opposed to judgments involving negative propositions, such as the proposition expressed by the sentence "It is not the case that Socrates is wise." The idea behind the distinction is that a contradiction results only if the theory entails:

(i) The round square is round

and

(ii) Not-the round square is round.

Such a contradiction supposedly does not arise even if we construe "being square" as entailing "being not-round," since we can only derive (i) and

(iii) The round square is not-round.

But (iii) purportedly does not contradict (i), as (ii) does. The basic problem of all such views is the introduction of a notion of negation that is not the standard notion in the sense that it is not a truth-functional concept.

Suppose one takes the pair of predicates "is Φ" and "is not-Φ" to indicate two properties or concepts that are the "negations" of each other. If one then distinguishes "It is not the case that x is Φ" from "x is not-Φ," it is not at all clear in what sense the predicate "is not-Φ" represents a property that is a negative property—the negation of Φ. It does not help to say that "x is not-Φ" and "not-x is Φ" are "equivalent" when x exists, but not when x does not exist. For it is still not clear in what sense negation is involved in the latter case. Nor does it help to say that the concept of existence, as well as of negation, can have a double role that allows "The existent golden mountain does not exist" to be true along with "The existent golden mountain exists." For, aside from the obvious verbal juggling involved, one must make the same moves with modal concepts. Thus we face "The possible round square is a possible object and the possible round square is not a possible object," "The impossible possible golden mountain is impossible" and so forth. Of course one can construct "formal" systems with rules that avoid contradictions or even make contradictions tolerable in a sense (by adjusting the logical rules so that they do not allow for the derivation of every proposition from a contradiction, for example), but the philosophical point is lost in the myopic focus on the formal game. One also loses the import of what appears to be the guiding ontological principle of Meinong's theory: what is thinkable *is*, in some sense of "is" that is not a mere synonym for "can be thought of." This means that "is thinkable" is construed as being a characteristic, and for such a characteristic to be truly instanced requires an instantiating subject or term. Such a principle cannot simply be pronounced. If it is taken to be basic, there is no further argument to be offered. Russell can then be seen as challenging such a principle by proposing alternative analyses of thought and reference.

Consider the general claim:

(I) If and only if an object exists, the assertion that it is not-Φ is equivalent to the assertion that it is not the case that it is Φ.

That is sometimes offered in Meinong's defense. But it will not do for all the cases involved, since, by what is called "Meinong's *Sosein* (so-being or being such and so) Principle," objects of thought, irrespective of whether they exist or not, are such that: for any concept F the statement "The object that is both F and G is F" is true (1983, 61-62). Moreover, taking that principle together with Meinong's principle of the "non-limitation of Assumption"—a principle that places no limitations on what can be an object of thought, be "assumed" in thought, and thus allows inconsistent objects—it follows that "The existent round square exists" is true. Yet, of course, there is no such thing, and (I) does not remove the problem. Meinong's distinction between *so-being* and *being* is then developed to distinguish, in the tradition of Aquinas' and Kant's separating existence from characterizing properties of objects, between so-called "nuclear" concepts, like golden, and non-nuclear concepts, like existence. And, to avoid Russell's problem, one is led to insist that "exists" cannot occur within expressions describing objects, like "the existent golden mountain," as it is not that kind of predicable—existence is not a constitutive (nuclear) property or concept, as being golden is. [There are questions among scholars as to whether Meinong was influenced by his student E. Mally or whether the influence went in the other direction, regarding the independence of so-being from being (Mally, 1904).]

Meinong's focus on definite descriptions of non-existent objects is connected to a more general concern of his—the attempt to analyze judgments like "A high mountain is an obstacle" and "The mountain is high" by answering the question: How does one construe these as subject-predicate judgments taking "a mountain" and "the mountain" as subject terms? The problem he raised is more obvious in the case of the indefinite description. For what is the subject one is judging about that is indicated by the phrase "a mountain"? This led Meinong to hold that when one used the indefinite article in such a context the subject was an "incomplete object." Being such an incomplete object meant that it could not be said to be either brown or not-brown, rocky or not-rocky, etc., though it could truly be said to be a mountain (1907, 121; 1915, 171-73). His view was put forth in opposition to the imagist construal of thought of the British Empiricists as well as the Humean view, defended by H. Cornelius, that the mind creates general ideas by acts of comparison involving similarity (1914, 465-75). Recall Berkeley ridiculing the idea that one could think of "a triangle" without thinking of it as being of a definite kind (isosceles, scalene or equilateral), of a horse that was not of a particular color, etc. Meinong's way of thinking of an incomplete object took it as a pure object where existence or non-existence was not relevant to its role as an object of thought. A triangle, as an incomplete object, and hence as not determinate with respect to properties like scalene, could not be taken to exist but could be apprehended in thought.

If Meinong is construed as holding that the golden mountain is golden, since golden is a constituent concept (property) of the complex concept golden mountain, his *Sosein* principle then preserves the apparent trivial truth that the golden mountain is golden by changing what it appears to state or by taking the non-existent object as a certain complex of concepts. Alternatively it can be seen as changing the assertion to the generality that any object that is both golden and a mountain is golden. Either way of putting the matter is something critics of Meinong can put up with. Moreover, one can preserve the crucial ideas behind Russell's theory of descriptions and yet abandon his familiar transcriptions of the relevant ordinary language sentences. For one can take what Meinong is getting at to be captured by rendering "The golden mountain is golden" as "Anything that is a golden mountain is golden." And this is trivially true whether there are golden mountains or not. Alternatively, one can demystify Meinong a bit by recognizing that to say that "The golden mountain is golden" is true is simply a way of saying that being golden is a constituent concept of the complex concept being a golden mountain. One simply preserves the apparent trivial truth that the golden mountain is golden by not really predicating "being golden" of any subject, existent or not, but by relating concepts. Either triviality is acceptable.

What is really at issue between Russell and Meinong, as we will see it will be an issue between Russell and his critic P. Strawson half a century later, is Russell's taking "The golden mountain is golden" to be logically equivalent to "The golden mountain exists." It was just claimed above that we could preserve the philosophical ideas behind Russell's theory of descriptions and yet alter his standard transcriptions of the ordinary language sentences. For, in place of taking the ordinary language subject-predicate sentence (o) "The golden mountain is golden" to be an existential claim in Russell's fashion, we can construe it in terms of the generality (o*) "Anything that is identical with the golden mountain is golden." One can do this while treating the descriptive phrase in (o*) along Russell's lines. To put the above suggested transcription in Russell's symbolism, with "G" for "is golden," "M" for "is a mountain" and "(ι y)(Gy & My)" for "the golden mountain," we have "(x)[x=(ι y)(Gy & My) $\supset$ Gx]" stating that anything that is identical with the golden mountain is golden. Then, as earlier noted, the sentence "The golden mountain is golden" is true, whether there is such a thing or not. However, "The golden mountain is non-golden" is then also true. That does not fit, though "The golden-non-golden mountain is both golden and non-golden," and many other claims that lead to a Meinongian type view are also true. They lead to such a view, since they are taken to be obviously true, and Meinong's view provides a way of holding that they are so. But, to a certain extent, that can also be done, on Russell's analysis, without a problematic dual construal of negation.

The distinction between nuclear and non-nuclear properties is really a way of admitting that *existence* (being) is not a property among properties. Yet to accommodate certain thoughts and the freedom of assumption, it should be a property (concept). Hence, a categorial distinction among properties is introduced. The problematic nature of the treatment of *being* is clearly seen when Meinong distinguishes between the pure object and its objective of being (non-being)—that the golden mountain exists—as the latter has the pure object as a constituent, but no other constituent. For Meinong denies that *being* (whether existence, subsistence, or *Aussersein*) is a constituent of such an objective. It is as if there is the object as pure object and the objective of being. Then the object, as existent, is identified with the subsistence of the objective of being, while the object, as non-existent, is identified with the non-subsistence of the objective of being or with the subsistence of the objective of non-being. Though it is a matter of some controversy among those who write about Meinong as to whether his "objectives" are facts or things and whether they are simple or complex (Tegtmeier, 2000), I avoid such matters here and simply take them as correlates of Wittgenstein's states of affairs. It is worth noting that Meinong commented on his not being influenced by Bolzano's notion of a "Satz an sich" (sentence— proposition—as such) or by Stumpf's "states of affairs" (1983, 74). However one works out the terminology, given the ontological complications Meinong is forced into, we may conclude that Russell made his point.

1g. Predicates, Propositional Functions and Properties

In a recent book on Russell, the author casually, but incoherently, claims that any relation R can be reduced to a monadic property since any dyadic relational predication, as in "aRb" for example, can be construed in terms of one term, say a in this case, having a monadic property—standing in R to b (Griffin, 1991, 324). This resurrects a familiar them from Bosanquet and Bradley. Even if we ignore the obvious problems posed by the facts that monadic first order logic is decidable, while an extension with relational predicates is not, and that the dyadic predicate "R" occurs in the supposedly monadic predicate expression "standing in R to b," there remains a fundamental philosophical problem. All we need note is that treating dyadic relations in terms of monadic predicates involves replacing relations by functions of two distinct kinds—which amounts to construing functions, *qua* monadic functions, as being of two fundamentally different kinds. It will help to see the point if we use the standard lambda notation associated with what is called the "Lambda Calculus" to form predicate expressions from sentential contexts. Thus, given sentences like "aRb" we form "$(\lambda x)xRb$," for the purported function or "property" of having (standing in) R to b. Likewise, we can use either "$(\lambda y)(\lambda x)xRy$" or "$(\lambda x, y)xRy$" to express the two-term function or relation, in place of simply using "R." One reason for using this latter device to represent relations stems from wishing to distinguish what some speak of as an "open" sentence, "xRy," with free variables, from a sign for the relation itself. This reveals an implicit Fregean way of thinking—that predicates, both monadic and relational, are "incomplete" symbols and are more perspicuously represented by signs containing individual variables—as "$(\lambda x)Fx$" and "$(\lambda x, y)xRy$" and "Fx" and "xRy" all do. But it is awkward to allow signs like "Fx" and "xRy" to occupy subject place and write "Fx=Fx" or "xRy=xRy," which Frege did not allow. Hence one introduces a lambda "abstract"—a sign like "$(\lambda x)Fx$"—to represent the property or function. Russell"s early form of this device was to put a cap, "^," over the free variable.

What is then easily seen is, first, that one uses functions that take facts (or propositions or truth values) as values, given a term (or even a Fregean "sense") as argument. Second, one must employ functions that take other functions as values given a term as argument. Thus one arrives at a "fact" (or proposition or truth value)—a being an instance of $(\lambda x)xRb$—involving the monadic function or "property," by recognizing monadic functions of basically different kinds. But it makes no sense to think of one kind as being a monadic property, if one employs a function like $(\lambda y)((\lambda x)xRy)$, with b as the argument for the function, to obtain the further function $(\lambda x)xRb$ as value. The function $(\lambda y)((\lambda x)xRy)$ is clearly not a property instantiated by b, since its value, $(\lambda x)xRb$, is a function, not a fact. There is no fact represented, and to say "b instantiates $(\lambda y)((\lambda x)xRy)$" is to utter nonsense. However, the function $(\lambda x)xRb$ does have a fact, that a stands in R to b (or a proposition, or, even, a truth value) as a value, with a as argument. The difference illustrates that such lambda abstracts are not viable predicates representing monadic properties, since their combining with a subject term sometimes results in a sign for a function and sometimes a sign "representing" or expressing a fact, proposition or truth value.

Thinking of truth values as values of a function obscures a basic point. If one thinks in terms of facts, one easily sees that the function cannot be a constituent of the value, the fact, and also be what maps an argument onto such a value. The relevant constituent of a fact is a property or relation, while what maps a term onto a fact is a function. There is another blatant misconception involved in the procedure. One supposedly starts out with a relational predicate "R" representing a relation that is purportedly to be "reduced." Yet, as noted earlier, one uses, and must use, the predicate "R" all along in the function abstract signs employed in the purported reduction. An obvious question arises: What does "R" represent as used in "$(\lambda y)((\lambda x)xRy)$," "$(\lambda x)xRb$," "$(\lambda y)((\lambda x)xRy)b$," and, finally, in "aRb," the sentence ultimately arrived at by "lambda conversion"? The question makes it clear that to speak of reducing relations (or dyadic predicates) to monadic properties (predicates), via lambda abstracts, makes no philosophical (or common) sense. But that does not show that there are no relational properties, and some logician-philosophers seem to think there are such properties, since they can form monadic predicate abstracts, like "$(\lambda x)x=a$" and "$(\lambda x)xRb$," whose "extensions" differ from those of the dyadic abstracts "(λx, y)x=y" and "(λx, y)xRy."

If one recognizes properties represented by such abstracts, one has no reason to deny that abstracts like "(λy, x)(Fx & Gy)" represent relations, which is obviously wrong. There are further problematic consequences. Suppose there is a property represented by "(λx)x=a": the property of "being a." Then we have, by the same procedure, the property of being the property of being a, and so on *ad infinitum*. Thus, one generates an infinite hierarchy of properties, which is reminiscent of the hierarchy of Fregean senses that, we will see, Russell rightly found problematic. It is also absurd to take the fact that a has the property of standing in R to b to be distinct from the fact that a stands in the relation R to b. Moreover, one who insists on the difference should also hold that a's having the relational property of standing in R to a (itself) is distinct from a standing in the relation R to itself. But if we allow for monadic relational properties, we must allow for the formation of abstracts like (λx)xRx to represent the latter monadic property. This points to two mistakes. The first is not to realize that patterns like "xRx" are simply special cases of "xRy." Not to realize this can lead one to hold that, in addition to a relation like *is prior to*, there are the monadic properties of being self-prior and *being prior to* a. "Being self-identical" is an easier phrase to digest than are "being self-left-of" or "being self-prior-to," but the same absurdity is present in all cases—for it is not a question of the truth value of sentences, like "a = a" and "a is to the left of a," but of the sense of purported monadic predicate expressions "extracted" from such sentences. The second mistake is more interesting.

Those who accept relational properties may do so because they fail to distinguish between properties and relations, on the one hand, and propositional functions on the other. Russell clearly and explicitly distinguished the two in 1925, though he had earlier sometimes blurred the distinction and continued to do so at places. Monadic relational properties, if they are anything at all, are functions, not properties. Whether we take functions to comprise a further category or treat them as classes or in terms of relations, the property F must be distinguished from the function (λx)Fx. The failure to do so can explain how one can think that the relation R can be replaced by the function

(λx, y)xRy, even though the latter obviously presupposes the relation R to begin with.

The distinction between propositional functions, on the one hand, and properties and relations, on the other, allows us to arrive at one simple resolution of the Bradley-Frege problem about predication (we will consider others later). Let Φx be the logical form of a monadic atomic fact. We can give Bradley his due, as Moore did long ago, by acknowledging that such a fact cannot be reduced to the items involved in its "analysis." The supposed problem is that where we have a and F in the form Φx, we are forced to recognize that we really have a further fact analyzed in terms of a, F and Φx instantiating a further triadic form that would be the form of the fact that consists of F and a standing in the relation (tie, nexus) Φx. One then holds that that further fact must be construed in terms of yet another fact with four terms, etc. Thus we never arrive at the structure of the fact that is the truth ground of "Fa."

If we distinguish the form of the fact Fa, the form Φx, from the function ($\lambda\Phi$, x) Φx, where the latter, for the arguments F and a, has, as value, the fact Fa, we can recognize a further function that yields the same fact as value, for three arguments—the function ($\lambda\Phi$, x) Φx, the property F and the object a. But there is no further fact, or more complex form of a fact, involved. Distinguishing functions from forms of facts provides one way to block the Bradley regress. One can generate an unending series of functions, if one recognizes such functions as entities and takes them as arguments for further functions. But they all have the same value—the fact that a is F. There is no regress, just a useless series of increasingly complex linguistic patterns. What is crucial is to keep functions distinct from logical forms and properties—F from the propositional function (λx)Fx, which the Fregean pattern for writing predicates, using "Fx" in place of "F," that has been adopted by Quine and others, invites us to confuse. Even Russell, in 1924, expressed an extreme variant of that pattern:

> Attributes and relations, though they may not be susceptible of analysis, differ from substances by the fact that they suggest a structure, and that there can be no significant symbol which symbolizes them in isolation. All propositions in which an attribute or a relation *seems* to be the subject are only significant if they can be brought into a form in which the

attribute is attributed or the relation relates. If this were not the case, there would be significant propositions in which an attribute or a relation would occupy a position appropriate to a substance, which would be contrary to the doctrine of types, and would produce contradictions. (1956e, 337-38)

Like the other abstracts we have considered, $(\lambda x)(\exists y)(x=y)$ is a function, and not a monadic property of existence. If one introduces such a function, then one can allow for descriptions, like "the existent golden mountain," employing such a "predicate," as well as sentences like "The existent golden mountain is golden" and "The existent golden mountain exists," which will simply be false on Russell's standard treatment of them. Russell can allow for a sense in which "exists" is a predicate, but that does not mean that *existence* is taken as a property. In fact, without any *ad hoc* additions, we arrive at a viable distinction between nuclear and non-nuclear predicates, but not properties, and we can viably remove the predicate "existent" from Meinong's relevant "nucleus"—the description "the existent golden mountain." For, "The existent golden mountain exists" reduces to "The golden mountain exists" on Russell's analysis. We even get two negations, one true and one false: "$\neg$ E! (ι w)(Gw & Mw & $(\lambda x)((\exists y)(x=y))$w)" and "E! ($\iota$ w)(Gw & Mw & $\neg$ $(\lambda x)((\exists y)(x=y))$w)." In a sense, then, Russell can accommodate Meinong's golden mountain and have his theory of descriptions too.

1h. Reincarnating Meinong: Searle's Intentional Speech Acts

J. Searle, following J. L. Austin (1961, 220-239), promulgated what is known as the theory of speech acts. The theory emphasizes the role of language in communication and the intentions of speakers to communicate via performing various kinds of "speech acts" in diverse social settings. But it also amounts to a detailed development of a simple, and long familiar, observation from the medieval period to Frege, Bradley and Meinong. One notes that the same "content" can be asserted, denied, doubted, "assumed," etc. Thus, we can distinguish the "locutionary" aspect (Socrates is wise) from the "illocutionary" force (I doubt that ...) of a given "speech act." One can also note that certain utterances on certain occasions (saying "I do" at an appropriate moment during one's wedding) have a certain "performative" role that has to be taken into account in any discussion of "meaning." While speech act theory was in vogue for a time among philosophers of language, it now appears to be mostly of interest to academics in departments of rhetoric, literature and linguistics. Here I will simply focus on recent attempts by Searle to apply ideas from speech act theory to the problems raised by reference, truth, intentionality and meaning in the context of dealing with the intentional or "attitudinal" verbs—believes that, thinks that, etc. Searle sees Meinong and, apparently, most philosophers as being confused by the distinction between "intention-with-a-t" and "intension-with-an-s." This, he claims, leads them to mistake properties of reports (in sentences expressing intensional contexts, such as "John believes that ....") for properties of things reported (objects of intentional states—what is believed, such as, that King Arthur killed Sir Lancelot), in discussions of intentionality. For reports may be "intensional" while what is reported is "extensional." Thus, speaking about John's belief that King Arthur killed Sir Lancelot, he says: "It is completely extensional: it is true iff there is a unique x such that x=King Arthur, and there is a unique y such that y=Sir Lancelot, and x killed y. That is as extensional as anything can get" (1983, 24). But the claim that the belief, as opposed to the report of the belief, is completely extensional merely means that one gives the "truth condition" for the belief, by giving the truth condition for the sentence "King Arthur killed Sir Lancelot." Put simply, the sentence "King Arthur killed Sir Lancelot" does not raise the familiar issues about substitution raised by "John believes that King Arthur killed Sir Lancelot." This is true, but it is also an utterly trivial observation, and Searle's analysis of intentional contexts that lies behind it fails to adequately take up, let alone resolve, the issues.

One problem with Searle's analysis concerns his implicit appeal to propositional entities, for there is John's belief and Mary's belief and Henry's belief, but what they share or have in common is *the* belief. But what is the belief as a common feature of various individual intentional states? Searle's symbolic representation of an intentional state as "Believe (It is raining)" raises questions about the representational roles of both the parenthetical sentence and the juxtaposition of it and the term "Believe." That term represents what Searle calls a "mode," which plays the role of a generic universal property, distinguishing cases of belief from cases of doubt, imagining, etc. When Searle says that a state is composed of a content and a mode (derived from the earlier speech-act notions of "locutionary" and "illocutionary"), he is really talking of a kind of state, and not of John's particular state. But he tends to blur the distinction between the two. This leads him to think that "the" ontological issue is about what particular intentional states are—brain states, mental acts, dispositions—and that that issue can be resolved if particular mental states are taken to be states of the brain. This leads him to take the complex expression "Believe (It is raining)" to represent a complex property of such particular intentional states, individual states of belief—John's belief state as opposed to Mary's—and have the content expressed by "It is raining." Shying away from such ontological issues as the problem of universals, Searle does not put matters in such a straightforward way, but that is what his view involves.

In speaking as he does, Searle recognizes content properties or propositions, as common properties or kinds of states that are realized in individual brains. Different individuals have diverse intentional states with the same content, and hence such particular states are of a kind. When Searle speaks of an intentional state being realized, he thus speaks of such a common property of something, as one may say that a particular realizes a property by being an instance of it. The particulars, for Searle, are the brains that intentional states, as common properties, are "realized" in. He also claims that a belief is intrinsically or internally a representation of its conditions of satisfaction and that the content of a belief is intrinsic to the belief. One reason he speaks of an intrinsic connection is to avoid a regress that would result from introducing an act, state or agent to make the connection between a belief and its truth conditions. But Searle fails to provide an explication of his uses of "intrinsic" and "internal." One reason for this failure is that he uses "intrinsic" ("internal") in a three-fold way in speaking of the connection between a content and its conditions and of that between a content and an intentional state. In one sense a content (property) expressed by "It is raining" is intrinsic to the intentional state of belief, taken as a kind of state—a belief that it is raining. This is the sense in which the property of being-golden may be said to be intrinsic to the property of being-a-golden mountain. In a second sense the content property is intrinsic to a particular brain state in that the particular state is an instance of the property (kind) or a "realization" of it. In a third sense, a content is said to be intrinsically connected to the "conditions of satisfaction" it is "directed at." Searle's ambiguous use of "intrinsic" reflects his ambiguous use of "intentional state."

Searle sometimes takes an intentional state to be a particular state, John's for example; at other times he takes it as the kind of state that is realized (in John's brain). Following Searle's use of single letters to embody distinctions, I will refer to the kind of state as an "Intentional-with-a-capital-I-state" and to an instance of the kind as an "intentional-with-a-small-i-state." Searle not only blurs the distinction between particular states and kinds of states, but between corresponding diverse senses of "intrinsic" that he employs, for he shifts from talking of "intrinsic" in the sense of a content's being intrinsic to an intentional state to speaking of "intrinsic" in the sense of a content's connection to its condition(s) of satisfaction. Such shifts fail to hide his implicit appeal to non-obtaining states of affairs, disguised as extensional "conditions of satisfaction" or "truth conditions." His terminology may be responsible for his not noting that he does not resolve the basic problems of intentionality he discusses: (1) What do false beliefs represent, if one characterizes intentional states in terms of their representational connection to conditions of satisfaction? (2) Are there propositions or content properties that are the basis for individual mental (physiological, behavioral, etc.) states having the content they have? (3) What is the connection (relation) between contents (propositions, content properties, etc.) and their conditions of satisfaction (truth conditions, objects, etc.)? He thinks that since a condition of satisfaction is "extensional"—its existence or non-existence furnishes a condition of truth (for a belief's being true or false) or reference (for a purported referential "speech act" succeeding or failing). Thus a belief state, which is "intentional," may or may not represent an existent object or condition, but, since it is "intentional," it represents whether or not what it represents, its "extension," exists. But how does an intentional state manage to be a term of a representation relation when the other term does not exist? According to Searle, the answer is simple: that is what intentional states do—that is why they are intentional (with a "t")! That is all there is to it.

Searle's talk of intentional states of persons and of an intentional relation treats such states as terms of such a relation. But in virtue of what do intentional-with-a-capital-I states have a declared "internal" or intrinsic connection to their conditions of satisfaction? Distinct intentional-with-a-small-i states that are the same kind of intentional-with-a-capital-I state have the same conditions of satisfaction in virtue of being of that kind. Searle must therefore connect, extrinsically or intrinsically, a mental state that is an instance of such a content property and embodies an intentional mode to an appropriate truth ground or condition of satisfaction. He purports to do this in virtue of its "realizing" an appropriate content property or "proposition." But, then, we are back to the problem posed by the representation of a condition by a content or proposition, irrespective of whether such a condition obtains (exists) or not, as well as to a question about the nature of the connection between the content and the condition. To simply reply that there is an "internal" or "intrinsic" connection between intentional states and conditions of satisfaction will hardly do. But that is all Searle does. He labels, but never accounts for, the purported connection. Searle must take his intentional relation—x has as its conditions of satisfaction y—to obtain between a belief and its conditions, irrespective of whether the belief is true, or explain how a sentence of the form "xRy" is true when one term does not exist—how two terms stand in a relation, when there is only one term. He does neither.

Searle fails to deal with the problem Meinong raises. The reason is that he thinks the problem of recognizing Meinongian entities arises if one takes the representative content of an intentional state (with a-capital-I or a-small-i) to be what the intentional state is about (1983, 17). Of course such an intentional state is not about, i. e. it does not represent or intend, its content. Rather, it is about what it is about in virtue of the content it has. So Searle can conclude that an intentional state is about something, in the sense that it has a content, and not about something, if there is no intended object (no extension). But the problem is not what he takes it to be, and his solution is no solution. The problem is to account for a representative content being representative, and not merely to distinguish a content (proposition) from a condition (state of affairs), and to do so without having recourse to a Meinongian objective or a possible fact. As Moore once acknowledged a basic reference relation between beliefs and facts that was a formal or logical relation (1953, 267-68), Searle has a basic relation—x *has as conditions of satisfaction* y—that is a purported internal relation, between contents and their conditions. But he thinks his distinction between intentionality-with-a-t and intensionality-with-an-s allows him to avoid the representation of non-existent conditions of satisfaction. A false belief (belief content) does not represent anything since it involves intentionality-with-a-t. It can do so since that is what it is to be a case of intentionality-with-a-t, as opposed to intensionality-with-an-s. No more need be said, and nothing more is said. .

Searle raises the obvious question: "What kind of relation is named by 'Intentionality' anyhow and how can we explain Intentionality without using metaphors like 'directed'?" (1983, 4) He answers this question by telling us that the intentional connection is internal and is something we have "fairly clear intuitions about." But, clearly, this either recognizes a fundamental relation between what is intentional (propositions, intentional states, etc.) and what is intended—what "intentions" are "directed at"—(conditions, objects, etc.) or does not. To speak of such cases as involving intentionality-with-a-t and the intentional connection as intrinsic adds nothing. In fact, some things Searle writes suggest that he takes the intentional connection to simply be a relation that need not relate—i. e. to be a one-term relation in certain cases (reminiscent of the medieval notion of a "one-sided" relation indicating ontological dependence). Thus an intentional state manages to represent—even though it fails to relate.

Speaking of "representing truth conditions," of "features of the objects or states of affairs represented" and of "truth conditions" that do not "hold," Searle asserts that "Intentional states represent objects and states of affairs in the same sense of 'represent' that speech acts represent objects and states of affairs" (1983, 4). This paradoxically adopts a Meinongian view and fails to recognize the obvious questions that arise. In virtue of what does the "intentional content" represent its "truth condition"? How does it do that when the latter does not exist? It is possible that Searle fails to see that he does not dissolve Meinong's problem due to being overly impressed with his distinguishing the "ontological" and the "logical" problems of intentionality—something he claims his predecessors have failed to recognize. The ontological problem concerns what intentional, with a "t," states are and is resolved by taking intentional states to be "realized" in brains—to be brain states. The logical problem, Meinong's problem, is purportedly resolved by distinguishing between intentionality-with-a-t and intensionality-with-an-s and holding that beliefs (judgments, etc.) are intentional with a "t," while being both extensional, in that they have conditions of satisfaction, and intensional, in that sentential reports of belief states are not truth preserving in the familiar cases of substitution. But nothing has been resolved. We are left with: (a) propositions (contents) in the form of properties of brain states; (b) a problem about the representation of non-existent "conditions" of satisfaction by such properties and, derivatively, being "intended" by individual intentional states (brain states) that "realize" such properties.

CHAPTER 2

DESCRIBING AND DENOTING

2a. Russell's Critique of Frege

Russell's criticism of Frege, which he set out in his own analysis of definite descriptions in 1905, occurs in a puzzling passage of "On Denoting." The passage has occasioned much commentary and even some abuse. According to Searle (1968), Russell's discussion is obscure, unclear, confusing, slipshod, either superfluous or irrelevant to Frege's view, inconsistent, involves a misstatement of Frege's position that is "combined with a persistent confusion between the notions of occurring as a part of a proposition ... and being referred to by a proposition"(1968, 342), "nonsensical" and mistakenly states the negation of Frege's theory instead of Frege's theory (1968, 344). Rarely has a philosopher of Russell's undeniable stature been so ridiculously caricatured. Yet, it is ironic, as Searle simply doesn't grasp the lines of argument that he is so contemptuous of. Geach, a Russell scholar, surprisingly agreed (1970, 209-212) that Searle had demonstrated the irrelevance of Russell's criticism of Frege and explained that as the result of an excusable confusion, on Russell's part, of Frege's theory with Russell's own earlier views in *Principles of Mathematics*. According to Geach, Russell was not really arguing against Frege's view but was led to think that he was since "Russell, like Aristotle, so often distorts others' thought into his own mold..." (1970, 212). Geach, unwisely, advises the reader of "On Denoting" to ignore the use of Frege's name. To Church, Russell is merely confused about "use" and "mention" (1943, 302), while Carnap, politely and correctly, finds Russell obscure (1956, 140).

Though obscure at some crucial places, the text of Russell's paper shows quite clearly that he is arguing with Frege, given the explicit references to Frege and his characterization of Frege's distinction between "meaning" and "denotation":

> Frege distinguishes the two elements of meaning and denotation everywhere, and not only in complex denoting phrases. Thus it is the meanings of the constituents of a denoting complex that enter into its *meaning*, not their *denotation*. In the proposition "Mont Blanc is over 1, 000 meters high," it is, according to him, the meaning of "Mont Blanc," not the actual mountain, that is a constituent of the *meaning* of the proposition. (1956a, 46)

Here we can take "proposition" to be used as "sentence" and not as a term for what a sentence means or expresses. Another footnote reads:

> In this theory, we shall say that the denoting phrase *expresses* a meaning; and we shall say both of the phrase and the meaning that they *denote* a denotation. In the other theory, which I advocate, there is no *meaning*, and only sometimes a *denotation*. (1956a, 46)

This makes it obvious that Russell is considering the notions of meaning and denotation to be involved in Frege's discussion, and, I add, does so correctly. The suggestion that Russell is not really arguing against Frege's view is simply not plausible. He was not only clearly arguing against that view, but pointing to basic problems of it.

Russell focuses on a purportedly required connection between "the meaning" and "the denotation" of an expression, on a view which involves both:

> The relation of the meaning to the denotation involves certain rather curious difficulties, which seem in themselves sufficient to prove that the theory which leads to such difficulties must be wrong. (1956a, 48)

This specifies the target of his criticism, and he proceeds to note that a natural way of talking about the meaning of a denoting phrase is to put the phrase in inverted commas. This contrasts with our simply using the phrase itself to denote the denotation. Where the name "Fido" names the dog Fido, we simply use the name, as I just did, to speak of the dog. Thus he writes:

> (1) The first line of Gray's Elegy states a proposition.
> (2) 'The first line of Gray's Elegy' does not state a proposition.

What (2) says is that the meaning of the phrase ("the first line Gray's Elegy") does not state a proposition, for meanings of such phrases are not the sorts of things that state propositions. Here he uses "proposition" as what is expressed by a sentence and not in the sense of "sentence." His two-fold use was not only common in 1905, when one was not so conscious of linguistic distinctions, but still is. More important, the double use does not affect his discussion, for it is almost always clear which sense of the term is relevant.

While I am using double quotes to speak about a phrase, as we normally do, Russell, in (2), is using single quotes around a phrase to form an expression that denotes the meaning (sense) of the phrase, and he simply says, about that sense, that it does not state a proposition. This is not problematic. A problem does arise when Russell proceeds to write:

> Thus taking any denoting phrase, say C, we wish to consider the relation between C and 'C,' where the difference of the two is of the kind exemplified in the above two instances. (1956a, 49)

A reader is easily led to think that when Russell speaks of "the relation between C and 'C'" he is talking about the relation between a phrase and something else. But he is not doing that. Instead, he is raising the question about the relation between the denotation and the meaning of a phrase, any denoting phrase, for he uses the letter "C" as a variable denoting phrase—as any unspecified denoting phrase. Suppose we take the capitalized third letter of the English alphabet to *abbreviate* some denoting phrase. Then that letter *is* taken as the denoting phrase, in abbreviated form—it *does not* stand for the phrase. Thus,

> C = the denotation of "C"

is true, just as

the man in the iron mask = the denotation of the phrase "the man in the iron mask"

is true. Keep in mind that Russell has told us that putting inverted commas (single quotes) around a denoting phrase (as he does with the letter "C") forms an expression denoting the meaning (sense) of the letter, where the letter itself is taken *to be* an arbitrary denoting phrase. Thus, it is also true, using single quotes as Russell does, that:

'C' = the meaning of the denoting phrase "C" (the denoting phrase is the letter "C").

We can then understand what Russell is saying in the quotation just above. Moreover, since he is using the letter "C" as a variable and does not want to talk about the letter, but about any arbitrary denoting phrase, he cannot put quotes around the letter, which is a familiar way of forming an expression that is used to denote the letter itself. That is why I spoke of the letter itself as a variable denoting phrase. Part of the problem is precisely the kind of difficulty that led to Quine's use of corner quotation marks in *Mathematical Logic*—a device that allows one to have a sign for any arbitrary value of a variable, instead of having a sign that is commonly used to denote the variable itself. The sort of problem is clearly seen in the context of talking about a truth predicate and Tarski's familiar Convention-T. Where "p" is a standard sentential variable, and using double quotes, one cannot simply write

"p" is true if and only if p

to express what is involved. For to the left of the phrase "if and only if" we have a sign that denotes the letter, and thus we do not state what we want to state—the general pattern, of which

"Snow is white" is true if and only if snow is white

is an appropriate instance. We must resort to a more complicated device, as Tarski in fact did, or, to take another example, think of what is involved in using Gödel numbers.

The simplest way of putting Russell's statement, given his concerns in 1905, is the way he does put it. This need assume neither charity nor sympathy on the part of the reader—merely expending minimal effort to understand him. Russell proceeds to make a claim that will form the heart of his criticism of Frege:

> ...the relation of meaning and denotation is not merely linguistic through the phrase: there must be a logical relation involved, which we express by saying that the meaning denotes the denotation. (1956a, 49)

This is interesting in two respects. First, he takes the relation between what denotes and what is denoted to be a "logical" relation; second, he claims that the relation cannot be "merely linguistic"—meaning by that that we cannot understand the relation of denotation, as a relation which holds between a sense and a denotation on Frege's account, merely in terms of relations between signs and non-linguistic items. The point will become clear as we unpack his much misunderstood criticism. That criticism, and the conclusion of his argument, is simply put.

> But the difficulty which confronts us is that we cannot succeed in *both* preserving the connexion of meaning and denotation *and* preventing them from being one and the same; also that the meaning cannot be got at except by means of denoting phrases. (1956a, 49)

On Frege's view, or any view that accepts some entity as a meaning (sense), as distinct from a referent, for a denoting phrase, we have a phrase associated with two entities, when there is something denoted. Thus, where the sign "Scott" is the denoting expression, we have:

> The sense of the sign "Scott" is not the denotation of "Scott"

and

>   Scott is the denotation of "Scott."

Russell's argument is simple. The problem he sees is that there must be a relation between the denotation, Scott, and the sense of the expression that cannot be made comprehensible on a Fregean type view. That is because such a relation is understood in terms of the merely "linguistic relations" between the phrase, on the one hand, and the entities involved, on the other. For we have a relation between the sense of the name "Scott" and its denotation, Scott, which we can call "R." But, if we ask what relation R is, Frege can only reply by asserting that to say that the sense stands in R to the denotation is simply to say that there is a denoting phrase which expresses the sense and denotes the denotation. (Keep in mind that both phrases and senses are said to denote on Frege's view.) He thus explains "denoting," as a relation between a sense and a denotation, in terms of, first, "denoting" as a relation between a phrase and a denotation and, second, "expressing" as another linguistic relation between a phrase and a sense. Russell is arguing that such a response will not do as a proposed analysis since it turns R into a "merely linguistic" relation between the sense and what it denotes. What he means by that is simply that the predicate, "R," indicating the relation, is defined in terms of dyadic predicates standing for relations between a linguistic item, a denoting phrase, and a non-linguistic item, either a sense or a denotation—that there is a phrase that means one and denotes the other. This does not express a significant relation holding between the two "entities," since R connects the two entities solely by means of their purported different connections to the same sign. Something is specified in a "merely linguistic" way if it is described by phrases that depend on speaking about a sign, as

>   the meaning of the name "Scott"

and

>   the denotation of the name "Scott,"

do. But Frege requires a relation that is independent of linguistic usage, since the sense and the denotation are not "linguistic" objects but non-linguistic entities. Understanding R as he does, Frege does not furnish a viable account of

R as a relation between two non-linguistic entities—a Fregean sense and a denoted object. Yet, no other account is feasible on Frege's view. Russell's detailed exposition of this in "On Denoting" attempts to show that to take the relation R as non-linguistic fails. But to understand R as Frege must do trivializes his view. Moreover, it is inconsistent with Frege's own statement of his view, since Frege holds that a phrase denotes an object in virtue of its expressing a sense that denotes that object. Thus Frege writes:

> The regular connection between a sign, its sense, and its reference is of such a kind that to the sign there corresponds a definite sense and to that in turn a definite reference, while to a given reference (an object) there does not belong only a single sign. (1970, 58)

The point is clear. On the type of theory involved a sign denotes derivatively, via its sense or meaning, since the sense or meaning is what basically denotes an object. But, as Russell sees it, all Frege really does is take the sense of the denoting phrase to be specified by the denoting phrase "the sense of the expression ...." In Frege's words:

> In order to speak of the sense of an expression "A" one may simply use the phrase "the sense of the expression "A"." (1970, 59)

The problem is about just what a sense is and how we are to specify or identify it. If we could provide a description of a sense in terms of R and the denoting relation between a sign and an object that problem would not arise, assuming we understand denotation as being a relation between a sign and an object. It would not arise precisely because we can specify the denotation of a sign by other than merely "linguistic" means—by descriptions that do not describe the denotation simply by using expressions like "the denotation of the denoting phrase ...." But this kind of alternative is not open in the case of a Fregean sense, and we cannot make use of the denotation in order to specify the sense or meaning, since, as Russell, like Frege, notes:

> ... there is no backward road from denotation to meaning, because every object can be denoted by an infinite number of different denoting phrases. (1956a, 50)

Thus we cannot describe the sense of the term "Scott" as "the sense of the expression that denotes Scott." We can only describe the sense as "the sense of the expression 'Scott'." [Here single quotes are not used in Russell's special way but in the standard way for separating quotes within quotes by the use of single and double quotation marks.] But we do not know what that sense is, aside from its being described as the sense of an expression. Thus we do not know, really, what we claim when we hold that the sense of "Scott" denotes Scott. R, the denotation relation between a sense and a denotation, is therefore mysterious, as is the relation between a denoting phrase and its sense. What one appears to do is simply postulate the existence of senses and a relation between such things and "ordinary" denoted objects. If we ask what the sense is, we are told that it is what is expressed by the term "Scott"—it is what *is expressed by* a word or phrase. If we ask about the relation of *expressing*, we are told that it is the relation that holds between a word or phrase and its sense. This is much like what the neo-Fregeans Hale and Wright do with respect to the function *the-number-of-Φs* and numbers, taken as values of the function for concepts as arguments, as was noted above in Chapter 1.

The key point to note is the difference between "expresses," on the one hand, and "denotes" on the other. To speak of the denotation of the name "Scott" is simply to speak of Scott, the person. There is no problem, of the sort that arises about senses, regarding knowing what is denoted. Nor is there a corresponding problem about the relation that holds between a term and its referent, even if one takes reference or designation as a primitive or basic relation. Russell takes objects and properties, such as colors, to be directly apprehended entities that we are directly acquainted with. And he takes *reference* to be a relation that we directly apprehend when we refer to objects of acquaintance. I know what colors are by acquaintance, and I know what it is to refer to something—to point it out and use a demonstrative (referring) expression, such as "that," or use a primitive referring term, such as a proper name or undefined predicate. Whether the objects referred to are familiar objects of experience or "sense data" is irrelevant here. The point is that the relation is supposedly directly known. This is not the case either with Fregean senses or with the relation of *expressing* or of *denoting* as a relation between a sense and a denotation. This is why the latter turn out to be "merely linguistic" and purported "senses" are mysterious entities.

Russell is not merely arguing against Frege's view but, as Geach noted, against his own earlier account in *Principles of Mathematics*, where he had held that definite descriptive phrases, denoting phrases occurring in sentences, corresponded to denoting complexes in the propositions (as non-linguistic entities) expressed by the sentences. He contrasted such linguistic expressions with proper names like "Scott." For the proposition expressed by the sentence "Scott is human" contained the referent, Scott, as a constituent (1956, 43), and he added:

> ... But a proposition, unless it happens to be linguistic, does not itself contain words, it contains the entities indicated by words. (1956, 47)

Here he is not confusing facts with propositions (as one might think from the earlier quotation referring to Mont Blanc) but simply reflecting his view about propositions at the turn of the century—as his views about facts, as the things that "make propositions true," will only gradually emerge. Russell's views about meaning and denotation in 1905 are quite clear, as it is clear that he then holds what will come to be called a "direct reference" theory about (logically) proper names (as he did in 1903). It is also clear that he speaks of both linguistic phrases and their "meanings" as being "denoting complexes," on a Fregean style view that recognizes senses (meanings) as distinct from the referents of terms. This no more illustrates that he is confused than is his speaking in a way that has led his critics, such as Searle, to accuse him of making the elementary confusion between signs and the things they are used to represent. The latter can be dispelled by simply reading Russell—not even carefully, merely casually:

> It may be expressed as the distinction between verbs and substantives, or, more correctly, between the objects denoted by verbs and the objects denoted by substantives. (Since this more correct expression is long and cumbrous, I shall generally use the shorter phrase to mean the same thing. Thus, when I speak of verbs, I mean the objects denoted by verbs .... (1956a, 107-108)

Though Russell's basic argument against Frege is simple, he gets enmeshed in a complex presentation to demonstrate the simple point that we cannot use a denoting expression like "the meaning of Scott" (i. e. thus talking of the meaning of the man Scott—not the meaning of the word "Scott") to denote, and hence speak about, an entity such as a sense. For by using a phrase like "the meaning of Scott" we then refer to the meaning of a sign's referent—which is absurd in this case, for the man, Scott, does not have a meaning (in the relevant sense), and we do not wish to speak about the meaning (significance) of the man in any case. Much has been made of the unfortunately complex manner of the presentation of this simple, obvious point, while ignoring or missing the point.

Russell goes on to argue that to speak about the meanings of denoting expressions involves introducing further denoting expressions that both express meanings and denote meanings. Most important is the point that the meaning *expressed* by the denoting phrase "the meaning of the expression 'Scott'" cannot be the same as the meaning expressed by "Scott," for the latter meaning denotes Scott, an object that is not a meaning. Just consider the expression:

(a) the sense of the name "Scott."

On Frege's view that expression denotes the sense that the name "Scott" normally expresses—a sense that, in turn, denotes the man. Hence the meanings *expressed* by the name "Scott" and the denoting expression (a) must be different—as are the denotations of (a) and "Scott." Thus Frege is forced to recognize an unending series of entities—meanings (senses) of expressions—that are generated from one sign, a name or a denoting phrase. Russell, rightly, finds such a view problematic. Much of the further complexity of Russell's argument in his paper simply purports to show that as the meanings of the expressions (a) and "Scott" cannot be identified, one is forced to recognize such an unending series. For, if one blocks the infinite series that is generated by identifying the sense of (a) with the sense of the name "Scott," one identifies what those meanings denote, and hence identifies Scott, the man, with a sense that denotes Scott.

Almost a century later Davidson would criticize Frege's theory for allowing a term to have infinitely many "senses" given such a series. On Davidson's view of meaning it would not then follow from finitely many semantic axioms what the "sense" of a denoting expression was. As far as his criticism is viable it amounts to Russell's objection to the infinite number of entities generated by a sign (hence it is not like the hierarchy of unit sets one gets from an element or set in set theory, not from a sign for an element) and a theory of meaning. Davidson's complaint about a finite number of axioms not doing is not viable, for the Fregean series is an iterative one, like that generated by a successor function. Just think of successively iterating by using Russell's device of pairs of single quotes. If the first element is not problematic, then neither should the "successors" be, since each sign produced, as well as its sense, is unique. Russell's earlier argument, unlike Davidson's, was directed against the very first element introduced, as being mysterious and merely "linguistic." The mystery simply grows with the successive elements in the series.

Recall that one line of Russell's criticism is that Frege's relations of expressing, as a relation between a phrase and a sense, and denoting, as a relation between a sense and its denotation, are mysterious or "merely linguistic." On Russell's alternative view a relation of direct reference, in the case of proper names, and the connection between an object and the properties that the object has, in the case of definite descriptions, replaces the appeal to expressing and denoting as Frege uses those notions. Assuming that neither the relation of reference, between a name and what is named, nor the relation of instantiation, between an object and a property that characterizes it, are problematic, Russell dispenses with problematic Fregean notions by employing non-problematic concepts. Moreover, even if the latter relations involve problems, we must resolve them in any case if we recognize direct reference and the instantiation of properties and relations.

2b. Facts and the Analysis of Judgment

In "On Denoting" Russell wrote:

> If 'aRb' stands for 'a has the relation R to b', then when aRb is true, there is such an entity as the relation R between a and b; when aRb is false, there is no such entity. Thus out of any proposition we can make a denoting phrase, which denotes an entity if the proposition is true,

but does not denote an entity if the proposition is false. E. g., it is true (at least we will suppose so) that the earth revolves around the sun, and false that the sun revolves around the earth; hence 'the revolution of the earth round the sun' denotes an entity, while 'the revolution of the sun round the earth' does not denote an entity. (1956a, 53-4)

Here, when he speaks of "such an entity as the relation R between a and b," he is not talking about the relation, R, but the holding of the relation R between a and b, which he speaks of as an "entity." What exists, if it does, is not just the relation, such as the relation "revolves around," but the obtaining of an instance of it, which is to say—a being in R to b. Though he does seem to speak as if he talks of an object rather than a fact, the question being raised concerns the representation of a situation by a sentence, where one takes the existence ("being") of something to be the truth ground for the sentence. Thus, if one thinks of the sentence "aRb" as representing the situation that a stands in R to b, irrespective of the truth value of the sentence, as Meinong and Searle do in there respective ways, when the sentence is false it appears to represent a non-existent entity or complex (state of affairs, possibility, fact). Russell is suggesting, as early as 1905, that his theory of definite descriptions will resolve a fundamental problem about false statements and false belief. He is not however limiting the propositions considered to atomic ones. In 1913 he in effect will do that (Hochberg, 2000). It is worth noting, in this connection, something Russell writes in 1924: "...if Plato loves Socrates, there is not an entity 'Plato's love for Socrates', but only the fact that Plato loves Socrates" (1956e, 337).

In 4.022 of the *Tractatus* Wittgenstein stated the problem simply by asserting that a proposition "shows" how things stand "if" it is true and "says" that they do so stand. An atomic proposition represents a situation, irrespective of its truth or falsity, and asserts that the represented situation obtains or exists. Thus whether or not the situation exists, it is represented by the proposition, and thus recognized. But the use of Russell's theory of descriptions to avoid such a conclusion faces a difficulty that does not arise when it is used to avoid recognizing a non-existent golden mountain.

Consider "denotes" to be a relational predicate used in sentences containing linguistic patterns like:

"Russell" denotes the author of "On Denoting."
The phrase "the sage of Monticello" denotes Thomas Jefferson.

Russell's analysis of definite descriptions implies that a sentence like

(1) "the golden mountain" denotes the golden mountain

is false, since his analysis of (1) is:

(2) There is one and only one golden mountain and "the golden mountain" denotes that object.

Since the descriptive phrase, as it occurs within the quotes in (2), is not used, but merely mentioned (or spoken about, as opposed to being used to speak about a purported denotation), no question arises about the expansion of that occurrence of the phrase within the quotation marks. Taking definite descriptions to be contextually meaningful signs, Russell can still adhere to a reference theory of meaning for the non-logical zero-level constants of a schema, signs that are, logically considered, proper names—logically proper names. Thus, where "a" is a logically proper name, we have: (3) "a" refers to (designates) a. For (3) to be true—more accurately, to be meaningful—a must exist, since genuine, or logically proper names, unlike the grammatically proper names of ordinary language, such as "Zeus," must name. The use of "must" reflects the fact that, in a clarified language or schema, (3) is a formal or logical truth if it is a meaningful pattern or sentence—what Carnap will take to be a semantical rule and characterize as L-True. If the sign "a" has not been paired with or assigned to an object, (3) is not a meaningful pattern of the schema, while if "a" has been interpreted, (3) is a trivial theorem—by a stipulated rule. The same kind of rule can be taken to hold for the primitive predicates of a schema, taking them to be interpreted in terms of properties and relations. But to take simple sentences, such as "aRb," to be coordinated to states of affairs as names and predicates are to particulars and properties (relations) raises the problem about the recognition of non-existent states of affairs—a problem Russell seeks to resolve. Part of the solution lies in the implicit distinction between "denotes," on the one hand, and "designates" (or "refers to"), as I have used those expressions in the present discussion.

Russell employs a denoting expression, like "the fact (or complex) of a standing in R to b," to speak of what the sentence purportedly denotes, as in,

(4) "aRb" denotes the complex consisting of a-standing-in-R-to-b.

This expresses the connection between an atomic sentence, "aRb," and its truth ground, while supposedly avoiding non-existent states of affairs. In short, sentences like "aRb" are not to be treated, as names are treated, as requiring an object that is referred to in order to be meaningful expressions. What they purportedly denote can be expressed by using definite descriptions. It is as if "aRb" is taken as elliptical for a description —the fact that a stands in R to b—to phrase it differently. If one thinks of atomic sentences in terms of definite descriptions, as Russell thought of "apparent" names like "Zeus," then one can explicitly separate the two roles Wittgenstein ascribed to such sentences in *Tractatus* 4. 022. What "aRb" *shows* is expressed by the description used in (4). What "aRb" *states* (is used to assert) is expressed by:

(5) The fact of a-standing-in-R-to-b exists.

But, no matter how it is phrased, Russell's analysis faces obvious problems. One problem is the use of sentential or sentence-like expressions—"R holding between a and b" or "a-standing-in-R-to-b"—in descriptions like those in (4) and (5). Russell does not raise this question in "On Denoting," though there is an obvious difference between using definite descriptions of states of affairs and descriptions like "the golden mountain." Upon the expansion of the latter definite description in context, the apparent subject sign is eliminated, and no apparent singular term remains as a subject sign. By contrast, in (4) and (5) one still employs a sentential or sentence-like pattern in the expansion of the description along Russell's lines, aside from any question about just how to expand it. Russell returned to the problem in 1913 and we shall shortly do so as well in developing a version of a correspondence account of truth, and hence a form of Realism.

Shortly after the publication of "On Denoting," Russell developed his multiple relation analysis of intentional contexts, of statements like "S judges that a stands in R to b." This rejected treating sentences like (i) "Othello believes that Desdemona loves Cassio" in terms of a dyadic relation (believes that), in Fregean style, holding between Othello and what was "represented" or "expressed" (a proposition or content) by the embedded sentence "Desdemona loves Cassio." On Russell's view the belief statement was perspicuously construed along the lines of "Believes (Othello, Desdemona, loves, Cassio)," where "believes" functions as a predicate representing a four-term relation and no linguistic term in the sentence is itself a sentence. Thus we supposedly avoid a Fregean-style propositional entity as a term of a dyadic belief relation. For we need no longer ask what an embedded sentence "represents" or "expresses," as such apparent sentences simply disappear, just as the definite descriptive phrase does in the case of "The golden mountain is in Austria."

Russell thus recognized, as Quine (1971) did many years later, a number of belief relations, three-term, four-term, etc. (to speak of one "multi-grade" relation, as Quine will do, merely puts the matter differently). For the analysis of "Othello believes that Desdemona is a liar" will involve a triadic belief relation that relates Othello to Desdemona and the property of being a liar, in an appropriate order. This is reminiscent of the recognition of various identity relations, "types" of truth, etc. on Russellian style type theories. He also needed to recognize functions like $(\exists x)\prod yx$ to handle sentences like (ii) "Othello believes that Desdemona loves someone" in terms of "B(Othello, $(\exists x)\prod yx$, loves, Desdemona)," though he also recognized such functions independently of any use in the analysis of intentional contexts. But while the use of a function sign like "$(\exists x)\prod yx$" as a predicate in sentences like "$(\exists x)\prod yx$(loves, Desdemona)" is elliptical for "$(\exists x)$ Desdemona loves x," or "$(\exists x)$loves(Desdemona, x)," the function sign is not used in such a way in embedded sentential contexts like "B(Othello, $(\exists x)\prod yx$, loves, Desdemona)." For one cannot "saturate" the variables "$\prod$" and "y" by the predicate and subject term, respectively. If one did, by some special rule, we would arrive at "B(Othello, $(\exists x)$Desdemona loves x)," which clearly suggests that Russell has simply developed a strange notation, while holding a view that is merely a disguised variant of a Fregean-style analysis. This is one way of understanding Wittgenstein's cryptic critique of Russell in Tractatus 5.5422 and in the letter to Russell of June, 1913 (1969, 121). The simple point is that one cannot make use of patterns like "B(Othello, x, $\prod$, y)" without an understood rule that the terms replacing "x," "$\prod$" and "y" must be combinable into a meaningful sentential pattern. The question is whether this implicit appeal to meaningful sentential patterns shows that Russell's relational theory is really a disguised version of an analysis that surreptitiously appeals to propositional entities—of an analysis that, in effect, duplicates Frege's.

Suppose we change the construal of "B," along the lines of Quine's later "semantically ascended" version of Russell's view, and read (ii) in terms of a claim about the application of a predicate, rather than as employing a predicate to represent a relation (or property):

> Othello believes that (the predicate) "x loves y" is true of <Desdemona, Cassio>,

where "... believes that _ _ _is true of ---" is the predicate and the sign "<Desdemona, Cassio>" is a sign for the obvious ordered pair (Quine, 1971). We still force the appropriate type of term into the appropriate place, as a singular term must occupy the first place, a name of a predicate the second place and an appropriate subject term the third place. Moreover, since the predicate is no longer simply "...believes that _ _ _," but "...believes that _ _ _is true of ---," we virtually recreate the propositional analysis. For "_ _ _is true of---" is explicitly a propositional form that requires a sign denoting a predicate (or a predicate itself) to occupy the first place. In a way Quine's version of Russell's relational view helps us to see the force of Wittgenstein's criticism, since it transparently employs an expression that is proposition-like. Quine's alternative rendition of his "semantically ascended" view, employing "...believes that _ _ _ is true," along with the explicit use of sentences or names of them as terms, simply emphasizes Wittgenstein's point.

Besides the problem Wittgenstein raised, Russell's relational analysis faces another major difficulty. In keeping with his adherence to a correspondence theory of truth in setting out of his relational analysis, Russell took a truth predicate as a predicate that would combine with terms indicating belief facts, and hence as a predicate representing an attribute of such complexes (assuming that it is taken to represent an attribute at all). The belief fact, that Othello believes that Desdemona loves Cassio, would be true if and only if another fact (complex), Desdemona-loving-Cassio existed. But, Russell failed to recognize that he must connect the first fact to the second, whose existence supplies the truth ground for the belief. He failed to do so for a fundamental reason.

On Russell's early form of the relational analysis of belief—the view prior to his work on the 1913 manuscript *Theory of Knowledge*—he construed Othello's belief that Desdemona loves Cassio as a complex or fact that contains all the constituents, Desdemona, the relation of loving and Cassio, in the right order, that the complex, Desdemona-loving-Cassio, contains. Russell thought that sufficed to establish the connection between the belief and its truth ground, since he focused on the problem of uniquely specifying the truth ground for the belief. But that does not suffice, for one must take the first complex to be "about" the second, so that the existence of the second will ground the truth of the first. It also does not suffice in that he did not then see the problem posed by specifying "the order." Recognizing the problem posed by distinguishing a complex like Desdemona-loving-Cassio from one like Cassio-loving-Desdemona in 1913, he proposed an analysis of relational order, in effect introducing ordering relations into relational facts. He took that, together with the addition of logical forms, such as $\prod xy$, to belief facts, to be a key to resolving the problem of linking a belief fact to its purported ground of truth. What he then did was return to the idea expressed in the 1905 paper and employ a definite description of the fact that, when it existed, was the ground of truth for the belief (Hochberg, 2000). But he did not develop the idea and abandoned the manuscript.

Aside from the seemingly odd feature of construing the fact that obtains when one has a belief that a and b stand in R in terms of a four-term relation relating a person to a, b and R, Russell's account faces another problem. For he does not acknowledge a sense of "believe" in terms of which the truth ground for "Othello believes that Desdemona loves Cassio" differs from the truth ground for "Othello believes that Desdemona loves Cassito," where "Cassito" is another name for Cassio. Given his analysis that removes the embedded sentence, one can simply substitute one name for another if the identity holds, unless one simply rules that out for contexts involving certain relations, like "believes." He did not take up this question of the substitution of different names in "On Denoting," since he simply distinguished intentional contexts with definite descriptions in embedded sentences from contexts with proper names and focused on the different scopes descriptions could have in such contexts. Descriptions thus logically differed from names in that names did not involve differences of scope in embedded sentences.

The distinction between the use of primary and secondary scope in intentional contexts is also relevant to his own relational analysis of belief. Suppose Cassio (=c) is the man with Desdemona's (=d) scarf, $(\iota x)(Sx)$. Employing both Russell's relational analysis of belief and his theory of descriptions, we have, with "o" abbreviating "Othello":

B(o, loves, d, c)
$c = (\iota x)(Sx)$
therefore, B(o, loves, d, $(\iota x)(Sx)$)

as a valid argument pattern. For, on Russell's relational analysis, a description in such a context does not occur in a way that allows for the use of secondary scope. The relational analysis treats such contexts as "extensional," and, thus, in effect, allows for the substitution of definite descriptions, given the requisite identity premise, in such "atomic" contexts. For though one cannot make the substitution based on the "apparent" identity statement, there is a corresponding valid pattern that does not depend on such a substitution in such contexts. (One motive for the relational analysis was that such intentional contexts become extensional (as opposed to "intensional") in just that sense, and *Principia Mathematica* deals only with extensional contexts. The relational analysis was developed in the years between 1906 and the publication of *Principia*.) If we slightly complicate the context to:

¬ B(o, loves, d, c)
$c = (\iota x)(Sx)$
therefore, ¬ B[o, loves, d, $(\iota x)(Sx)$],

the question of scope appears to become relevant and we arrive at a version of a case Quine has made familiar in contemporary discussions of belief. (Such cases simply involve referring to or denoting someone or something in diverse ways in circumstances where it is not known that one talks about the same object.) With the description in the conclusion given primary scope, the argument is valid if we adopt both Russell's theory of descriptions and his relational analysis. Moreover, even with the description in the conclusion taken as having secondary scope, the argument remains valid, for, when the premises are true, the alternative renditions of the conclusion are equivalent. Russell's account thus fails to allow for a sense of "believe" in which it is plausible to hold that Othello does not believe that Desdemona loves Cassio, but does believe that she loves the man with her scarf, given that Cassio is that man.

Ignoring Russell's relational analysis of belief, his theory of descriptions, employing scope differences, would allow for the distinction in the context of a propositional analysis of the Fregean type—an analysis of the kind Russell seems to have held in 1905. Moreover, the difference between primary and secondary scope is related to Quine's more recent concerns about "quantifying in" (1971). These concerns have to do with the question of the scope of an existential quantifier, where one generalizes from the occurrence of a name in a context like (i), if that context is construed as containing an embedded sentential component. Thus, the question concerns the relation of (i) to (ii), where (ii) is taken as "There is an individual such that Othello believes Desdemona loves that individual." This is an analogue of the question that arises for the scope of a description on a Fregean-style analysis recognizing propositional entities. Construing "believes that" in such a Fregean manner, we then construe the first argument as:

> Othello believes that-Desdemona loves Cassio
> Cassio=the man with the scarf, therefore
> Othello believes that-Desdemona loves the man with the scarf.

But, given the propositional component in the conclusion of the argument, that conclusion can be taken in two ways by varying the scope of the description. If the scope is taken as primary, the argument can be taken to be valid, on Russell's theory of descriptions. For, if the premises are true, it can be claimed that there is a man, and only one, with Desdemona's scarf and Othello believes that that man (whether Othello knows or not that the man is unique in having her scarf) is loved by Desdemona.

If the scope is taken as secondary, then the conclusion is transcribed as:

> Othello believes that-there is a man, and only one, who has her scarf and Desdemona loves that man.

Thus, the belief relation is taken to relate Othello to whatever is expressed or represented by the existential sentence. Whether one then takes the conclusion, so transcribed, to be true, given the truth of the premises, will depend on other aspects of one's analysis of belief contexts. But, it should be obvious that there are certain senses of "believe" in which one may deny the conclusion, while affirming the premises. Russell's theory of definite descriptions, taken in connection with a propositional analysis of belief contexts, as opposed to his relational analysis, would allow for using scope distinctions to provide alternative ways of construing intentional contexts like "Othello believes that Desdemona loves the man with the scarf"—with such intentional contexts no longer taken as "extensional." In "On Denoting" Russell appears to have thought that definite descriptions could be expanded in intentional contexts. But, in cases where a secondary scope is involved, the replacement of the description in accordance with Russell's theory of descriptions is problematic. Such problems about substitution in belief contexts, whether involving descriptions and questions of scope or names and questions about quantification "into" such contexts, have generated numerous discussions.

One widely discussed variant of such problems, involving names and negation and reminiscent of our earlier discussion of Meinong, is a purported puzzle Kripke has raised that involves someone using two names for the same thing without realizing or knowing that they name the same thing. Kripke makes use of names in different languages, "London" and "Londres." Pierre, not knowing that London is Londres, believes that London is not pretty, while convinced that Londres est tres jolie. What it all comes down to is whether or not one can say that a person P has contradictory beliefs, since P believes what is expressed by "a is F" and by "b is not F," but does not know that a = b. Kripke's version stresses that one who gives an account of Pierre's beliefs appears forced to make a contradictory claim by having to hold that Pierre both believes and does not believe that London is pretty. This is derived from several assumptions.

First, there is a criterion for determining that P has a belief—sincerely asserting a token of a relevant sentence, etc. This is not crucial as we can simply take P to have a belief state with the content expressed by the sentence. Second, there is the "translation" theme—if a statement is true, then its translation into another language is also true ("in that language"). What this supposedly amounts to is that London is pretty if and only if Londres is pretty—to mix languages to simplify matters. What it really amounts to is covering the substitution of diverse names for the same thing in intentional contexts. Third, there is the idea that if P believes that ß is not-Φ then P does not believe that ß is Φ, for suitably simple contexts and assuming P has an appropriate degree of "logicality." Then one must hold that Pierre does and does not believe that London is pretty, given the purportedly reasonable assumptions. But no puzzle is involved, as the key assumptions are problematic, however reasonable sounding. One thing we must do is recognize that having a state of belief with the content that ß is not-Φ does not entail that one does not have a state of belief that ß is Φ. There is obviously a sense in which Pierre does, and a sense in which he does not, believe that London is pretty. The fact that he has a belief state with a content expressed by "London is not pretty" does not entail that he does not have a state with a content expressed by "London is pretty," unless that is simply stipulated under the condition of possessing sufficient "logicality." There is no reason to accept such a stipulation, as the context is quite different from the attempts to defend Meinong by introducing "two negations." The entailment recalls the old issue regarding how one could have an "idea" of negation—of what is not. Holding that one cannot have a concept of negation, some claimed that when one is said to believe that ß is not-Φ one really disbelieves that ß is Φ. That turned negation into a characteristic of an intentional state, as being a belief is such a characteristic, since we had no "idea" of negation to enter into the content of the thought. It is as if negation was shifted out of the embedded sentence into the surrounding context. Kripke's assumption that to believe that ß is not-Φ entails not believing that ß is Φ is no more viable than the earlier treatment of negative contents—talk of appropriate degrees of logicality not withstanding. The appeal to an appropriate "degree of logicality" is in the vein of Davidson's (following Quine) principles governing interpretation. Thus we supposedly have *a priori* knowledge of the normative principle that one who believes that-London is pretty ought not to also believe that-it is not the case that London is pretty (ignoring the language the latter is expressed in). If one does one is not appropriately logical.

A second thing one must do is raise the obvious questions about belief contexts and the use of diverse names for the same thing whether or not we know that they are names of one object, which are covered over by the "translation" hypothesis (Hintikka, 1962, 1967). One simple way of dispensing with the purported problem is to recognize that the use of different expressions to refer to something involves a different "mode" or manner of reference. This is a simple and clear way of understanding Frege's notion of "ways" of denoting, a theme we shall return to in Chapter 4. Pierre simply has two ways of referring to London. This does not mean that he does and does not have a belief state with a specific content.

In recent years Kripke has misleadingly promulgated the idea that there is a Frege-Russell account of proper names, which contrasts with what he takes to be his own direct reference account that harks back to Mill (but which is essentially a replica of Russell's view)—the theme that names directly refer without the intermediation of a definite description or connotation or sense specifying what is named in terms of identifying properties. When, in 1905, Russell contrasted a name like "Scott" with a definite description like "the author of *Waverley*," he indicated at the end of "On Denoting" that he embraced what would come to be called a Principle of Acquaintance, requiring that all primitive names and predicates of a logically correct language refer to objects and properties that one is acquainted with. Thus he held that the names of ordinary language were generally not genuine names, since he did not believe, due to his views about perception and acquaintance, that we are acquainted with physical objects or with other minds. Holding that the only particulars (as opposed to universals) that one is acquainted with are sense data, mental acts and other such "private" objects, he was led to hold that "logically proper names" could only name such objects. Later, in the logical atomism lectures, to emphasize his view, he took demonstratives like "this" and "that" to be prototypes of proper names, since he was considering direct reference to particulars like sense data—the direct data of sense experience.

But his view was clear. From the first decades of the century to 1940 he rejected the elimination of proper names, via descriptions or anything else. In a letter to Frege, dated December 12, 1904, he wrote:

> In the case of a simple proper name like "Socrates," I cannot distinguish between sense and denotation; I see only the idea, which is psychological, and the object. Or better: I do not admit the sense at all, but only the idea and the denotation.

This was before the question of a Principle of Acquaintance complicated matters. But even in subsequent works, he reiterated the main theme repeatedly—in "The Philosophy of Logical Atomism" (1968, 197-198); in *Introduction to Mathematical Philosophy* (1953, 174), where it is interesting to note, in connection with Kripke's later talk about rigid designation and the fixing of reference, that Russell speaks of meaning (reference) being "already fixed"; and in *An Inquiry into Meaning and Truth* (1940, 117, 118-19). In a well known passage about Bismarck, Russell (1946, 56-57) held that even people who know Bismarck well, including, presumably, Mrs. Bismarck, cannot refer to Bismarck directly in the way that Bismarck can, if there is such a thing as "the self." This theme had already occurred in "On Denoting":

> ... and the minds of other people are known to us only by denoting phrases, i. e. we are not acquainted with them, but we know them as what has such and such properties. (1956a, 56)

In the *Inquiry*, proper names named qualities, due to Russell's view that ordinary particulars were "bundles" of compresent qualities. Hence the lowest level terms of his schema were signs for qualities like "red" that functioned only as subject terms for predicates. This had nothing to do with his sometimes holding that the proper names of ordinary language are to be construed as descriptions. It is worth emphasizing that Russell took primitive predicates to directly refer to qualities and relations in the early years of the century as well as in his later works in the 1940s, since he was at no point a nominalist denying the existence of qualities and relations. Moreover he took a "logically perfect" language to employ one name or primitive predicate "and no more" as a label for each object or property. Thus he precluded, as philosophical matters, the familiar problems arising from substitutions based on true identity statements employing two names of the same thing. But, more important, he clearly rejected the replacement of all logically proper names by definite descriptions.

Since any attempt to replace all directly referring terms by definite descriptions is doomed to failure, as the very same problem of replacement arises for constant predicates used in such definite descriptions, the basic question is begged by the use of primitive predicates without "ontological commitment." When one recognizes the significance of such a theme in the context of the present discussion, the philosophical poverty of Quine's notorious notion of ontological commitment becomes transparent. What is also transparent is that Kripke's direct reference view about names, ignoring whether causal chains or direct acquaintance provides the link, repeats Russell's direct reference view for the simple predicates and proper names of an ideal language. Russell, consistently being a realist about properties, clearly rejected, and had to reject, what Kripke calls the Frege-Russell view. Moreover, in the years since 1905 various philosophers have held such a direct reference account of names—an account clearly employed in Carnap's *Introduction to Semantics*. It is thus strange to note that in the recent literature there has been an ongoing, and heated, dispute about whether Kripke or R. Barcan (Marcus) discovered the "tag" theory of names—i. e. Russell's direct reference theory. What has perhaps confused some recent writers is that Russell and, subsequently, many others took simple predicates, as well as logically proper names, to "directly refer to," "designate," "label," "tag," etc. primitive properties and relations. Though, in the logical atomism lectures of 1918, Russell, in Fregean fashion, speaks of names and primitive predicates referring in different ways, what he had in mind was that predicates, like "F^1" or "Fx" and "R^2" or "Rxy," revealed the logical form of the sentences they entered into as predicates, by showing that they were monadic, dyadic, etc. In these essays Russell, like Frege, does not take predicates to be terms that can stand in subject place in "higher order" statements, like "Red is a color." Such a statement would be transcribed as "Everything that is red is colored."

2c. Referring to Facts

Speaking of Russell's 1913 manuscript, Jaakko Hintikka writes:

> This pinpoints Wittgenstein's *Tractatus* precisely in relation to Russell. The *Tractatus* is nothing more and nothing less than Russell's 1913 theory *sans* logical forms as object of acquaintance. This relationship was for a long time obscured by philosophers' unawareness of Russell's long time unpublished book. Wittgenstein himself was never the less fully aware of this relation:

> My fundamental thought is that "logical constants" do not represent [anything]. (*Tractatus* 4.0312)
>
> Here it becomes clear that there are no such things as "logical objects" or "logical constants" (in the sense of Frege and Russell). (*Tractatus* 5. 4) (2000, 19)

Hintikka's claim is fundamentally flawed. For he overlooks the radical move Russell made in 1913 regarding the linking of atomic statements to their truth grounds (truth makers), which he had already suggested in 1905. A more accurate assessment would be that awareness of Russell's 1913 manuscript is essential for understanding the *Tractatus*. For Wittgenstein's book not only shows that he adopted many crucial themes from Russell but that he was reacting against various other Russellian themes, including the one regarding logical forms. Hintikka also misses a crucial point in his discussion of Wittgenstein's views about logical form:

> If a proposition is not held together by the "logical glue" provided by logical form as actually existing objects of acquaintance, what does hold it together? Wittgenstein's answer was: A proposition is held together, not by any additional "tie" or "glue" but by the forms of its constituents. Objects are connected with each other in a proposition, not like tiles cemented together, but like jigsaw-puzzle pieces held in place by their form:
>
> > In a proposition objects hang together like links in a chain.
>
> More literally speaking,
>
> > The logical form of the proposition must already be given by the forms of the component parts. (*Notebooks 1914-16*, p. 23) (2000, 19)

But all that this amounts to is the Fregean thesis regarding the "incompleteness" of predicate terms being extended to subject terms, as both "concepts" and "objects" are taken to carry their logical form. Thus, a proper name like "a" is more perspicuously rendered by "Φa," as a predicate like "F" is rendered by "Fx." Then the idea, simply put, is that the two go together like the "links in a chain" as the "F" fits into the "Φ" place as the "a" does in the "x" place—without any need for an additional connecting link or relation. There is a complication, however, since names can enter into a variety of atomic sentences of different logical form, i. e. combine with one-term predicates, two-term relational predicates, etc., as subject signs for such predicates, while predicates can only enter into one kind of atomic sentence as the predicate term. Thus, either the "Φ" in "Φa" is a place-holder for monadic, dyadic, etc. predicates, or one must have various signs for "a"—" Φa," "∏ay," etc. This is not the case with "x" in "Fx" in the context of a first order predicate logic, where constants like "a" are the only kind of constant signs that can replace the variable "x." Hintikka's discussion also ignores the rejection of propositional entities in the *Tractatus*, where linguistic propositions (atomic sentences) are directly linked to the states of affairs (possible facts) that they represent.

To speak of the logical forms (either of the signs or of the objects and properties they represent) determining the possibilities of combination, as Wittgenstein did, does not resolve the problem of linking a proposition to the state of affairs it represents. It merely packs the representational role of the sentence (proposition, belief, thought) into the "logical" roles of the constituent elements. An interpretation rule is required that takes the juxtaposition of signs to form a sentence that represents the situation of a-being-red, whether the latter exists or not. Thus Wittgenstein not only does not resolve the problem of linking an atomic sentence to the situation that it represents, he does not avoid recognizing such situations or "possibilities" by speaking of "logical form" and "links in a chain," as Russell does not avoid it by his multiple relation analysis of belief, though avoiding it is one motive for that analysis (Hochberg, 2000).

These are the same problems Searle faces almost a century later and their respective patterns are not fundamentally different from Meinong's recognition of non-subsistent objectives. But the solution indicated by Russell in 1905, a solution he tried to develop in 1913 but abandoned under Wittgenstein's influence, contains an idea that does suggest a way of avoiding the recognition of such possible facts, as we noted in section (2b) above. It employs his theory of definite descriptions to describe facts and is illustrated by:

(R) "Fa" is true if and only if the fact consisting of a and F exists. (1984, 144-45)

In (R) the implicit existential quantifier ranges over existent facts, not possibilities, as Russell's existential quantifier for particulars ranges over existent individuals. (R) does three crucial things. First, it makes no use of a basic representational or "intentional" relation—designates, represents, refers to—

connecting a sentence to a complex, a purported state of affairs. Instead, it employs a Russellian definite description that "purports to denote" an existent complex, as "the winged horse" purports to denote, by being a description, but fails to denote without introducing Meinongian non-existent objects. Second, it specifies a truth condition for a sentence by means of an explicit use of the predicate "is true." By so doing, it, third, follows the basic pattern of Russell's use of definite descriptions and seeks to avoid any implicit reference to non-existent entities by employing an existential statement as the right side of the biconditional. But as it stands (R) is not satisfactory, given the use of "the fact" and "consisting of," which require further clarification. More about that in due course.

2d. Strawson's Critique of Russell

In a well known critique of Russell's account of definite descriptions, P. Strawson (1950) ironically resurrected aspects of Frege's theory as a key theme. Strawson's critique was also a criticism of Russell's account of proper names, his conception of reference and his reference theory of meaning. Though Strawson is adverse to approaching issues in philosophy by considering an artificial schema (a "perspicuous" or "ideal" language in the tradition of Russell, the Wittgenstein of the *Tractatus*, Carnap, Sellars and others, including Frege), it is easiest to see the issues that arise between Russell and Strawson in terms of a simple such schema. Consider the signs "a," "b," "F" and "G," where we take the first two as belonging to the category of subject signs and the second pair as being predicate signs. Thus we will admit strings of signs like "Fa" and "Gb" as syntactically well-formed formulae or grammatically admissible strings, while strings like "aa," "aF," etc. will not be counted among such grammatically correct strings. Suppose we further hold that the signs "a" and "b," if interpreted, will be interpreted by correlating them to individual or particular objects and the predicate signs "F" and "G" will be correlated with (interpreted in terms of) non-relational properties. If we then say that "a" and "b" are proper names, we use the phrase "proper name" as some use "individual constant" or "zero-level constant" in logic texts and, hence, as taking a proper name to be a sign that belongs to a certain grammatical (syntactical) category and not as a sign that has in fact been interpreted as referring to some object. In this sense of "name" ("proper name"), names need not name. Moreover, knowing that such signs are names in this sense and knowing the grammatical rules of the schema, we may be said to know how to use the signs. Since we know what kind of sign "a" is and, perhaps, what kinds of things we will use such a sign to refer to, without knowing what specific object it will be taken to refer to or be interpreted in terms of, we may even say we know, in that sense, the "meaning" of the sign. If we then use the sign "a" to refer to various objects on different occasions—give it various interpretations—we may say that the name, as such, does not name one thing but is used to name various objects on different occasions, as we use demonstrative terms like "this" and "that" to indicate various things at various times. In noting this we can distinguish between the sign, as a physical mark (or class of such) or as such a mark taken together with *the* appropriate a-sound (or the various utterances of the appropriate a-sound), and "the" sign together with its interpretation in a particular use, where using it to refer to an object is to give it a specific interpretation. The sign, taken as a type rather than as a token, can also be said to have various interpretations. We might then consider "it" to be a different name on the different occasions on which "it" is used to refer to different objects. This emphasizes different senses of "name" that are involved in disputes about use, meaning and reference. It also recalls Wittgenstein's distinction, in the *Tractatus*, between a sign and a symbol—the latter being the sign taken with its interpretation that provides its "projective relation to the world."

While Strawson has claimed that Russell's views about reference and meaning are confused, it is clear that Russell did not confuse the two senses of "meaning" we just noted. What one might, more reasonably, claim is that speaking of meaning, reference and names as Strawson chooses to do is closer to the way we normally use "names" or speak about naming. One could then claim that Russell would be wrong to take his views to record or reflect common usage of English expressions such as "means," "refers to," etc. But Russell did not seem to think he was explicating or reflecting such common usage, in spite of his sometimes speaking as if he is. Rather, Russell seems to have been concerned with proposing solutions to certain philosophical problems that arise in connection with our ordinary usage of language—as many philosophical problems appear to do. Consider one such problem about names and reference. Let "a" name some object and "F" refer to the color white. With the appropriate syntactical or grammatical rules, the sign sequence "Fa" may be used to assert that the object, designated by "a," is white. Suppose, however, that the sequence of signs is written (or uttered) without an interpretation of the sign "a" having been made. It is clear that in such a case the token of the sequence would not have been used to assert what was asserted in the first case—in fact, one might say that something was not said in the sense that something was said on the first occasion. Strawson and Russell agree about this. Strawson, however, holds that the "sentence" is significant (meaningful) but that an assertion was not made. Russell denies that the sign sequence, in the second case, is a meaningful or significant sentence. One reason for his doing so might be a desire to avoid introducing "assertions," which, in this context, are clearly reminiscent of Fregean "thoughts" or classical propositions. There are other reasons for doing so.

Suppose "a" is not interpreted and hence is not taken to refer to anything. An obvious question arises about its occurrence in patterns that are those of standard logical truths, such as "a=a." The latter seemingly follows from what is sometimes called a "law" of identity—"(x)(x=x)." One subsequently derives "(∃x)(x=a)" from "a=a," which either makes no sense, if "a" is simply a non-referring constant sign, or is false if it is a term like "Pegasus" that has a context of myth, a "story," guiding its use. Russell sought to avoid such problems by not acknowledging "Fa ∨ ¬ Fa," "Fa," "¬ Fa" and "a=a" as meaningful sentences when "a" did not designate. He did that by requiring that names name—for a sign being a name "presupposed" that it did in fact name (designate). If one allows terms to function as primitive subject signs while not being interpreted, names that do not name, and patterns containing them are recognized as significant sentences, something else must be done. One may limit existential generalization to cases where the sign involved, "a" for example, does designate. One could then distinguish, syntactically, two kinds of zero-level constants and require that only signs of one kind designate (be interpreted). The problematic inferences can then be avoided by restricting existential generalization to constant signs of that latter kind—the names (syntactical) that did name (were interpreted).

Another alternative would be to stipulate that sentences like "Fa," "¬ Fa," "a=a" and (some or all) molecular compounds containing them are neither true nor false, and hence no problems concerning inferences to or from them arise. In effect, Strawson adopts this alternative by means of his distinction between sentences (utterances of sentence tokens) and their use to make assertions and claiming that the sentences "Fa" and "¬ Fa" are used to make true or false assertions only if "a" does in fact designate. In his terminology, the use of such sentences to make a true or false assertion "presupposes" that "a" does refer to something—that a exists. By speaking of "presupposing" as he does, Strawson does something that amounts to what Russell does: he neutralizes the troublesome sentences. Only he does it by allowing the problematic names to occur, and hence the problematic sentences, and holding that the sentences containing such terms are not used (in the relevant cases) to make true or false assertions. The problematic inferences are avoided since even if one allows standard logical inference patterns to apply to such sentences, rather than to assertions, we could still not infer that the troublesome existential sentences were true (or used to make true assertions), since the sentences "Fa" and "¬ Fa" were not so used. Thus Strawson, like Russell, avoids the problematic inferences, but in a different way.

Russell specifies a meta-linguistic criterion for a term's being a name of a clarified linguistic schema. It is a logical consequence of that criterion that if a sign is a logically proper name there is a unique object that it designates. The claim that a sign's being a name "presupposes" that it designates or names something then simply means its being a name entails, in a standard sense of "entails," that it does in fact name. This use of "presupposes" contrasts with Strawson's use of that term. For Strawson, to say that the use of "Fa" to make a true or false assertion "presupposes" that "a" designates is not to assert a standard logical truth. Strawson sets down a general claim about language and its use. But it is hardly an empirical generalization. Nor does he appear to take it as a mere stipulation. Rather, he seems to think of it as a kind of "conceptual" or "logical" truth in unanalyzed senses of those terms. Even if one specifies a set of axioms for Strawson's use of "presupposes," which some have attempted to do, this would simply correspond to a set of stipulations, without any explication beyond that of the context supplied by the axioms themselves. But, aside from any problems regarding the explication of Strawson's use of "presupposes," one might hold, as he certainly suggests, that his view is closer to, and supported by, our ordinary linguistic usage, as opposed to Russell's view, which purportedly conflicts with such usage. For we commonly use names that do not name, which Russell bans from a clarified or "idealized" language and thereby suggests that ordinary language is problematic—it does not "take care of itself," to turn Wittgenstein's phrase. But this is misleading, as Russell's point can be made even if we allow non-naming names in a formal or "clarified" language schema.

One can allow such signs, so long as the distinction between names that name and names that do not is preserved, and avoid the problematic inferences (to existential statements for example). However, the question of the truth value of subject-predicate sentences containing non-designating names remains. Quine has suggested that one can simply take all such atomic sentences to be false, and their negations true. This would allow one to adhere to (1) all (indicative) sentences are either true or false, and (2) a sentence is true if and only if its negation is false. Strawson, by his appeal to "assertions," denies (1); but, in effect, he accepts (2), since he can hold that an assertion is true if and only if its negation is false. Assertions, like classical propositions, are of two kinds in two ways—in the sense of being true and being false and in the sense of being positive and negative. This aspect of Strawson's view was altered, to meet certain objections, in a later paper where he apparently held that some assertions may be neither true nor false, and thus the doctrine of presuppositions was altered to require that existential presuppositions must be fulfilled for a sentence to be used to make an assertion with a truth value (1964, 103-105, 106).

The later version of Strawson's view allows for assertions that are the negations of each other with neither being true or false. It also complicates the doctrine of assertions to meet a problem posed by the apparent difference, as Strawson sees it, between sentences like "Peter Strawson is the present king of France" and "The present king of France is Peter Strawson." The former appears to make an "identifying reference" to someone, Strawson, and is thus used to make a false assertion about that person—the existential condition of presupposition having been fulfilled. The latter, however, fails to make such an identifying reference, and thus fails to fulfill the required presupposition for making an assertion with a truth value. Thus apparent identity statements—as two-term relational statements—are transformed, in the manner of Bradley and the Absolute Idealists, into subject-predicate statements and questions about truth values thus depend on the sentential role of the purportedly "denoting expression." On Strawson's later view, negation, as operating with assertions, is not truth functional in some contexts. Moreover, on either the earlier or the later view, negative sentences were taken as meaningful but not used to make assertions with truth values. Such sentential uses of negation are not truth functional. We thus have a correlate of Strawson's unexplicated use of "presupposition"—an unexplicated notion of "negation." In fact Strawson can be considered as presenting a modified version of a three-valued logic that applies to sentences and simply ignores assertions. Let "Fa" take one of three values—T, F or N. If "a" does not designate anything, "Fa" takes the value N and "$\neg$" then yields the value T, F or N, depending on whether its argument has the value F, T or N. But the negation function retains the standard two-valued truth table when "a" does designate.

Given non-designating names, say "a," and atomic sentences containing them, like "Fa," it makes little difference if we take such sentences to be without a truth value or assign them a "value" like N. The point is that we take neither the sentences nor their negations as true or as false. What Russell does, by contrast, is remove the problematic sentences and allow for the preservation of the standard treatment of negation and the retention of standard logical rules and truths. Yet, supposedly, Strawson's analysis reflects ordinary language usage in a way that Russell's does not, though to preserve this fit he pays the philosophical price of introducing assertions, an unexplicated use of "presupposes," a non-truth functional use of negation, or an odd variant of a three-valued system (the use of "odd" will be explained shortly) and, finally, a philosophically peculiar notion of "secondary reference," for terms in stories, for example. (Is it reference or isn't it?) But the purported strength of Strawson's analysis, its supposed fit with ordinary usage, is specious.

Consider the sign "a" as belonging to a certain grammatical (syntactical) category of signs in a schema (logically proper names, zero-level constants, individual labels). To keep various issues apart, we do not take such signs to be used, on different occasions, to represent different things but simply take them, if they refer (are interpreted) at all to refer to one and only one thing. If it so refers we will call it a "referring name." We can establish this referential connection in various ways: by a gesture, a coordination procedure (as in mathematical contexts) or by giving a definite description of an object, "$(\iota\ x)(Gx)$." The gesture, the procedure and the definite description do the same job—they are used to link a sign to an object in order that the sign may then be used to, or simply be taken to, represent the object. But there is a radical difference between the different ways of establishing such a coordination. We can assert "$a = (\iota\ x)(Gx)$" but not that the gesture is identical with a or, even, "a = this." For the last sentence is useless without an accompanying gesture (or an appropriate context playing the role of the gesture). Given that the description serves to connect the name to its referent, the sentence "$a = (\iota\ x)(Gx)$" plays the same role as a stipulation like "Let 'a' stand for this," where an utterance of that pattern is accompanied by an appropriate gesture or occurs in an appropriate context, or a stipulation like "Let 'a' stand for b," where we know what "b" refers to. In short, we deal with a conventional assignment of a sign to an object. Thus "$a = (\iota\ x)(Gx)$" is better expressed by a designation rule—or semantic rule as in Carnap's *Meaning and Necessity*—along the lines of: (R) "a" designates $(\iota\ x)(Gx)$. The apparent identity statement may then be taken as a simple consequence of the rule of interpretation or even as an alternative rendition of (R), since it is not an ordinary statement of identity, as "Russell is the most significant twentieth century philosopher" can be taken to be.

Assume, then, that there is an appropriate object and that the sign "a" is coordinated to it by such a statement or by (R). We can call the object the "referent meaning" of the sign "a" and contrast that with the "grammatical meaning" of the sign, where the latter is provided by the implicit or explicit rules governing the use of the sign, including those specifying what kind of referent meaning it may be given, if it is given one. We may also take the definite descriptive phrase "$(\iota\ x)(Gx)$" as the "semantical meaning" of the sign "a." Suppose, now, that there is not in fact an object that "a" is coordinated with, since "(ι x)(Gx)" does not "denote" anything. We may then say that while the sign "a" has both a semantical and a grammatical meaning, it has no referential meaning. This would simply emphasize that aside from the rules specifying the grammatical role of "a" we have only the sign "(ι x)(Gx)" and not an object denoted by the description to provide "meaning" or "significance" for "a." Since (ι x)(Gx) does not exist, we may take Russell to hold that the descriptive phrase gives the meaning of "a" and even that the latter is defined by or merely abbreviates the descriptive phrase—since a definition is often said to specify the meaning of a term solely in terms of other signs. Strawson, by contrast, can be seen as claiming that the grammatical rules provide the meaning. We can understand Russell's view in that (R), or "a = "(ι x)(Gx)," which introduces "a" into the linguistic schema is like a definition in that respect. and is, in any case, a stipulation. Just consider, for example, the familiar introduction of a predicate into a schema by a formula like "H = (ιΦ)(x)[Φx ≡ (Fx & Gx)]." In an obvious sense that formula introduces "H" into the schema in the same way "a" was introduced. The similarity may reinforce the idea that "a" is defined by means of a description. The distinctions we have made should enable us to see what is reasonable in the claim. Given the distinctions, one can point out that the sign has the same semantical and grammatical meaning whether or not it has a referential meaning. In that sense it has the same meaning, whether or not the purported referent exists, just as a sentence means the same thing whether it is true or false. What is emphasized by putting matters this way is the difference between introducing a sign by means of a definite description in the same schema as opposed to directly coordinating it to an object by the use of a demonstrative like "this" or another indexical label, another name that names, whether in the schema or in the meta-language for it.

Yet one can also understand why someone would hold that the description does not "define" the name "a." For, although it is correct to say that an interpretation provides or gives referential meaning to a sign, one cannot hold that the interpreted sign is an "abbreviation" for its interpretation. There is really nothing to argue about. So long as we recognize (1) that we can distinguish the diverse ways of "introducing" or "interpreting" signs; (2) that a sentence like "a = (ι x)(Gx)" is quite different from a true sentence like "a = (ι x)(Fx)," where the latter does not introduce "a" into the schema; and (3) that an "ostensive definition" can only be given where there is an object to be co-ordinated to the sign, the points made by Russell's account of purported names that do not name can be granted. The disputes about whether such "names" are really names or not, about the "meaning" of names like "a" that are introduced by definite descriptions and about whether "a" is really a name or a "disguised" description are specious. But there is another aspect to the question posed by the introduction of "a" via a description like "(ι x)(Gx)" when there is not a unique object that is G.

Whether we deal with a designation rule, (R), or an identity postulate, "a = (ι x)(Gx)," it would seem that the statement, expanded along Russell's lines, is false, even though it is a stipulated rule or postulate. Simply put, if the object does not exist, nothing is identical with "it" nor can a sign stand for "it." Thus one must introduce such signs by more complex rules, following the lines of Russell's definitions in context in *Principia Mathematica*. We could use "introductory" postulates like:

a = (ι x)(Gx) ≡ G(ι x)(Gx)
Φa ≡ Φ (ι x)(Gx)
"a" =df "(ι x)(Gx)"
E! a ≡ E! (ι x)(Gx).

None of these affect the basic issue, for the fundamental difference between "b = (ι x)(Gx)" and "a = (ι x)(Gx)," where "b" is a name that names and is not interpreted by means of "(ι x)(Gx)" but "a" is interpreted or introduced in terms of "(ι x)(Gx)," would be preserved, whether (ι x)(Gx) exists or not.

The above discussion also points to the utter emptiness of contemporary lengthy disputes regarding descriptions and "rigid designators" denoting objects in possible worlds. Supposedly a name, being a "rigid designator," designates the same object in all possible worlds, since an object is necessarily identical with itself. On the other hand, a definite description could apply to (denote) one thing in one possible world and another in a "different world." After all, Gödel might not have discovered his famous first incompleteness theorem, given that many were looking for such a result, and Tarski might have beat him to it. So a description based on a reference to the theorem might have denoted Tarski, but Gödel could not have been Tarski. Again, we have much ado about absolutely nothing. That Gödel is Gödel is an instance of a logical law, the law of identity. That Gödel proved the most celebrated theorem in logic that bears his name is not an instance of a logical law. That one claim applies a "contingent" property to Gödel, while the other does not is another factor involved. In the case of "being Gödel" or "x=Gödel" we do not deal with or attribute a property at all, let alone an "essential" or "necessary" property. For neither being self-identical nor being identical with Gödel are properties, of Gödel or anything. Moreover, if a sign, "a" say, is introduced into a schema via a semantical rule, such as "a" =df "$(\iota x)(Gx)$," "Ga" may follow from the rules of the schema. That is all there is to it. Whether one chooses to speak of "a" as an abbreviation of a description or as a "name" is irrelevant. There is not an issue worth fussing about nor possible worlds to argue about. Is Gödel necessarily Gödel in diverse possible worlds or are there merely "counterparts" of Gödel in other possible worlds? That too is not a real question, though there are basic, and classical, problems about individuation and identity that must be dealt with—but that is another matter. The real questions, about the grounds of individuation and identity, tend to be ignored or dismissed by those who discuss "rigid designators," "counterparts" in other worlds and "trans-world" identity, as we will note in later considering some aspects of Kripke's view about the purported analytic *a posteriori*.

As the above issues about names and descriptions are specious, so are the claims regarding Russell's supposed unfaithfulness to ordinary usage and Strawson's view supposedly fitting such usage. Consider the ordinary language name "Pegasus." On Russell's analysis, a sentence such as "Pegasus does not exist" would be correlated to a sentence of a formal schema which contains a definite description rather than a logically proper name. This is one thing that can be meant by the claim that "Pegasus" is really a disguised description. But this does not mean that Strawson's retention of the term "Pegasus," on his analysis, more faithfully reflects ordinary usage, since "Pegasus" is a grammatically proper name in ordinary usage. Strawson seeks to deal with the same puzzles that Russell does regarding logical inferences involving, and truth values of, sentences like "Pegasus = Pegasus," while the ordinary user of ordinary language is not concerned with such matters. Strawson's claim about the term being a proper name is made within a certain contextual background of philosophical puzzles, and that is not a context the ordinary user of language employs or, generally, is aware of. This is clear from Strawson's notion of "secondary reference." What lies behind that notion is that we do speak about Pegasus and Hamlet, and speak truly or falsely, even "theoretically," as in the case of psychoanalytic accounts of Hamlet, his mother and his proverbial hesitation. But, of course, all that is involved is that one treats the play "as if" it were about some person. Thus the evidence, or what there is of it, for Hamlet's Oedipus complex consists solely of sentences in a manuscript. This may be all that Strawson intends, but then the use of the term "reference" is misleading, for to speak of a sign referring is to speak of two things, the sign and its referent, connected in a certain way. In the case of secondary reference there is no object and hence no connection—that is why, after all, it is "secondary" and part of Strawson's attempt to deal with the same puzzles Russell deals with. To be sure, in ordinary usage "Hamlet," "Pegasus" and "Peter" are proper names—grammatically proper names. Russell can easily accommodate, in various ways, a category of signs in a logically clarified *Principia*-type language that would be names that do not name (as Frege could, but considered doing so to be useless). But all that aside, Strawson distinguishes between names that do and do not name in that, forgetting secondary reference, one does not use names that do not name to make true or false assertions in the way one does with names that do name. These are logical, not grammatical, distinctions that match Russell's distinctions between the use of definite descriptions and logically proper names in inference patterns. For, in a sense, one can say that definite descriptions of particulars and logically proper names belong to the same grammatical category in that they both combine with predicates to form sentences. Thus the question of whether "Pegasus" is really a name or not, or, perhaps better, *should be* construed as a name or not, is a question asked in the context of the philosophical dispute between Russell and Strawson. To raise the question is to ask which philosophical analysis is to be preferred. It is not to ask the trivial question of whether "Pegasus" is really a grammatically proper name in an ordinary language (British English, American English, German, etc.). Consider another example.

The sentence "This is red" may be used on various occasions to speak about various objects, some red and some not red. Strawson might argue that such a feature of ordinary usage presupposes that assertions, not sentences, are the bearers of truth and falsity, since otherwise the "same" sentence would be both true and false. On the other hand, by distinguishing the sign design type from its various tokens, one can easily hold that the different tokens of the same sign design type can be used as different sentences. If we are concerned with more than the "grammatical meaning" of the sign, we must consider the interpretation of the sign design or particular token of that design, as well as the grammatical rules, in order to understand the meaning of and determine the truth value of the sentence.

It is true that, in one sense, anyone who understands English understands what is said if an utterance of "This is red" is overheard coming from behind a closed door. But there is another clear sense in which the eavesdropper doesn't quite know what is being said by not knowing what is being referred to. Again, there is no point in quibbling about how to use the terms "understand" and "meaning." What is crucial is to note that our ordinary usage does not dictate the answer that assertions, not meaningful sentences (i. e. interpreted well-formed formulae of an appropriate kind) are the bearers of truth and falsity. The questions we are raising about sentences, sign design types, tokens, meaning, interpretation and assertions do not arise in an ordinary context. In such a context we might well be satisfied with noting that *the* sentence is sometimes true, sometimes false and sometimes unclear. Strawson offers one solution to certain puzzles that arise; Russell offers another. Imagine a linguistic schema of a Russellian kind where the proper names have different interpretations at different times. If by "same name" and "same sentence" we mean the sign design type, then the same sentence, like "the" name, may have many interpretations. If one includes the interpretation in what one means by "same name" and "same sentence"—what Wittgenstein called the sign's "projective relation" to the world—then neither the same name nor the same sentence can be said to have diverse interpretations. But our ordinary use of phrases like "same sentence" have nothing to do with contexts in which such distinctions are made and taken to be relevant to philosophical problems about language. Thus Strawson's view that on diverse occasions the same sentence was uttered but used to make different assertions does not mean that Strawson is reproducing an ordinary observation about the "same sentence" being uttered. For the phrase "same sentence" doesn't mean the same thing in the quite different contexts—one in which certain distinctions are made and one in which they are not. What is crucial to note is that Strawson introduces "assertions," makes problematic use of notions like "presuppose" and "negation" and introduces the idea of "secondary reference" to fictional entities (1960, 35, 40). Russell avoids assertions, uses "presuppose" in the sense of "logically entails," retains a standard use of negation and avoids introducing secondary reference.

To get at Strawson's attack on Russell's analysis of definite descriptive phrases, we can simplify matters by avoiding talk about assertions and simply take Strawson to hold that subject-predicate sentences containing unfulfilled descriptions as subject phrases are neither true nor false—either lacking a truth value or having the "third" value N. Strawson then holds that: (1) sentences of the form "The Φ is Ψ" are not existential sentences but subject-predicate in form; (2) such sentences being true or false presuppose the truth of an existential sentence stating that the described object exists (or simply, presuppose that the described object exists); (3) definite descriptions are referring expressions like proper names. Again Strawson's use of "presupposes," as different from that of standard logical entailment, plays a key role. For Russell, given the contextual definitions of "The Φ is Ψ," the statement "The Φ exists" trivially follows from it. Hence,

(R) The Φ is $\Psi \supset$ The Φ exists

is a logical truth in a standard sense. For Strawson, we have:

(S1) "The Φ is Ψ" being true (false) presupposes that the Φ exists.

But as "presupposes" is a basic notion that he employs, there is no corresponding standard logical truth (assuming a suitable truth predicate) like:

(S2) "The Φ is Ψ" is true $\supset$ The Φ exists.

Yet, as he understands "presupposes," (S2) "follows" from (S1) by the meaning of that term. Thus one major difference between Strawson and Russell is that for Russell (R) is an ordinary logical truth, while for Strawson (S2) follows from (S1), where (S1) is clearly not a logical truth itself, but a "conceptual" truth. And the use of "follows from" in the previous sentence is merely a way of expressing what is involved in the notion of "presupposes" in (S1). One might say (S1) simply reflects Strawson's use of the term "presupposes" and thus operates as an axiom (theorem) of his "theory." Moreover, given the use of the third value N, a question arises about

(S3) The Φ is Ψ $\supset$ The Φ exists

when the Φ does not exist, and hence the right side is false and the left side is then N (or, if one prefers, without a truth value). Not surprisingly Strawson cannot, as he does not, take the conditional to have the standard truth table. This bears on not being able to have "'The Φ is Ψ' is true $\equiv$ The Φ is Ψ" and thus satisfy Tarski's Convention-T. That is characteristic of attempts to use "gaps" to handle "the liar paradox." Thus his revisions extend beyond matters having to do with Russell's analysis of definite descriptions and fit with his attack on "modern" logicians and the use of the standard conditional. But there is an oddity to Strawson's view that borders on the paradoxical.

Whether we consider "The Φ is Ψ" in terms of having the value N or a truth gap when the Φ does not exist, an existential sentence like "The Φ exists" will be true or false, never N or with a gap. This is the odd feature, mentioned earlier, of Strawson's account, if we consider it in terms of a three-valued schema. Only some sentences would take one of three values, while others take only the standard truth values. This, in itself, is awkward. But there is a paradoxical feature as well. In ordinary usage "The Φ exists" is a subject-predicate sentence with "exists" as a predicate. This is obvious not only in grammatical terms but from the history of philosophy and the various attempts to show, as Russell argued, that "exists" is not, logically considered, a predicate applicable to particular objects. But, on Strawson's analysis of definite descriptions, if we consider "The Φ exists" to be of subject-predicate form, then, for it to have a truth value, the presupposition must be fulfilled. So "The Φ exists" can only have a truth value, or take either the value T or F rather than N, if the described object exists. Thus it could only be false if it were true. The same is the case with non-naming names and sentences like "Pegasus does not exist" on Strawson's account of names and presupposition. So what is Strawson to do? Remarkably, he argues that this shows that "exists" is not really a predicate! Thus he corrects ordinary language, by appeal to his analysis, rather than have his analysis fit ordinary language. Ironically, he transcribes "The Φ exists" much as Russell did, and not as a subject-predicate sentence. (1964a, 191) This is precisely what he accused Russell of doing in criticizing Russell's analysis of definite descriptive phrases.

There is another odd consequence of Strawson's treatment of "existence." It leads him to hold that when we say that a class exists it is not clear what we mean if we do not mean that the class has members (1964a, 191 ff.). He must say this, since we cannot transform the apparent subject-predicate sentence "The class of Φs exists," along the lines of "The Φ exists," into "There is one and only one Φ." Hence, aside from any question about the existence of classes or of the null class, we cannot even assert "The class of Φs exists" or "The null class exists" in anything like the standard sense of those statements.

As he attacks Russell, Strawson attacks "logicians" by applying his notion of *presupposition* to the use of the conditional sign (1964a, 85). Following a line that motivates the development of so-called "relevance" logics, Strawson argues that a sentence like "All my children are blond" can be taken to be true or false only if the existential presupposition is fulfilled—that I have children. He thus condemns the standard construal of the conditional and the Aristotelian "A" proposition in terms of a universal generalization employing that conditional. But note something about the conditional and "modern" logic. Consider "All mermaids are blond" and "No mermaids are blond," construed as "(x)(Mx ⊃ Bx)" and "(x)(Mx ⊃ ¬ Bx)," respectively. Both are true as there are no mermaids. Strawson, like others, finds this paradoxical. But the conjunction of the two conditionals is logically equivalent, using standard logic, to "¬ (∃x) Mx"—i. e. to "There are no mermaids." Thus the "modern logician" can be seen as merely "asserting" that there are no mermaids, by accepting *both* conditionals, which is hardly paradoxical and is why "both" is italicized.

There is a last feature of Strawson's argument worth noting. Consider three sentences. (1) The golden mountain is high; (2) The one and only golden mountain is high; (3) The one and only existent golden mountain is high. One might reasonably hold that (2) makes explicit what is implicit in (1) But does that mean that what is stated in (2) is "presupposed" by asserting (1) or that it is implicitly asserted in using (1)? How could one make clear what the question is about without going into the issues that lead to the dispute between Strawson and Russell? If one brings in ordinary usage, one may reasonably claim that, by ordinary usage, (2) makes explicit what is implicit in (1). But both Russell and Strawson have ways of construing that feature of ordinary usage. (3) may well strike one as puzzling, since one does not ordinarily talk about non-existent objects (forgetting stories and secondary reference). But (3) may be seen as puzzling in that it makes explicit an even more obvious condition implicit in (1). But, again, how is "implicit" to be taken? Russell's analysis actually makes quite clear one feature of our puzzlement. Recalling a point made in connection with Meinong's golden mountain, we could construe the English sentence "The golden mountain is high" in terms of "Anything that is uniquely a golden mountain is high." Then the English sentence would be taken to correspond to a sentence, in Russell's logically perspicuous schema, that is true, given that there is no such individual, for we have a universally quantified conditional where all instantiations would have a false antecedent. Thus any puzzlement about sentences like "The golden mountain is high" can be taken to be reflected by two things. First, the sentence can be construed in terms of a true universally quantified sentence or a false existential statement; second, the alternative transcriptions only differ in truth value if the definite description in the English sentence is not fulfilled.

Regarding the issue of whether his or Strawson's analysis is more faithful to ordinary usage, Russell made a point in his own inimitable way:

> ... although I have no wish to claim the support of common usage, I do not think he can claim it either. Suppose, for example, that in some country there was a law that no person could hold public office if he considered it false that the Ruler of the Universe is wise. I think an avowed atheist who took advantage of Mr. Strawson's doctrine to say that he did not hold this proposition false, would be regarded as a somewhat shifty character. (1973, 125)

2e. On Distinguishing Descriptive from Referential Use

K. Donellan added a postscript to Strawson's critique of Russell's analysis of the contextual use of definite descriptive phrases by distinguishing between the referential and the attributive use of a definite description—a distinction that neither Russell nor Strawson purportedly made (1966). His claim is simply put. Suppose I see Strawson holding a martini glass at a party and say to someone, whom I know not to have ever heard of Strawson, "The man with the martini is a philosopher." I have supposedly referred to Strawson by using the descriptive phrase. That is so even though Strawson may have sherry, and not a martini, in his martini glass. In such a situation it is clear to whom I refer, even though it would be false to say that the person referred to was having a martini—as opposed to holding a martini glass. Thus the Russellian transcription of "The man with the martini is a philosopher" would yield a false sentence. Yet, the sentence is true in that the man I refer to (succeed in referring to in a referential speech act) is a philosopher. This kind of use of a descriptive phrase supposedly contrasts with Sherlock Holmes saying, regarding an as yet unknown criminal, "The person who committed the crime left by the front door." Here one does not know to whom one refers and may even be said not to refer to a specific individual, in the sense that one does so refer in the first case. One simply claims that there is a unique individual characterized as "having committed the crime" and further claims that the individual, so characterized, exited by the front door. In the first case we have a referential use of a descriptive phrase and in the second case a supposedly attributive use, since we attribute a property to some "unknown" person. Russell's account of definite descriptions thus fails in failing to make the purported distinction. That purported distinction has generated much discussion, but it amounts to little, if anything, and is hardly a criticism of Russell's theory. It is easy to see why this is so.

In the case of proper names Russell clearly distinguished between logically proper names and grammatically proper names. The former were genuine names while the latter might or might not be. In the case of a grammatical name like "Pegasus," which is not a genuine or logically proper name in that it does not name anything, we have a term that can be construed as an abbreviation of a definite description. In the case of definite descriptions Russell did not clearly make a corresponding distinction. In the 1905 paper he simply characterized definite descriptions as phrases of the from "the so and so." But a corresponding distinction should be made and is implicit in his discussion of the context determining the scope of a description that we discussed earlier. Is one really to hold that Russell would be forced to say that a statement to Moore, after a meeting of the Apostles, asserting "The argument is invalid" would be false since Moore gave many arguments prior to the meeting, or since there are virtually countless arguments?

In the case of the purported description "the man with the martini," we either attribute "having a martini" to the individual, and hence do say something false; or, we do not ascribe the predicate in the phrase to anyone. If we do not use the predicate to attribute a property, then it is not functioning as a predicate, and hence the phrase is not functioning descriptively. What we have is not a case of a referential use of a definite description. Rather, we simply have a case where a grammatically descriptive phrase is not a genuine definite descriptive phrase. If one baptizes one's child "the present king of France" one has given the child an odd name, one has not used an expression that is, logically speaking, a definite description, though it is, grammatically speaking, a descriptive phrase. Nor has one, thereby, refuted Russell's account of definite descriptions. Such examples arise in everyday contexts as well. Just consider the parent who welcomes a college student to the dinner table with the statement "the professor has arrived." One is clearly not literally ascribing the attribute of being a professor, let alone being the only professor, to the student. Here, as in the odd imagined case, what is viable to hold is that a phrase, grammatically a descriptive phrase, is being used to refer to someone, but the phrase, so used, is not a definite description, logically speaking. The simple point is that one should apply to descriptive phrases a distinction paralleling that between logically proper names and grammatically proper names.

In the case of expressions of the form "the Φ" we may recognize that some of them are used as names or as labels. But, even in such cases, Donellan's distinction ignores the descriptive component present. For it is always appropriate to point out, or at least note, that an object does not have the property mentioned in the descriptive phrase and, consequently, that something false is stated or implied. There is nothing like that in the case of purely indicating labels—logically proper names. We can conclude that there is no purely referential use of definite descriptions. That there are referential uses of expressions that are grammatically descriptive phrases is an obvious sociolinguistic fact about usage. It marks another case where logical and grammatical form do not coincide in ordinary language usage. Aside from that, it has no philosophical significance. If one were to take a perspicuous schema to be a formal "mirror" of ordinary linguistic use, one could employ expressions like "$(\iota\ x)(\Phi x)$" as primitive signs like "a" and interpret the former as one interprets the latter. One could also use expressions like "$(\iota\ x)(\Phi x)$" as expressions defined in context in Russell's fashion. But, aside from duplicating an ambiguity of ordinary language, there would be no point to doing so. One point of employing perspicuous schemata is to avoid ambiguities that lead to philosophical perplexity and disputes. We should still note that if one introduces (some) expressions like "$(\iota\ x)(\Phi x)$" as primitive terms requiring interpretation, then one either ignores the occurrence of the predicate "Φ" in the expression (and what then is the point of using it?), as well as the imbedded sentential-form of expression "Φx," or one understands it to play a "descriptive" role. Doing the former, we would pointlessly be using esoteric names; doing the latter we do not merely use the expression as a name—a purely referring expression. Realizing this, we may safely relegate Donellan's distinction to the sociology, rather than the philosophy, of language. One must keep in mind that in spite of what he sometimes says Russell is concerned with a schema that will serve philosophical purposes—a framework for describing what there is—embodying science, mathematics and logic. A similar point applies to talk about descriptions "fossilizing" into "rigid designators"—a later expression embodying Russell's notion of a logically proper name (irrespective of its use in contexts involving modal logic and "trans-world" identity). Phrases like "the man in the iron mask" and "the sage of Monticello" can be said to "rigidly designate," i.e. function like proper names, as does a description like "$(\iota\ x)(x=a)$," where "a" is a proper name.

2f. Kripke's Causal Theory of Reference

Causal theories of reference became quite fashionable in the last quarter of the twentieth century as part of a general tendency blending "naturalism" with a neo-Wittgensteinian focus on ordinary usage that marks one strain of the "analytic turn." What such theories do, at most, is seek to provide necessary and sufficient causal conditions for a specific use of a term being spoken of as referring to a specified thing. They neither offer an analysis of reference nor acknowledge a primitive designation or representation relation. Dummett has rightly dismissed such theories out of hand, but for the wrong reason. Since, for him, one knows or "fixes" the reference of a term by knowing "the conditions for the truth of any sentence containing it," reference cannot "consist ... in the existence of a causal chain leading from the object in question to an utterance of the term" (1991, 192). He is right as to what it cannot be, but it is not at all clear as to what it actually is for him. In any case, causal theories are irrelevant to philosophical problems about what reference "is." Consequently, it will be no surprise, as we will later see, to find that causal accounts of reference share themes with attempts to "deflate" the concepts of truth and reference by means of so-called "semantic theories" of truth and reference. In defense of his version of a causal account, Kripke writes:

> A rough statement of a theory might be the following. An initial baptism takes place. Here the object may be named by ostension or the reference of the name may be fixed by a description. When the "name" is passed from link to link," the receiver of the name must, I think, intend when he learns it to use it with the same reference as the man from whom he heard it. (1980, 96-7)

But this not just a rough statement, it is not a statement at all in the sense of providing a philosophical analysis. The problem persists in the need to specify what it is to "intend to refer to" an object when one uses (or hears) a token of a term. Kripke is aware of the problem and continues:

> Notice that the preceding outline hardly *eliminates* the notion of reference; on the contrary, it takes the notion of intending to use the same reference as given. (97)

He concludes: "To repeat, I may not have presented a theory, but I do think that I have presented a better picture than that given by description theorists." But all he has done is reiterate, in different words, Russell's standard distinction between logically proper names that refer and definite descriptions that denote (but do not refer) and repeat Russell's claim that such names cannot be replaced, in Quine's fashion, by definite descriptions, or require a Fregean "sense," construed in terms of supplying a descriptive phrase (a "back up" description, as some speak). That he, like Strawson before him, disputes Russell's views as to what terms of ordinary language are genuine names is irrelevant. Unfortunately, Russell's empiricism, which is logically independent of his accounts of reference and description, complicated matters for later philosophers who derived their theories from his writings. Holding that acquaintance was required to link a name to its referent (or a predicate to the property it represented), he insisted that one must be acquainted with an object (or property) to refer to it by the use of a purely indexical term—such as a logically proper name, demonstrative term or primitive predicate. Logically proper names were what many have later called "labels," others "pure indexicals" and what some would eventually come to speak of, years later, as "tags." Arguing that we were not acquainted with physical objects or other "persons," on standard empiricist grounds, Russell also held that we could not refer to them by names or labels but must denote them by definite descriptions. This has led many to misleadingly place Russell among those philosophers who have advocated the replacement of names by definite descriptions or requiring having a "back up" description for using a proper name. This Russell did not do, and Kripke has misleadingly invented the idea of a "Frege-Russell Theory" of proper names.

Many philosophers, influenced by the development of ordinary language philosophy, reject acquaintance with an object as a suitable "link" for using a term to refer to that object. After all, as we normally speak, we refer to Plato, Aristotle and Ramses the Great—objects that no sane contemporary philosopher is acquainted with. Thus the causal chain, whereby the name "is passed from link to link," has been substituted for Russell's appeal to direct acquaintance. But this simply introduces the commonsense triviality that we learn who Aristotle, Plato and Ramses the Great were from books and statements, employing tokens of the appropriate terms, derived, in turn, from other books, etc. until one supposedly goes back to a situation that plays the role of Russell's experience of an object—a "baptism." But the fundamental philosophical problems surrounding reference and intentionality are either not raised or simply discarded.

Whether one offers an account like Sellars's (Chapter 3 below) or a causal theory like Kripke's, two simple questions arise. How does one justify the claim that one refers to a historical figure, Aristotle say, when one uses a token of the term "Aristotle" in a way that accords with the account? On what grounds does one hold that one then refers to Aristotle in the same sense that one refers to a presented object by a token of a demonstrative term? As we commonly speak, we say we refer to Aristotle, as we assume I just did, rather than Plato, under certain conditions. That is obvious. When Kripke and Sellars take the providing of a set of necessary and sufficient conditions to provide a theory of reference that omits a basic representation relation, all they are entitled to say is that they provide a set of necessary and sufficient conditions that pick out the same cases that we normally speak of as being cases where a reference was made. To do this is not to give an analysis of reference. It does not even show that, on a viable notion of reference, we actually refer to objects when we "ordinarily" are said to do so, nor does it pick out those cases where we do in fact refer. Just as in cases of "knowledge," "identity" and "perception," it is one thing to set out criteria that pick out cases where we ordinarily speak about knowing something to be true or of something being the same object or of perceiving a physical object—it is another thing to offer philosophical analyses to resolve familiar philosophical problems, as opposed to dismissing the latter. In the case of reference there is an added problem. Given a causal theory like Kripke's or an account of Sellars's kind, one must show that one uses "refers to" in the same sense when one speaks of referring to Aristotle by using a token of "Aristotle" and of referring to a presented object by using a demonstrative token or name (label). Unfortunately the legacy of the linguistic turn has led many philosophers to uncritically accept common speech as the embodiment of philosophical wisdom, whether it is in the relatively simple style of Kripke's ordinary language based analysis or in the inordinately complex manner of Sellars's attempt to sketch out a socio-psychological account of linguistic behavior that we will shortly take up.

To give a causal account of reference is to do no more than reiterate how we learn a language or specify criteria for determining when we take someone to have referred to some specific thing rather than something else. Thus we merely try to specify criteria that will pick out the object that we would normally say was referred to, cases fitting our "ordinary" use of "refers to." One is satisfied with criteria that are extensionally equivalent (more or less), as Tarski was satisfied with a definition of a "truth" predicate that had the appropriate extension. Giving criteria that are extensionally equivalent to a concept is not to give a philosophical analysis. To do the latter is to specify and analyze the state of affairs that obtains when one intends or refers to something.

Causal considerations are irrelevant for a simple reason: they do not account in any way for the intentionality that is involved in initial cases of reference. That is why one often hears of "baptizing" an object or of "attaching" a name to an object or of "fixing" the referent. Nor do such causal accounts deal with a crucial question: Is the direct reference or direct intention that occurs in cases where the object referred to is directly apprehended also involved in cases where the object is not so apprehended? This question is never faced by those who offer causal accounts. Kripke might argue that just as any natural number greater than 0 can be said to be a natural number, since 0 is a number and anything that is in the line of succession from 0 (in the "posterity" of 0) is a number, so, given an initial reference to Aristotle (or "baptism" ceremony), and the existence of a causal chain from that initial reference to a present occurrence of a token of "Aristotle," or thought involving it, one refers to Aristotle in such a case. This must assume, as Kripke says, that one "intended" to use the term in the way it was used by the one it was learned from—where what it is to intend to refer is not explained but is taken as given. Yet, clearly, one cannot take the class of references to Aristotle as the "posterity" of an initial reference, as one specifies the class of natural numbers as the posterity of 0. Reference in an initial case involves a basic relation of direct reference or direct intention. One can then stipulate a definition of "refers to" or "intends," as a new disjunctive predicate that will apply to both initial cases and "descendants" of such. This does not show at all that the basic relation of direct reference or intention that is involved in the initial case holds between a descendent token and the object. Kripke avoids the fundamental issue when he takes the "notion of intending to use the same reference as a given" and offers neither an analysis of the situation nor an argument for the claim (1980, 97). As Hume questioned ordinary assumptions about causality, perception and knowledge, others are concerned, as Brentano was, with what is involved in a thought being about an object or state of affairs. Such a question is not resolved by setting forth a report on the usage of "refer" or finding conditions that match, more or less, what we would ordinarily say about a reference being made or not and to what.

One use of causal theories of reference and, generally, of meaning, has been to provide a recent means of disposing of philosophical issues along positivistic lines by "naturalizing" them. Thus, consider the classic problem of universals, where realists take (some) predicates to refer to universal properties. Given a causal theory of reference, the obvious question that is raised is how universals, assumed not to be spatio-temporal entities, can be causally linked to our use of predicates. Not having such causal links such objects are dismissed in favor of talk of behavioral responses, including utterances of linguistic tokens, to appropriate stimuli. In a way the issue is simply a contemporary version of the classical questions about "abstraction" and the origin of ideas that led Plato to his doctrine of "recollection," a form of the doctrine of innate ideas, Augustine to divine illumination and Descartes to his variant of innate ideas for some ideas (infinity being an interesting one). Some realists about universals hold that universals are in space but are "multiply located." This, however, becomes difficult to hold for relations, especially spatial and temporal relations, and, in the monadic case, seems to amount to little more than holding that particulars that instantiate them are spatial. Russell, when he construed "ordinary" particulars as "bundles" of qualities in the 1940s, took qualities to be at multiple locations, but characterized them as "particulars" since, unlike relations, they were not exemplified by objects but were "constituents" of such objects, which were complexes of "compresent" qualities.

In contemporary parlance the causal theory has led to the so-called problem of "access" to abstract entities, particularly in connection with the philosophy of mathematics. In that context it is an issue that requires no knowledge of mathematics and reflects little appreciation of the history of the general issue in philosophy. For the same problem arises about the natural numbers (as well as sets and other mathematical "objects") that supposedly arises about purported universals, like the color *red* and the relation of *prior to*.

There is often a physicalist tinge to the discussion of the issue and an implicit, or explicit, suggestion that only physical objects and events can be causes, as we will note when we return to the problem in Chapter 4. For the present, it is worth recalling that Russell and Moore claimed to be directly acquainted with, or directly apprehend, universals—often universals that characterized non-physical entities like sense-data. Does such direct apprehension count as a "causal" factor? Surely if I do so apprehend a universal property, then it would seem to be a cause of my doing so in the sense that its existence is a condition of my apprehending it. However, one can hold, as many realists about universals do, that universals must be instantiated. Thus the universals one recognizes are "grounded," so to speak, in the experience of particular objects instantiating them—in the apprehension of facts involving them. Just what the notion of "causality" is that enters into causal theories of reference and meaning is conveniently not made clear, as those who advocate them do not seem to inquire about the, or several, causal relations themselves. But an obvious question arises. How is one to be in causal contact with the relation of causal connection (forgetting questions about just what that is as well as the name of Hume)? How does one specify the meaning of "causes" and what could one possibly mean by claiming to be in causal contact with the (or a) relation of causality? One may claim to perceive causality, as some causal realists do, Armstrong for example; but this seems more in the nature of a declaration than a report of experience.

That aside, one surely comprehends abstract logical "forms" and concepts—monadic and dyadic predication, negation, quantification, and so forth. Again, one can talk about seeing that *all* the books that are on the table are red, that *not* one is green, that there are *three* books, and so forth. One can even speak of apprehending in such cases, or even of seeing colors and not just colored objects, but is one in causal contact with red, green, negation, generality, and the number three? Trivially, of course, a cause of my seeing three books is that there are three books. Is that all that is meant? But then my abstracting the logical form of a fact is a cause of my apprehending it. And my apprehending it presupposes that there is something to apprehend. Thus we return to the old issues about "abstracting" and "apprehending." For even if one holds that one experiences objects, properties and facts, surely one does not experience logical forms, say monadic predication, even though one experiences facts of that form. In that sense one can perhaps say we experience instances of them. Perhaps all one would mean is that we learn the meaning of the appropriate terms and "concepts" from having certain experiences, irrespective of how one analyzes the concept of causality. If one adds that other terms and concepts, not so tied to experience, are meaningful in terms of those that are, we are on the verge of repeating classical empiricist accounts of meaning. Alternatively, one can be led, like some of the logical positivists and, later, Quine, to talk of a "web of belief" or nomological "net" of concepts and statements that are "anchored" to experience at certain points. Thus many are led to "holistic" theories focusing on the "internal" role such terms, concepts and statements play in a conceptual framework and to thinking of meaning in terms of such roles.

Kripke is often said to have discovered the "analytic *a posteriori*," (and seems to suggest that himself, 1980, 34-40), since Kant is generally taken to have used his well known dichotomies, analytic-synthetic and *a priori-a posteriori*, in a way that did not allow for propositions that were analytic, yet *a posteriori*. The classic twentieth century cases of analytic *a posteriori* propositions are provided by true identities like "Russell= Russell." For it is supposedly a necessary truth, yet one that is dependent on a "non-necessary" empirical condition, Russell's existence. This matter also relates to the supposed further discovery of "rigid designators" of which much is written, as much is written about "deflating" truth and reference. There is an interesting passage in Kant's *Prolegomena to Any Future Metaphysics* that bears on the matters and shows Kant to be quite aware of the questions involved.

> For this very reason all analytic judgments are *a priori* even when the concepts are empirical, as, for example, "Gold is a yellow metal"; for to know this I require no experience beyond my concept of gold, which contained the thought that this body is yellow and metal. It is, in fact, this thought that constituted my concept; and I need only analyze it, without looking beyond it elsewhere. (1977, 12-13)

Before considering Kant's statement, note Russell's relevant claim:

> We know *a priori* that two things and two other things together make four things, but we do not know *a priori* that if Brown and Jones are two, and Robinson and Smith are two, then Brown and Jones and Robinson and Smith are four. The reason is that this proposition cannot be understood at all unless we know that there are such people as Brown and Jones and Robinson and Smith, and this we can only know by experience. Hence, although our general proposition is *a priori*, all its applications to actual particulars involve experience and therefore contain an empirical element. (1946, 105)

The common theme of Russell and Kant is, to alter Kant's example, that "π=π" is *a priori*, and analytic, where "π" is a variable covering genuine names and meaningful predicates. Thus "Gold is Gold" is *a priori*, though, to put it in more contemporary terms, it may be said to involve the empirical presupposition that "Gold" expresses a meaningful concept that is derived from experience. For Russell, one cannot simply infer "Gold = Gold" from "(π)(π=π)"—ignoring issues of "type"—without an additional premise, a premise much on the order of the existential premise needed to make inferences from universal quantifications to definite descriptions. What is interesting is that Kripke hasn't discovered anything at all. He has expressed a point Kant made long ago, and Russell reiterated later, by packaging the issue in a manner that combines familiar Kantian terms in a seemingly paradoxical manner (paradoxical given Kant's well known views). This is also the sort of issue that gives rise to the use of names that do not name and so-called "free logics"—logics that essentially borrow the restrictions on inferences that Russell employs for definite descriptions and apply them to proper names, so that one can allow "non-naming" names. All we need note is that to have the statement "Smith=Smith" in a perspicuous schema, to shift the example to a simpler case along the lines of Russell's discussion, would require not just the "analytic" or "*a priori*" law of identity but the semantic rule interpreting the term—coordinating it to a referent. Such simple points avoid the endless and useless discussions of whether "Smith=Smith" is necessarily true if true.

Kripke cites Kant's statement but ignores the interesting point it involves while focusing on criticizing Kant.

> Kant (someone just pointed out to me) gives as an example [of an analytic statement] 'Gold is a yellow metal', which seems to me an extraordinary one, because its something I think that can turn out to be false. At any rate, lets just make it a matter of stipulation ....(1980, 39)

Of course it should be a "matter of stipulation," in Kripke's terms, since for Kant an analytic judgment with regards to a "subject A" is one where "the predicate is (covertly) contained in this concept A" (Kant, 1958, 48). And, "To meet with this predicate, I have merely to analyze the concept...." (48-

49). Kant's discussion is just a variant of the problem posed by having "$(\pi)(\pi=\pi)$" as a logical truth or "logical law"—a law of identity—deriving "Smith=Smith" from it by instantiation and proceeding to "$(\exists \pi)(\pi=$ Smith$)$" by generalization. Reading the latter as "Something is identical with Smith," and hence a way of saying, or presupposing, that Smith exists, appears to allow the derivation of an obviously "contingent" statement from the logical law of identity. Thus some are led to "free logics" and the requirement that such consequences follow not from "$(\pi)(\pi=\pi)$" alone but from the conjunction "$(\pi)(\pi=\pi)$ & $(\exists \pi)(\pi=$Smith$)$," which renders the inference harmless and trivial. But that is unnecessary as the problem is really disposed of by recognizing that semantical rules are involved that coordinate names to objects—hence the very occurrence of the name in a logically perspicuous schema involves there being an object designated by the name. While semantical rules can be considered among the logical rules, Carnap's L-rules, they are of a different sort than standard logical rules as they bridge the gap between the linguistic schema and the objects and properties that are among the "ontological commitments" that the schema (or its use) involves. This, of course, employs a quite different notion of "ontological commitment" than Quine's. Kant clearly takes "Gold is a yellow metal" to be true in virtue of a "relation among ideas" (to borrow a phrase from Hume) or relation among concepts—while recognizing that the concept of gold is dependent on experience in being analyzed in terms of empirical concepts like metal, yellow, etc. If he were to take gold to be an empirical concept in that the term "gold" represents a property found in experience, there would be a problem about "Gold is a yellow metal" being held to be analytic. For the statement would then simply link three empirical properties, assuming "yellow" and "metal" are also taken to represent such properties. But he apparently means, or should, that we deal with an "analysis"—that the predicate "gold" is understood or defined (has its meaning stipulated) in terms of other predicates that are empirical concepts. Thus Kant's example involves the appeal to a *conceptual* truth "$(x)(\theta x \supset (\Phi x \& \Psi x))$," based on the purported meaning of the expression "θ," and an "analytic" pattern of the form "$(x)((\Phi x \& \Psi x) \supset \Phi x).$" Applying the patterns to the case of gold involves properties exemplified by objects of experience and, hence, connections to experience. In principle, it is no different from the case of the law of identity. One need not fuss about the terminology. We have the logical law of identity (or non-diversity). Given that "Russell" is a genuine name, and its being so is not a matter of a logical law, we have "Russell=Russell." That identity statement is a consequence of the interpretation rules (semantic rules) and the logical laws. To add that Russell is necessarily Russell, or that if "Russell=Russell" is true it is necessarily true or that Russell is Russell in all possible worlds simply reiterates what was said in the previous sentence. The basic point is simple. Once there is the concept, Kant speaks of a judgment being analytic, even though one deals with "empirical" concepts, since one does not have "to go beyond the concept" which is connected to the "subject" term of the judgment (1958, 48). Experience is, of course, required in order to have empirical concepts. Descriptive (non-logical) signs, names and (some) predicates, must be interpreted, to put it another way. Kant ignores this aspect in stressing what is analytic and *a priori*, since he covers the matter by talking about the concept being "empirical." Kripke so uses the relevant terms that one can speak of the judgment being an *a posteriori* matter, since, in Kant's terms, an empirical concept is involved. It is one of those frequent cases in philosophy where we have much ado about nothing generated by a purely verbal dispute—not a discovery of anything. To put matters at their simplest, what concerns Kripke is what, in Kantian terms, is addressed by the difference between *a priori* propositions that are "pure" and *a priori* propositions that are "not pure":

> *A priori* modes of knowledge are entitled pure when there is no admixture of anything empirical. Thus, for instance, the proposition 'every alteration has its cause', while an *a priori* proposition, is not a pure proposition; because alteration is a concept which can be derived only from experience. (1958, 43)

Kant was quite explicit about the basic point in the sentences immediately preceding the short passage about "gold" being an empirical concept.

> All analytic judgments depend wholly on the principle of contradiction, and are in their nature *a priori* cognitions, whether the concepts that supply them with matter be empirical or not. For the predicate of an affirmative analytic judgment is already thought in the concept of the subject, of which it cannot be denied without contradiction. (1977, 12)

He goes on to cite the example of "gold" to illustrate what he here means.

The phrase "rigid designator" has come into common usage in connection with talk of possible worlds. The idea is simple. The name "Russell," as a "rigid designator," designates Russell not only in this world but in other possible worlds where he might not have written "On Denoting." So, the descriptive phrase "the author of 'On Denoting'" might not designate Russell in such a possible world, and hence is not a "rigid designator." This is tied to the idea that "Russell=Russell" is a necessary truth (and hence not false in any possible world), while "Russell authored 'On Denoting'" is not a necessary truth and hence is false in some possible world, such as the one imagined just above. Again thinking in terms of a perspicuous schema, and not taking seriously either talk of possible worlds in general or alternative views about them—disputes as to whether it would not be Russell in another possible world, but a "counterpart" of him—there is no real issue of philosophical significance. The term "Russell," taken as a logically proper name in a perspicuous schema, is interpreted by means of a semantical designation rule—the descriptive phrase is not. Thus "Russell=the author of 'On Denoting'" is not an L-truth of the schema, but a matter of fact, while "Russell=Russell" is a consequence of the logical and semantical rules. [Like Russell, I take "Russell=the author of 'On Denoting'" to be an existential statement and not an "identity." Thus we may ignore the pseudo-issues generated by talk of such an "identity" being necessarily true if true. For all the latter talk amounts to is that an object is necessarily identical with itself.] That descriptions like "the x such that x=Russell" will function much like proper names, in that "(ɩ x)(x=Russell)=Russell" will be a consequence of the logical rules, including definitions, is of no import. However, if one wishes a general phrase to cover such descriptions and logically proper names, "rigid designator" will do for such a role. Likewise, the complications posed by the familiar problems associated with notions like "natural kind" and "metaphysical necessity," as well as the facts of ordinary language usage whereby certain descriptions become fossilized into functioning somewhat like proper names, such as "the sage of Monticello" and "the father of our country," pose no real problems, or even interesting philosophical questions. Though, such matters are of interest to those interested in the sociology, history and anthropology of language, as well as in linguistics as opposed to philosophy, or even in the psychology of language use and so-called "cognitive science."

Kripke's subsequent lengthy discussion of the case of gold (1980, 116-125) simply takes "natural kind" terms to be "much closer to proper names than is ordinarily supposed" and involves a number of stipulations —and that is all they are—about essential properties, gold being necessarily of atomic number 79 and water being H_2O. What is surprising is that so much discussion has been generated about these so-called Kripkean necessities. For all that is involved is that the sort of thing we have called "water," understood as something having a number of macro properties and standing in certain relations, has been discovered to have a certain molecular structure. One then stipulates that anything with a different molecular structure, but which, nevertheless, has the same macro properties and relations (or a significant number of them) is simply not water, as water is necessarily of that molecular structure. Alternatively one could stipulate just the opposite, keeping in mind that if there turns out to be a different structure for water (standard water) we would have found out that what had the macro properties was of that different structure and not that what had one (supposed) structure also had the different structure. It is not an accident that Kripke's manner of talking about necessity has been picked up by those who speak of "the concept of water," rather than of macro properties, as guiding how we characterize water. For speaking of concepts allows one to think in terms of a sort of "stuff" that we apply the term "water" to and which we later discover to have a certain molecular structure. In typical neo-Wittgensteinian fashion, as one finds in various ways in writings of Dummett, Strawson, Geach and Searle, having a concept is knowing how to use a word in a variety of contexts. Thus, for Kripke, we find out that our concept applies to things of a certain micro structure, and thereby discover what it really is. Thinking along such lines has helped prepare the way for materialism. We have a concept of (or speak of) someone being in a certain mental state. We later discover that people to whom we apply the concept (or speak about in such a way) are in a certain neurophysiological state. Thus we discover what it "really is" that we apply the concept (phrase) to—as we discover what gold and water really are in discovering their micro structure.

Kripke's ordinary language dismissal of philosophical problems is nicely illustrated by his dismissal of the real issues that lie behind the various debates among discussants of possible worlds and the supposed problems of "trans-world identity" (Is Russell the same individual in another possible world? What is the ground of identity for such cases?)

> It is often said that, if a counterfactual situation is described as one which would have happened to Nixon, and if it is not assumed that such a description is reduced to a purely qualitative one then, mysterious 'bare particulars' are assumed, property less substrata underlying the qualities. ... What I do deny is that a particular is nothing but 'a bundle of qualities', whatever that may mean. If a quality is an abstract object, a bundle of qualities is an object of an even higher degree of abstraction, not a particular. ...this table is wooden, brown, in the room, etc. It has all these properties and is not a thing without properties, behind them; but it should not therefore be identified with the set, or 'bundle', of its properties, nor with the subset of its essential properties. Don't ask: how can I identify this table in another possible world, except by its properties? I have the table in my hands; I can point to it, and when I ask whether *it* might have been in another room, I am talking, by definition, about *it*. (1980, 52-3)

What is interesting is that one theme here reproduces the simple kind of mistake that led Bradley to identify a complex of concepts with a complex concept. Kripke simply stipulates that a bundle of qualities must be an "abstract" object (of an even "higher degree of abstraction") if qualities are "abstract objects." He obviously thinks of bundles as classes, and thus, as classes are abstract objects, a class of x's is "more abstract" than an x is—somewhat like being of a higher Russellian type. It is interesting, in this connection, that when Russell took particulars to be bundles of qualities in the 1940s, to dispense with "bare substrata," he took particulars to be of the same logical kind as basic qualities—they were thus complex qualities as well as complexes of qualities. [That he called basic qualities, like colors, "particulars" is another matter, as that simply reflected their not being "predicables" but constituents of the complexes that "ordinary" particulars were taken to be.] What is more to the point is that the above passage simply denies or is obstinately oblivious to the traditional philosophical problems centering on individuation, exemplification, the nature of qualities and the connection between particulars and qualities. To be sure, things are what they are and not other things, as Bishop Butler informed us long ago. Just as surely, there are presidents, cabbages and kings—and cabbages are vegetables, presidents are human beings and kings (generally speaking) are male human beings. As that is that and we know the difference between someone being president and something being a statue of a president, the philosophical issues one may raise about things and kinds are dismissed by the neo-Wittgensteinian injunction: Don't ask! It is no wonder that Kripke can go on to talk of "necessity," of what sorts of things can "possibly" have what properties and of what properties are "necessarily" had by what things without any hint of either the nature or the history of the problems. This is quite in the manner of Dummett's taking there to obviously be abstract objects, and noting that you even find them written about in the daily newspapers in stories about air pollution, economic prosperity and national hatreds. In the same manner, it is obvious that I am now writing about Kripke and Dummett (not "by definition," whatever that might possibly mean), but that takes us nowhere when we deal with the philosophical issues surrounding reference, intentionality and description.

CHAPTER 3

MEANING, TRUTH AND ANTI-REALISM

3a. Tarski's Conception of Truth: Twisting the Linguistic Turn

Tarski set out what has become known as "Convention-T" as an equivalence condition for the introduction of a truth predicate into a linguistic schema (Tarski, 1956). It requires that a "formally correct definition" of a truth predicate introduced into or defined in a meta-language for a schema L, will be "adequate" if, for any statement of L, it has as a consequence a biconditional holding between a meta-linguistic transcription of the statement and a meta-linguistic sentence ascribing the truth predicate to the statement (Tarski, 1956, 187-88). In his early paper, as well as in a later paper, Tarski linked Convention-T to both "the classical Aristotelian conception of truth" expressed in Aristotle's assertion:

> To say of what is that it is not, or of what is not that it is, is false, while to say of what is that it is, or of what is not that it is not, is true. (Tarski, 1956, 155; 1944, 342-43)

and the notion that the truth of a sentence is determined by its correspondence to reality (1944, 343).

Tarski did not think that the "the pragmatic conception" and "the coherence theory" of truth had "been put so far in an intelligible and unequivocal form" (1944, 356). But we can go further, as Convention-T provides a ground for rejecting coherence theories and for accepting a correspondence theory that is in keeping with Aristotle's concise, but explicit, realism. The arguments for these claims involve explicating the concepts of correspondence and truth condition in a way that construes a theory of truth quite differently than Tarski does. They will also naturally lead to evaluating Davidson's attempt to provide a theory of meaning based on Tarski's semantic conception of truth.

To see why coherence theories cannot satisfy Convention-T, consider an atomic sentence "aRb" or the proposition that one may take it to express, which we can designate by "<aRb>." As the distinction between sentences and propositions makes no difference for the present issue, we can use the latter sign design to represent the sentence or what is "expressed by" or "meant by" the sentence. Thus, we can consider "aRb" to belong to a basic language L and "<aRb>" to belong to a meta-language for (or a suitably stratified extension of) L, L*. We will confine the contexts to atomic sentences in order to facilitate the setting out of a version of a correspondence theory to contrast with a coherence theory that will suffice for the discussion.

We take a coherence theory to hold that <aRb> is true if and only if there is some class of propositions C, such that <aRb> coheres with C. This involves recognizing a coherence relation obtaining between <aRb> and the class C (or a sub-set of C, or a conjunction of members of C, etc.). Then, with "T" for "is true," we have:

(D1) T<aRb> ≡ <aRb> coheres with C.

We need not further specify the relation *coheres with*, for we can take it to be as strong as *entails* or as weak as is *consistent with*. However it is taken, (D1) will not allow us to derive the biconditional required by Convention-T, i. e. the T-sentence:

(E) T<aRb> ≡ aRb.

If we add C (the members of C) to the assumptions or axioms of the schema L* (or take C to consist of logical truths), then (E) may be obtained, with "coheres with" taken as "is entailed by." But, doing this would raise an obvious and familiar problem Russell noted. For, if the members of C are added to the assumptions, then we take those propositions to be true in a different and basic sense. It is irrelevant that each member of C is then trivially entailed by the basic set of assumptions. If "coheres with" is not taken as "entails," but as indicating a basic coherence relation, or is simply understood as "is consistent with" (or "probabilifies," in some sense), (E) is not obtainable on the basis of (D1). To obtain (E), without taking "coheres with" in terms of entailment, one would have to assume

(A1) <aRb> coheres with C ≡ aRb

(or something equivalent or stronger). Even if one makes use of logical entailment, one still faces Russell's argument that the logical truths (rules) are then taken to be true (correct) on grounds other than that they "cohere with" some set of propositions. As we will see below, Davidson, commenting on his once advocating a coherence theory of truth takes coherence simply in terms of *is logically consistent with*. Bradley sometimes did that as well, while at other times suggesting that *coheres with* or *connects with* was a basic concept.

Tarski's statement about a correspondence theory suggests expressing such a theory, for atomic propositions, in terms of a generalized version of (E):

(D2) T<...> ≡ ...,

where any atomic sentence may replace both occurrences of the dots. But, (D2) will only express such a theory for atomic sentences if we understand that the occurrence of the same sentence, within and without brackets, is used to express the connection between an atomic proposition (sentence) and a situation or possibility (state of affairs). The existence of such a situation then furnishes the truth ground for the sentence on the right side of the biconditional and, hence, by (D2), for the left side of the biconditional as well.

Convention-T is then trivially satisfied by <aRb>, as well as by every atomic sentence, given the adoption of the schema (D2) for the atomic sentences of L, with the interpretation we have just given to that pattern. We might note that Tarski's well known admonition that Convention-T does not furnish a definition of a truth predicate, but, rather, a criterion for determining the viability of purported definitions, is not germane here. His type of definition in terms of "satisfaction" is designed to deal with complex formulae, particularly sentential patterns with free variables (so called "open sentences") that are not sentences and do not have truth values, whose quantified closures are sentences with truth values. It is trivially fulfilled by an atomic sentence which is satisfied (vacuously) by all objects of the domain if and only if its meta-linguistic transcription holds (is true).

The above interpretation of (D2) clearly involves more than simply stating a general pattern for a T-sentence. It is made explicit if we replace (D2) by the schema:

(D3) T<...> ≡ (<...> represents ... & ...).

Given a specific instance of (D3), such as:

T<aRb> ≡ (<aRb> represents aRb & aRb),

the sentence "aRb" is understood to represent a situation or possibility when it occurs without brackets, while the complex sign consisting of the sentence within brackets is taken to stand for a proposition (or to be a meta-linguistic sign designating the sentence). The first clause of the conjunction reflects taking an atomic proposition to represent a situation, while the second clause is used to assert that the represented situation obtains or exists.

In place of a schema like (D3), with the understood role of the brackets and dots, one could express the view by using variables ranging over suitable entities, as in:

T(x) ≡ (∃p)(x represents p & p).

Here "p" ranges over atomic situations, both obtaining and non-obtaining, while "x" ranges over atomic sentences or propositions. Moreover, given the reading of "(∃p)(x represents p & p)" as "There is a situation represented by x and that situation obtains," one would read "(∃p)p" as "There is a situation that obtains," just as in the case of existentially generalizing from "aRb" in "<aRb> represents aRb & aRb."

Using (D3) we can derive (E). Clearly, we have "T<aRb> ⊃ aRb"; and, understanding that "<aRb> represents aRb" is a theorem (or true by the semantic rules) of a suitable schema, we also have "aRb ⊃ T<aRb>." This was implicit in the use of the same sentence within and without brackets in (D2). However, such a pattern involves the recognition of situations that may or may not obtain (exist, be actual). Thus, Aristotle's stating that we speak truly when we say "of what is not that it is not" and Wittgenstein's statements in the *Tractatus* about negative facts, taken literally, are involved in such a view:

> 2. 06 The existence and non-existence of states of affairs is reality.
> (We also call the existence of states of affairs a positive fact, and their non-existence a negative fact.)
> 4.1 Propositions represent the existence and non-existence of states of affairs.

These statements clearly bring out two themes that are implicit in various versions of a correspondence theory of truth. Such a theory is not stated simply by means of definitional patterns for a truth predicate but is expressed by means of statements made about a pattern like (D3) and, consequently, about the interpretation of the elementary sentences of a linguistic schema. Second, two senses of the term "correspond" are involved. In one sense, an atomic sentence (proposition) may be said to correspond to a situation irrespective of its truth or falsity, and, hence, irrespective of whether the situation obtains or exists. In a second sense, an atomic sentence is said to correspond to a fact, which is to say a situation that obtains or exists. This two-fold sense of "corresponds" points to one ambiguity in the notion of a truth condition. In one sense a condition of truth is the situation that the atomic sentence or proposition represents, irrespective of the latter's truth value. In another sense the truth condition is the obtaining of such a situation, the existence of a fact. To avoid that ambiguity, we have the suggestive phrase "truth ground," or the presently more popular "truth maker," for this latter sense of "truth condition."

The point can be emphasized by recalling a construal of "is true" that Moore used to express a correspondence theory:

(D4) $<...>$ is true $\equiv (\exists p)(<...>$ is directly proven by p),

where the variable "p" ranges over existent situations or facts. This has virtually been duplicated in recent years by various writers who are concerned with "truth maker" theory, a notion that reflects Russell's 1918 use of the phrase "makes true," and replace Moore's "directly proven by" in (D4) with "is made true by." Thus, they construe "truth" in terms of:

(D5) <...> is true ≡ (∃α)(α is a truth maker for <...>),

where "α" can be an atomic fact, a conjunctive fact, an object, a pair of objects, etc.—anything that is taken as a "truth maker," which depends on one's view of what sorts of things truth makers are. Yet, whatever phrase one uses, or whatever one allows as a ground of truth, a statement of the form of (D4) or (D5) does not allow us to derive a T-sentence unless we also assume a pattern like:

(A2) (∃p)(<...> is made true by p) ≡ ... ,

or something from which (A2) follows. Thus, such a way of stating a correspondence theory faces the same problem that a coherence theory does.

The coherence theory faces an even more basic problem in that the truth ground of a statement or proposition is said to be its coherence with a set of sentences or propositions, C. But, this raises a question as to what a truth ground is on a coherence theory. The expression "coheres with" appears to be a relational predicate, but the coherence theorist cannot take "<aRb> coheres with C" to represent the fact that the relation *coheres with* holds between <aRb> and C without abandoning the theory. Thus, such a theorist is forced to hold that the ground of truth for the proposition <aRb> is the truth of the further proposition that <aRb> coheres with C, and not the existence of a fact. But, according to the coherence theory, such a claim must be taken to mean that the "truth ground" for <aRb> is given by the statement:

<<aRb> coheres with C> coheres with C*,

where C and C* may be the same. Whether or not they are the same, a non-terminating series arises, since the truth ground for a proposition (sentence) is always the truth of another proposition. Of course one can hold that one is not providing a "truth ground" by specifying that a proposition "coheres with" C, which is basically what Davidson does in his version of a coherence theory. But this abandons the classical account and, in Davidson's case, the notion of coherence is taken as "nothing but consistency" (2001, 155) which runs into the earlier mentioned objection of Russell's regarding there being no grounds to choose between competing coherent systems (1946, 122-23). In simplest terms, if {p, q} is a consistent set of propositions so is {¬ p, ¬ q}, so long as logical truths are excluded. Moreover, if we exclude logical truths from inclusion in the "coherent system," we recognize some truths that are so "absolutely" in that we judge "consistency" in terms of them (i. e. by employing a system of logic). If we do not exclude them we face the kinds of problems we shall take up in connection with Dummett's and Davidson's views that lead us into more extreme forms of idealism than Bradley's—given that Bradley seems to have recognized logical "consistency" as either the basis for "coherence" or as a condition for it. Thus Bradley's "idealism" was not tinged with the "relativism" that has come to characterize the contemporary variants of idealism that comprise twists in "the linguistic turn." This is one reason the view of Bradley and Bosanquet was "Absolute" Idealism and not "subjective" idealism.

A viable correspondence theory cannot merely satisfy Convention-T, for it must articulate the representational role of propositions *and the nature* of the grounds of truth. In spite of some passages in Tarski's original paper and the way the "semantic conception" of truth is sometimes discussed:

> ... the clause "t is in K" explicitly describes the state of affairs which the sentence T(t*) of A is to express. The statement (T) strongly resembles traditional definitions of truth as *adaequatio rei et intellectus*. (Beth, 1959, 340)

it is misleading to link Tarski's views with the correspondence theory. Tarski quite explicitly held that taking sentences to designate "states of affairs is the kind of formulation that leads 'to various misunderstandings' since it is not sufficiently precise and clear" (1944, 343). The difference between a correspondence theorist's use of Convention-T, as a mere condition to be satisfied, and Tarski's use of that convention is vividly illustrated by:

> If the language investigated only contained a finite number of sentences fixed from the beginning, and if we could enumerate all these sen-

tences, then the problem of the construction of a correct definition of truth would present no difficulties. For this purpose it would suffice to complete the following scheme: x ∈ Tr if and only if either x=x_1 and p_1, or x=x_2 and p_2,... or x=x_n and p_n, the symbols "x_1," "x_2," ..., "x_n" being replaced by structural descriptive names of all the sentences of the language investigated and "p_1," "p_2," ..., "p_n" by the corresponding translation of these sentences into the metalanguage. (1956, 188)

In short, no analysis of truth need be given in the traditional sense of specifying truth grounds —facts, coherence, a basic property of (or relation in) propositions, etc. All that is needed is an extensionally equivalent condition for applying a predicate to sentences of a schema that are evaluated in a certain way. Consider an artificially simple case. Let us assume that we have only two atomic sentences, "Fa" and "Ga," in L, and no logical signs to enable the formation of non-atomic sentences. We can, then, understanding the use of variables in a suitable way in the meta-language for L, follow Tarski's suggestion and define a truth predicate for L by:

$$x \in T \equiv ((x=\text{``Fa''} \ \& \ a \text{ is } F) \vee (x=\text{``Ga''} \ \& \ a \text{ is } G)).$$

Thus, we get:

$$\text{``Fa''} \in T \equiv ((\text{``Fa''} = \text{``Fa''} \ \& \ a \text{ is } F) \vee (\text{``Fa''}=\text{``Ga''} \ \& \ a \text{ is } G)).$$

In the present discussion I follow Tarski''s use of "∈." It is worth noting that Tarski also offers a definition of the "semantical concept" *designates* such that: α designates π if and only if ß = π , where "α" is a meta-linguistic name of the sign "ß" (Tarski, 1944, 373, n. 2). As we will shortly see, this footnote will later be turned into a deflationary theory of reference by P. Horwich, illustrating a recent tendency in "analytic philosophy" that seeks to employ aspects of Tarski's semantic analyses to support neo-Wittgensteinian attempts to dismiss and avoid serious philosophical issues.

Since the identity in the second disjunct is trivially false, we obtain:

$$\text{``Fa''} \in T \equiv (\text{``Fa''} = \text{``Fa''} \ \& \ a \text{ is } F).$$

As the conjunct "'Fa'= 'Fa'" may be taken as a logical or formal truth, we arrive at the requisite T-sentence and Convention-T is satisfied, but nothing at all is said about what it is that grounds the truth of "Fa." This contrasts with a correspondence theory, where, taking "Fa" to be true if a certain fact exists, one specifies a ground of truth and what constitutes a ground of truth—an atomic fact in the present case. Thus one may well ask: What is the point of transcribing a predicate like "T," as defined just above, in terms of "is true"?

Tarski was not concerned to say anything further about "a is F." In fact, he seems to have thought that nothing intelligible remains to be said:

> I have heard it remarked that the formal definition of truth has nothing to do with "the philosophical problem of truth." However, nobody has ever pointed out to me in an intelligible way just what this problem is…. In general, I do not believe that there is such a thing as "the philosophical problem of truth." (1944, 361)

As Aristotle may be taken to have done so long ago, a correspondence theorist purports to tell us what it is that grounds the truth of a sentence. Tarski showed that his type of definition of a predicate can satisfy Convention-T, but such a definition does not capture the import of the Aristotelian conception of truth. At most, Tarski set forth a criterion one might require a viable truth predicate to satisfy, since the connection of his semantic conception with "truth" seems to amount to the fact that we generally take a statement that is true (false) and a statement stating that it is true to have the same truth value.

Ignoring philosophical problems, Tarski was concerned with the evaluation of complex linguistic patterns, given evaluations of simpler patterns, and the apparent problem posed by the "liar" paradox (1944, 353). But what he did is relevant to the construction of a correspondence theory, for the correspondence theorist faces questions about the truth and representational role of non-atomic sentences. A correspondence theorist may attempt to use the techniques logicians employ for truth functional compounds and quantified contexts to attempt to avoid recognizing molecular and existentially and universally quantified states of affairs. Negation, we will see, poses a special problem. There will also be issues concerning the meaning of the logical signs and the grounds, if any, of the logical rules and truths employed in dealing with molecular and quantified statements. But the host of philosophical problems that arise about truth and truth grounds are ignored by Tarski's semantic conception of truth, and, as we will see, its legacy in writers like Davidson. In Tarski's case it is clear from his comment: "Therefore every definition of truth which is materially adequate would necessarily be equivalent to that actually constructed." For Tarski, any predicate that is coextensive with the predicate he has defined or provided axioms for (for the particular schema in question) will do. And this is merely a matter of what statements are taken to be true (in a sense that we must already understand) and neither a matter of specifying what grounds of truth are nor providing an analysis of the philosophical issues surrounding the concept of "truth."

3b: Positivism and Pragmatism in Carnap and Sellars

Carnap's two celebrated distinctions—that between "internal" and "external" questions and that between the "formal" and "material" modes of speech—and the idea of a "pseudo-statement" that they are tied to, are hallmarks of logical positivism. For Sellars, Carnap's pair of distinctions would be transformed into the device of "semantic ascent" that turns apparent statements about suspect purported entities into statements about "linguistic roles" involving language rules of basically two kinds—language-world connections and intra-linguistic connections. These would involve the complexities of the psychological stories of stimulus-response and of the social network governed by "norms" and "practices," including norms governing language, and described by empirical generalizations about communal linguistic practices.

Sellars had long been taken to claim that the employment of a perspicuous schema that did not contain predicates forestalled the need to ask what predicates represented. Though he explicitly denied that that was an argument he used against property realism, it became clear in *Naturalism and Ontology* that that indeed was an argument he employed. In that book Sellars made three claims relevant to the issue: first, that his perspicuous schema, which he ironically, or perhaps self-consciously, labeled "Jumbelese," does not contain predicates; second, that since it does not he had avoided a "commitment" to properties and relations as opposed to particulars, though such particulars were qualited; third, that recognizing qualited and "arranged" particulars does not involve recognizing qualities or relations as entities.

His ideas develop a thought casually stated in Russell's logical atomism lectures and, depending on one's interpretation, can be taken to be expressed in an often quoted passage of Wittgenstein's *Tractatus*. In place of "aRb," as a sentence expressing that a stands in R to b, one can state what "aRb" is used to state by an arrangement of the names "a" and "b." Russell did not take that possibility to be of any philosophical significance, and, moreover, thought that it would lead to exceedingly cumbersome, if not unfeasible, linguistic schemata. But Sellars took it to allow for a perspicuous representation of the relation between the objects a and b, and such a perspicuous representation had philosophical consequences. As we only have an arrangement of the signs "a" and "b," on the linguistic side, we only have an arrangement of the things a and b on the object side—the "world" side of what Sellars called the "word-world" relationship. That was the obvious lesson of his perspicuous representation. That arrangements of entities are not further entities was the less obvious philosophical lesson. That is, the "arrangements," as well as the qualities of objects, were not entities, though the arranged and qualitied objects were.

The first two claims go together, for if predicates have not been avoided then the second issue does not even arise. Since it is obvious that Jumbelese does not contain standard predicates, we must ask whether Sellars employs other forms of predicates. It is clear that he does. Moreover, Sellars has no argument that those predicates do not involve the same sort of commitments made by the use of other, standard predicates. Here it is important to recall that Sellars consistently declined to travel the royal road to ontological minimalism—what many now call "ostrich nominalism"—taken by Quine and his followers, based on the arbitrary declaration that using predicates does not involve commitments to qualities and relations, so long as one stays within the confines of first-order languages.

Sellars's idea is simple. Instead of "aRb" and "cRd," he employs a spatial arrangement of the names—"a" and "b" in the one case, "c" and "d" in the other—to state what others take "aRb" and "cRd" to state. He then insists that we must not think that the relation (arrangement) common to the respective pairs of signs is "doing the job" that "R" does in "aRb" and "cRd." For in the latter cases, in spite of using the relational predicate "R," one still employs the common "arrangement" between "a," "b" and "R," in the one case, and "c," "d" and "R," in the other. Thus he has successfully removed one element of the representing pattern by moving to Jumbelese. The implicit argument is that he has, then, removed the need to account for the representing role of what has been removed.

To appreciate what is going on here we have to go back to Frege. We noted earlier that Frege, to avoid the "Bradley paradox," treated predicates as "incomplete" or "unsaturated" in that the concepts (properties) they represented (expressed) were incomplete or unsaturated entities. Hence, they are more perspicuously represented by signs like "Fx" and "xRy," where the attached individual variables reveal the need for completion. This is a fundamental way in which properties and relations differ from particulars. The Fregean pattern clearly involves taking each property and relation (concept) to have a two-fold role, by providing conceptual content as well as the connection in a proposition (fact). In Quine's more picturesque version in *Methods of Logic*, he used signs like "F0," with the subscripted "0" indicating a gap or place that required filling. Frege can be seen as taking Plato to have merely introduced forms as different kinds of "objects." What was required was the more radical idea that forms (concepts) were not objects but entities of a basically different kind that enabled propositions (facts) to be formed without their constituents being "connected." Frege's concepts were thus combinations of a "content" and a "predicative form." Sellars carries this basic idea of Frege's to an extreme. Instead of taking the logical form and combinatorial connection as internal to the concept in Frege's fashion, Sellars gives the form the role of the relational and monadic properties. This is a radical move in the sense that when you do that you appear to be in a position to argue that, as the form is not "something," neither properties nor relations are anything at all. For what the form is the form of is dispensed with.

As Sellars puts it:

Thus, one who is simply struck by the fact that we *could* use "a"
b
to say that a is larger than b will be tempted to look for some aspect of

(6) a
     b   *which is doing the job done in*

(5) a larger than b

by "larger than," for example "the fact that 'a' is above 'b'" or "'a's being above 'b'." It is absolutely crucial to appreciate that *nothing* in (6), or *about* (6), is doing the job done in (5) by "larger than." Many philosophers have stared this point in the face and missed it, thus failing to grasp its significance. (1979, 108)

It is clear that Sellars is claiming that nothing is playing the role, in his ideal schema Jumbelese, of the predicate "larger than." The relation between the tokens in (5), or Sellars's (6), is not to be, and supposedly cannot be, taken in isolation. In his (6) the tokens stand in a certain spatial relation, and in his (5) the tokens of "a" and "b" occur in a certain spatial complex involving their relations to each other and to the token of "larger than." Thus we are not to think that we replace the predicate "larger than" by the relation between "a" and "b" in (6). Rather we replace the fact of tokens standing to another token in the relation of "having _ _ _ between - - - and ..." by a different relation holding of tokens. In (5) we have a rather complex relation between three tokens and in (6) we have a simpler relation between two tokens. Thus nothing in (6) plays the role of the token of "larger than," since the predicate expression has been eliminated by using a notation that does not employ a predicate sign or anything corresponding to such a predicate. But something is clearly wrong, for Sellars has obviously not made a convincing case for nominalism.

If from a token of "aRb" we withdraw the tokens of "a" and "b," a token of "R" remains. But if we withdraw the tokens of "a" and "b" from Sellars's notation, as used in (6), nothing remains. This does not show, as Sellars claims, that nothing plays the role of the token of "larger than." It merely emphasizes the fact that no sign plays the role of the expression "larger than," and that the spatial relation between the tokens of "a" and "b," which takes on the role of the predicate, disappears when the latter tokens disappear. If, in Sellars's (6), we replace the tokens of names by tokens of variables, we clearly have something like the Fregean "xRy" (or "Rxy") to play the role of the predicate. Nevertheless, Sellars has gone Frege one better. For the obvious problem with the Fregean notation is that there is the sign "R" as an "independent" sign, in that it can remain when the subject signs, the variables in this case, are "removed." Thus in spite of taking the predicate to be "incomplete" and properly written as "xRy" rather than "R," "xRy" contains "R" as a constituent notational element. Sellars has created a notation where the predicates are not merely incomplete or unsaturated in Frege's sense, but where they disappear when the individual variables or constants are "withdrawn." To put it another way, predicates can only occur with subject signs—whether variables or constants. Thus we do not have a mere syntactical rule stipulating that "xRy," not "R," is "the predicate." Rather, we make use of the physical or geometrical fact: that to have a spatial relation between terms, you must have terms. But this does not mean that we cannot isolate what plays the role of "R" in "aRb." It means that what plays the role of "R" cannot be set down, as I just set down a token of "R," without setting down tokens of subject terms.

Sellars has failed to eliminate predicates. Thus, he has not removed the question of what they represent. So he must forestall the question in another way. This may be why he appealed to further arguments, involving a substitutional account of quantifiers, an attack on reference (for names as well as predicates) and an unclear appeal to qualited individuals. In the case of monadic predicates, he replaced predicates by characteristics of names (thickness of the sign, for example). Here too, as in the case of relations, one could not have a predicate without having a subject term. This led him to hold that while he did not recognize qualities, he did recognize qualited particulars. When "Fa" is true we have a kind-of-a, not a fact of a exemplifying F—a white spot and not the fact of a particular spot exemplifying whiteness (or containing a white trope). But it is not clear what this move involves, aside from the obvious fact that we can speak of "the white spot" as well as say "the spot is white." One can take the "truth maker" for the sentence to be the spot, rather than the spot exemplifying or having a quality, but it still is a "qualitied spot," and the problem about properties remains. However, one need not argue the pros or cons of this, as that strategy clearly does not work in the case of relations—there is nothing to be of the kind R, to be an R-kind of thing, unless Sellars introduces ordered pairs of individuals or some other entities as further individuals. And he does introduce something. This requires a long story about maps, pictures, rules, roles, picturing and representing. But we still have qualited and related things (1979, 122-138), and, to handle relations, he does shift to talking of complex, structured objects, such as a checkerboard (1979, 138-142). This provides an interesting historical twist. Russell developed his view of facts from an earlier notion of a complex unity, a-being-R-to-b, in the early years of the century. Sellars, to avoid facts, shifts from aRb to a complex object, a structure or configuration. Though Russell clearly saw that there was a relation involved in such "complex unities," one wonders if Sellars really thought he avoided relations like R by recognizing complex "things"— configurations of a and b. At a certain point argument ceases, but one thing is beyond doubt—Jumbelese has predicates—and another thing is of interest—the occurrence of the terms "configuration," "structure," "arrangement" and "manifold" in Sellars's discussion of projecting linguistic complexes onto complexes—arrangements and configurations— in the world (1979, 146).

There is also the familiar fallback provided by contemporary variants of the idealist's holist pattern. On Sellars's variant of holism, one does not take "Fa" to be true in virtue of the fact that a is F. Rather, one makes "the truth move"—what will later be spoken of as "deflation." When one commits oneself to "'Fa' is true," one commits oneself to "Fa" (1967, 137-40; 1979, 147). By semantically ascending we think in terms of a move from one linguistic item to another, from words to words, in talking of truth, and not of a move from words to the world. It is just a move in a story, a picture that, as a whole, is projected onto the world, taken as a complex configuration of objects—in which such objects are related and qualitied but where there are neither qualities nor relations among the objects. Altering the pattern a bit, one stresses the "normative" element of employing a language, as a social instrument, and the resultant "obligation" to make certain moves given one's commitment to other moves. This places the emphasis on the total social context within which the moves are made and from which they derive their "meaning."

The Frege-Bradley paradox of predication has played an important role in recent arguments about the viability of a correspondence or referential theory of truth, and it is a crucial aspect of Sellars's attack on the referential role of predicates and sentences. Bradley sometimes seems to have taken "the paradox" to involve constituents of an object, since he considered the problem in terms of a relation between a basic subject and a quality, both "in" an ordinary object, or in terms of a relation between two qualities of an object, construed as a complex of its qualities. In this vein, Bradley linked Zeno-like puzzles about time and space to his discussion of predication (1897, Chapters ii-iv). Like Zeno, Bradley took it to be problematic for an analysis to generate an infinite number of constituents in an object or apparent fact. The problem is that if the fact aRb is understood in terms of—(1) a and b exemplify R—with *exemplification* as a relational constituent of the fact, the realist fails to viably analyze that fact. For we assume two things, as Sellars did and as one can read Bradley as having done. The first is:

(A1) For any n-adic relation R, and terms $x_1, x_2, ...x_n$ (of any type), there is a fact consisting of such terms "in" the relation R only if the terms exemplify R, which is to say that the terms and R stand in an n+1-adic relation of exemplification. Thus R is a term, along with $x_1, x_2, ...x_n$, of the n+1-adic exemplification relation.

The second assumption Sellars makes is (A2): Exemplification is a relation in the range of R. Then, (1) is "analyzed" in terms of—(2) a, b and R exemplify exemplification—which, by the further application of (A1), forces us to analyze (2), etc. This is Sellars's version of the Bradleyian regress. We need not be concerned with the difference between taking different n-adic exemplification relations to be involved in (2), as opposed to one "multi-grade" relation, to use Quine's term, as an unnecessary complication that does not affect the real issues. Thus, supposedly, the correspondence theory is not only forced to recognize an infinite number of facts that "correspond" to "aRb," and possibly an infinite number of exemplification relations of different adicity, but, more crucially, fails to provide an analysis of the fact aRb. For we never arrive at the analysis of any element of the series, since each supplied truth ground requires a further fact as its analysis. Though recognizing an infinite number of facts can be taken to be a merely awkward consequence, not arriving at an end to the analysis is seen as refuting the view.

Before taking up Sellars's argument, it is instructive to consider an obvious mistake he makes in his presentation of the pattern. He writes:

> But it might be argued that the platonist could capture the conceptual tie between exemplification and truth with the claim that truth is to be defined in terms of exemplification, thus
> That Fa is true =df a exemplifies F.
> But this would be equally absurd, for it would be synonymous with
> That a exemplifies F is true =df a exemplifies F
> which, as a definition (though not as a necessary equivalence), is incoherent. (1979, 108)

Sellars is assuming that "Fa" and "a exemplifies F" are "identical in sense" and only differ in that "Fa" does not employ an "auxiliary expression." But he overlooks a simple point in making such a claim. What is being defined in the first definition is the predicate "is true"—not the predicative juxtaposition of "Fa." There is nothing incoherent about holding that

(I) "a exemplifies F" is true =df a exemplifies F.

The realist, by employng (I) is not incoherently using "exemplifies" in the definition of "exemplifies." This is easily seen when we write:

(II) "a exemplifies F"

rather than

(III) that a exemplifies F,

since (II) clearly shows that we use the name of an expression that contains the term "exemplifies" and do not use the term "exemplifies" to the left of the definition sign in (I). By identifying the sense of "Fa" with that of "a exemplifies F," Sellars substitutes the one expression for the other and arrives at the misleading claim that "exemplifies" is absurdly used in its own definition. He might just as well have used the identification of sense to arrive at the familiar:

(IV) "Fa" is true =df Fa,

which some find not only not absurd, but viable. In fact Sellars himself will offer a variant of the disquotational move embodied in (IV) as another thread in his refutation of realism (1963, 244-45)! Making this latter move, however, does not allow the realist to even state his view, but that is not the point here. The point is that as nothing is absurd or circular in using (II) in (I), there is nothing "incoherent" about (I). (I) would be incoherent only if the realist thought (I) is used to define "exemplifies" rather than to merely give what some call a *partial* definition of "is true."

There are, however, two formidable points that one can extract from Sellars's line of argument. One is the raising of the Bradley problem. The other is not so clearly seen, and Sellars probably did not see it. It concerns the realist being forced to use a three-fold biconditional in specifying both the linguistic role of predicative juxtaposition and the ground of truth for atomic sentences. Thus, something like

(ST) Fa ≡ "Fa" is true ≡ a exemplifies F

is involved, which Sellars would take to be problematic, though he does not clearly set out what the problem is. He cannot do so since he fuses a purported problem about (ST) being a three-fold biconditional with both the Bradley problem regarding a purported regress and the supposed incoherence we just discussed. We discussed an aspect of the Bradley problem in Chapter 1—in connection with distinguishing functions, forms and relations. Here we can note that an analysis that allows an unending generation of entities, as in (1), (2), etc., is *prima facie* implausible, whether paradoxical or not. And, such an account fails to provide, at any point in the series, a viable analysis of the initial fact. Hence, it purports to offer an analysis of an atomic fact, but fails to specify a sufficient truth ground for the initial atomic sentence. A viable theory will neither recognize such an infinite series of facts nor fail to specify the truth grounds for atomic sentences.

Some seek to accept an infinite chain of truths as non-problematic, as we took an infinite series of functions to pose no problem in Chapter 1. But they do so since the elements of the chain are supposedly merely deductive consequences of the original sentence and hence have the same initial fact as the truth ground. Thus, as in the case of the series of sentences (i) "p," "'p' is true," "' 'p" is true' is true," etc., one fact, the original fact, provides a truth ground for each sentence in a Bradley-type series. Hence, there is no series of facts to generate a regress. But this solution presupposes what it must establish, as it assumes that the purported series of sentences, "a exemplifies F," "a and F (or the ordered pair <a, F>) exemplify (exemplifies) the exemplification relation," etc., is like the series of sentences (i) in that one ground of truth suffices for the whole series. Alternatively, some simply hold that a generated infinite series of relational exemplifications do not comprise a "vicious" regress.[6] Sellars would point out that a realist cannot simply appeal to an analogy with "is true." For, while the predicate "is true," defined in a schema in a certain way, is not taken to represent a property, a realist who recognizes a tie or relation of exemplification does assume that "exemplifies" represents something, a nexus, relation, tie, connection, that is employed in the analysis of an atomic fact. Moreover, if one recognizes such a series of facts there is a problem, as each purported element of the series is "analyzed" in terms of the next element in the series—and thus one never arrives at a viable analysis.

It is also obvious that it is pointless to seek to represent exemplification by a relational predicate, say "Ex," for then we are forced to make use of sentence structure to also represent an exemplification connection when we employ such a relational predicate in a sentence like "Ex (a, F)." This point can also be seen when we note that if, abstracting from the sentence "Fa," we obtain the pattern "Φx" and take such a sign to be a dyadic predicate abstract (as we did earlier with lambda abstracts) that represents an exemplification connection (for particulars and monadic properties), we make a crucial mistake. For the sign "Φx" already incorporates sentential structure in an obvious way. The sign is more viably and more obviously taken to represent the "form" of a fact, such as a-being-F, and not a relational component in such a fact, given that "Φx" is a sentential pattern composed of two variables. This points to a difference between standard relational predicates and a sign like "Φx" that reveals a difference between a dyadic relation and a logical form like Φx. That is why one cannot viably argue that a and F must be taken to stand in, or exemplify, the logical form of monadic exemplification. Forms like Φx are

[6]Quine held such a view in a letter to C. Hartshorne written between 1952 and 1960:
"Bradley's point about the regress, which you take seriously ... never impressed me. Let every relation of the whole infinite series subsist: all are good, and there is no circularity of definition, nor any vicious regress."
I am indebted to I. Angelelli for showing me the letter Hartshorne had given to him.

common forms of monadic atomic facts, but they are neither monadic properties of such facts nor dyadic relations obtaining between the "constituents" of such facts. Exemplification, as a logical form, is represented by sentential structure and the formation rules of the schema, and thus derivatively by "Φx." As there are universal properties of objects, so there are common forms of facts, such as Φx and $\prod xy$ (or $x\prod y$). Sellars, as acknowledged in Chapter 1 in the discussion of Bradley, is right to insist that a fact is not a composite of its elements, nor is it reducible to or analyzable into such elements. Realists too often mistakenly take themselves to "analyze" a fact into elements in a connecting tie or relation, which is then, obviously, another element or arbitrarily declared not to be one to avoid the regress.

Facts can be said to be complex in one sense in that they have terms and attributes and are of a form. Thus the terms and attributes can be thought of as "components." But in that they are neither reducible to nor analyzable into such components, they are not complexes of them—and the form is not a component "in" the fact but a logical form of the fact—one can say "logical character of" but must not be misled into thinking that it is then a universal property exemplified by such facts. One might say that the peculiarity of a logical form like Φx is that it appears to be like a monadic property, a common feature of facts, while, structurally, it also appears to be like a dyadic function, and thus tempts one to think of it as a relation that connects a term and an attribute to or into a fact. Sellars, impressed by Bradley, can be seen as arguing that such a form must be taken as a further term, along with F and a, of a further fact, and so on. F. MacBride (2003) has raised the same kind of argument in taking the above construal of a logical form as a common universal attribute. As such, whether one takes it to be a monadic universal instantiated by the fact or a dyadic universal instantiated by the terms a and F one does not avoid the Frege-Bradley problem. I fail to see that one is compelled to do so. A logical form is quite different from a constituent term or attribute (relation), and one is not forced to think of it as a monadic attribute of the fact that yields a further fact. For it is not "external" to the fact. But we need not rest content with merely asserting that or depending on vague and question begging uses of terms like "internal" and "external." An argument can be presented for the claim that I am making. We can start with a point Bradley would likely have made, and, in his way, did make.

In considering a fact like a-being-F in terms of abstracting a term, an attribute and a form, Bradley would have suggested that we "falsify" the way things are. For we end up with a term, an attribute and a form, and not the fact from which we started. This is not paradoxical but it suggests that atomic facts are not to be thought of, along the lines of the logical atomism of the *Tractarian* Wittgenstein, as perspicuously mirrored by atomic sentences of a *Principia* type "ideal" linguistic schema. Suppose a is an F and that we, for the moment, ignore Wittgenstein's injunction against naming facts and take "[Fa]" to represent or name that fact. Let C be an unspecified relation, a kind of whole-part relation between the fact, on the one hand, and its term and attribute, on the other. We then have the truths "[Fa] C a" and "[Fa] C F" as trivial consequences of the rules introduced to govern the linguistic device of the square brackets "[...]," since such brackets are used to form names of existent atomic facts. There is clearly no need to take such sentences to have further facts, facts in addition to a's being F, as truth grounds. For, given the fact "named" by [Fa], "[Fa] C a" must be true! To put it another way, whatever "logical" rules one introduces to govern the square brackets and the relational predicate "C," it will have to be the case that they ensure the "derivation" of "[Fa] C a" from "Fa." Thus the truth ground, if any, is the original fact, not a further fact of which it is a term. If we recognize a relation like C, we can take it to be an "internal" or "formal" relation, relating atomic facts to their terms and attributes, in a precise sense of "internal" or "formal." Its holding between [Fa] and a is not a further relational fact that grounds the truth of "[Fa] C a" which is a consequence of the syntactic and semantical rules for the "[...]" brackets and the predicate "C." As the items involved in the analysis of the atomic facts we are considering are of diverse logical categories— particulars and first order attributes and relations, and, we can add, the fact is of a logical form, like Φx—we can recognize diverse formal relations that such "entities" have to facts, in place of C. This will enable us to develop an idea of Russell's that was noted earlier and avoid Wittgenstein's possibilities, Meinong's non-subsistent objectives and Searle's non-existent truth conditions— as well as enable us to develop a response to MacBride's Bradleyian objection.

Reference can also be taken to be an internal or formal relation in that statements of referential connection are semantical rules of a perspicuous linguistic schema, whether such statements involve interpreting names, predicates or sentences. Following Carnap's *Introduction to Semantics* that employed designation rules like:

(1) "a" designates Russell.
(2) "F" designates the property of being a philosopher.
(3) "Fa" designates the state of affairs of Russell's being a philosopher,

we may say that these are necessary or linguistic truths, or that "designates" represents an internal relation, in the simple and unproblematic sense that (1)-

(3) are semantical rules for a schema. That means that (3) would still be true, and hence the relation would hold, even if Russell were a linguist and not a philosopher. Thus one faces the familiar problem that Sellars requires the realist to solve without introducing non-actual states of affairs (objectives, situations). Believing that such a problem cannot be solved by the realist, Sellars had a reason for rejecting facts and a correspondence theory of truth. This reinforced his nominalism, for rejecting facts and a correspondence theory of truth fits with the rejection of properties and relations, as the latter are often taken as constituents of facts. But the problems posed by stating the truth grounds for atomic sentences can be resolved by a pattern derived from an idea Russell expressed in 1905, that we noted earlier, and which he articulated more fully in 1913 in a way that gave rise to a well known dispute with Wittgenstein (Hochberg, 2000). Whether the dispute did or did not lead Russell to abandon his 1913 manuscript, the manuscript clearly influenced Wittgenstein's *Tractatus*, since many themes of the latter are directed against Russell's 1913 ideas.

We may say that (1)-(3) are necessary truths, or that "designates" represents an internal relation, solely in the sense that they are semantical rules or postulates for a schema. Taking *designates* as a relation, as *refers to* was a relation for Moore, Carnap, like Moore, ignored the problem that false sentences raise. For the time, we will also ignore that and focus on the designation relation itself. For while we may say (1)-(3) are necessary in that they are stipulated rules, the fact that they are taken as such rules clearly points to a sense in which they are not necessary and may only be said to express "internal" connections, as interpretation rules, for a particular schema. As such rules, they are hardly necessary in the sense in which "a ≠ b" may be said to be necessary, given appropriate interpretations of "a" and "b." Calling the connection between "a" and Russell (or "Russell" and Russell) and between "Fa" and Russell's being a philosopher "internal" or "intrinsic" resolves none of the philosophical problems involved. Nor is the problem resolved by dismissing the issue, as many did, by thinking of it as stemming from a misapprehension of how language functions and a reference theory of meaning. Thus one heard Carnap's semantical views dismissed by derogatory references to the "'Fido'—Fido" principle.

(1), taken as a semantical rule, does not express a matter of fact. That such a rule is a rule of a particular schema is a matter of fact. The same sort of distinction applies to the "ordinary language" sentence (s) "'Russell' designates (names) Russell." Considered in a straightforward way, (s) belongs to the logic or semantical rules of a system or language. Considered as elliptical for a statement about the usage of the term and matters of sociology and history, (s) can be taken to express a number of matters of fact. This does not mean that (1), (2), (3) and (s), properly understood, express matters of fact and not matters of linguistic stipulation or of the "logic" of a "language" or semantical system. It only means that, taken as physical patterns, (1)-(3) and (s) can hardly be taken to state an "internal relation" in the sense that such a relation holds given the existence of the physical marks, Russell, the property of being a philosopher and the fact that Russell was a philosopher. But taken as "interpreted" signs—as symbols, in the sense of Wittgenstein's *Tractarian* distinction between a sign and a symbol—there is an internal relation expressed by all such semantical "truths" in a clear and unproblematic sense of "internal." For the symbols are interpreted signs, or signs taken together with an interpretation. As giving interpretations of symbols, (1)-(3) and (s) trivially express internal relations, as "formal" truths. For the symbols would not be the symbols they are without representing what they represent. That the objects can exist, as the objects they are, without the language (or conceptual structure) is irrelevant; as it is irrelevant that philosophers as diverse as N. Goodman and J. P. Sartre deny this obvious fact—a denial nicely summed up in J. Lacan's statement: "So I said to myself, addressing myself by my name... 'so that's why, after all, Jacques Lacan, your daughter isn't dumb; that's why your daughter is your daughter; because if we were dumb, she wouldn't be your daughter'." (In Roudinesco, 1997, 285) That natural language use involves a long and complex learning process does not change the basic logic of the situation. But there is a crucial difference between (1) and (3).

Let "T," "A" and "IN" be signs representing the relations *is a term in*, *is attributed in* and *informs* (is the form of), respectively, which, for the moment, I will simply claim are viably taken to be categorial or formal relations between atomic facts, on the one hand, and their terms, attributes (including relations) and logical forms, on the other. The truth grounds for monadic atomic sentences will be specified in terms that involve a modification of (3) that embodies Russell's idea and recalls (ST), in the above discussion of Sellars:

(T) "Fa" is true $\equiv$ Fa $\equiv$ E! $(\iota\ p)(T(a, p)\ \&\ A(F, p)\ \&\ IN(\Phi x, p\ ))$.

The sentence "Fa" is now included as one of three *equivalences*, and (T) is a tri-partite biconditional, since it functions as an interpretation rule for the sentence "Fa" and, in so doing, states the truth ground for that sentence—thereby linking "Fa" to the meta-linguistic statement that "Fa" is true. The key statement "the fact having a as a term, F as attribute and Φx as form exists"—the third element of the tri-partite biconditional (T)—provides both the interpretation rule for subject-predicate juxtaposition in the atomic sentence "Fa" and specifies the truth ground for that sentence—the latter being the existence of the described fact. If the sentence, when true, is taken to represent the atomic fact which then exists, one could express that by "($\exists$p)(p = [Fa])," where placing the "[...]" brackets around the sentence forms a sign used to denote such an existent fact, though one must keep in mind that the fact is not taken to provide an interpretation for the sentence in the way that objects and properties do for names and predicates, respectively. There is no designation rule for an atomic sentence, "Fa" for example, only the use of (T) as a semantical rule in place of a designation rule. One can then either limit a sign like "[...]" so that it can combine only with true atomic sentences or adopt an idea from Russell's theory of descriptions and treat the apparent name "[Fa]" as an abbreviation for the definite description "the fact having a as a term, F as attribute and Φx as form." Given the existence of the described fact and such a use of atomic sentences, we have "($\exists$p)(p = [Fa])" as true. But, where the fact does not exist, we do not have "[Fa]" as a sign denoting anything, as the description "the fact having a as a term, F as attribute and Φx as form" does not denote anything, since the described fact does not exist. This is why "[Fa]," no more than "Fa," can be taken as a "name." The familiar "picture theory of language" of Wittgenstein's *Tractatus* is thus misleading, for it involves a mixing of "Fa" with "[Fa]" and of the situation represented by "Fa" with the fact represented by "[Fa]" that is covered by the talk of "showing" and "stating." In spite of what he says, Wittgenstein took atomic sentences as names in the sense that they were taken to represent situations whether or not the latter existed.

As I noted above, (T) recalls the tripartite biconditional (ST) that was earlier taken to be implicitly involved in Sellars's version of the Bradley paradox. One can even say, with Sellars, that "Fa" and "the fact having a as a term, F as attribute and Φx as form exists" have the same sense, in one use of "same sense," since (T) is an interpretation rule for the subject-predicate juxtaposition in "Fa" as well as a description of the truth ground or truth maker for that sentence. This double role might lie behind the unfortunate talk of "truth conditions" being the "meanings" of sentences. That aside, there is nothing problematic about (T). Moreover, the sentence "Fa," when true, can be taken to represent or denote the atomic fact which then exists, so long as the fact is not taken to either be the "referent" of, or provide an interpretation for, the sentence, as objects and properties are so taken for names and predicates, respectively.

In that (T) is a further semantic (but not designation) rule or stipulation it belongs to the logic of the schema, as (3) did, and is "internal" or "logical" in the way that the designation rules (1) and (2) are, as semantic rules. Yet, it is not internal in a way that (1) and (2) are, since atomic sentences are not taken to represent facts as names and predicates are taken to represent objects and properties—by being terms of a basic representation or designation relation. It is this feature that allows us to not only avoid an implicit commitment to non-existent facts, but to avoid a basic "internal" or "intrinsic" referential connection between propositions and such problematic non-existents. Carnap's discussions of the existence of properties and his concern with the designative role of false sentences can be misleading, given his claim that his views "do not involve a hypostatization." In spite of the apparent realism of *Introduction to Semantics* at places in the text, Carnap reiterated a familiar positivist theme in "Empiricism, Semantics, and Ontology." Mentioning critics who had misunderstood him to be advocating some form of metaphysical realism, he sought to clarify his view:

> .... the external question is not a theoretical question but rather the practical question of whether or not to accept those linguistic forms. .... it is certainly wrong to regard my semantical method as involving a belief in the reality of abstract entities, since I reject a thesis of this kind as a metaphysical pseudo-statement (1956, 217-218).

It is in this vein that he will also problematically take "designates" to be implicitly defined by the semantic rules of the system—but that raises another set of issues. What is interesting to note is that his dismissal of metaphysical questions, while holding that the answer to internal questions about existence, of numbers for example, is "analytic and trivial," does not differ significantly, though it does verbally, from Dummett's views about the existence of, and our reference to, abstract entities like "the Equator" and "air pollution," and his criticism of "nominalists" who reject such entities (2002, 23).

Given (T), a fact, if it exists, is denoted by a definite description. If no such fact exists, we need no more recognize a Meinongian non-subsistent objective than a non-existent king of France. We also avoid having to take facts to be related to their constituents in further relational facts, and thus block a Bradley type regress. For "T" does not represent a relation that will be a constituent of a further relational fact with an object and a fact as its terms, and so on and on. It is easy to see that T, A and IN, as formal relations, are immune to such a regress. If we seek to specify the fact that would be a term of such a relational fact, we can only describe it. The relevant description is "the fact having a as a term, F as attribute and Φx as form." Thus, that a is a term of such a fact is then expressed by the claim: a stands in T to the fact having a as a term, F as attribute and Φx as form. And this is equivalent to saying that the fact exists, to "the fact having a as a term, F as attribute and Φx as form exists," on Russell's analysis of definite descriptions. Given that there is such a fact, it trivially follows that a is a term of it. For on Russell's theory we trivially have: E! (ɿ p)(T(a, p) & A(F, p) & IN(Φx, p)) ≡ T(a, (ɿ p)(T(a, p) & A(F, p) & IN(Φx, p))). It simply amounts to a variant of a familiar theorem of *Principia Mathematica*: E! (ɿ x)(Φx) ≡ Φ(ɿ x)(Φx). The same is true for the logical relations A and IN.

In view of this feature of such relations, they can viably be taken to be formal, or internal or logical relations in a perfectly clear sense of those terms—terms that are often used in vague and problematic senses. That is the argument I promised earlier and the justification of the use of terms like "formal" and "logical" to characterize such relations. The present pattern's use of Russellian definite descriptions resolves the puzzles of both Meinong and Bradley without simply declaring that certain relations are "special" or "supervenient" or "abnormal" or "non-entity" relations. An analysis and an argument have been offered. Moreover, one need not take the present view to deny the recognition of "exemplification." In that T, A and IN are formal relations, they can be said to be exemplified by pairs consisting of a term of a fact and the fact, an attribute of a fact and the fact, etc. The point is that such instances of exemplification do not give rise to further facts and are thus not cases of exemplification or instantiation in the sense that philosophers have held that the object a exemplifies the property F. This is all that is required to avoid the Frege-Bradley regress in a way that does not amount to a mere declaration that no further relations are needed. It follows from the very analysis of facts, from Russell's theory of descriptions and from the role of such logical relations that no additional facts are involved. This neither denies that atomic facts stand in formal relations to their constituent terms, attributes and relations nor that they have forms. What avoids the paradox of Bradley and Frege, and MacBride's reiteration of it, and the non-existent intentional objects of Meinong, while blunting Sellars's many pronged assault on Realism, is, first, that their standing in such relations does not give rise to further facts and, second, the use of (T) in place of (3). The role of such formal relations has not been stipulated to be different from that of normal universals but has been *shown to be so*, on the pattern developed above. This blocks Sellars's raising and MacBride's reraising of the Frege-Bradley regress.

Recently P. Horwich (1996) has repeated a pattern Sellars sought to use to dispose of a basic reference relation, even in the case of singular terms, including proper names. The pattern turns the footnote in Tarski's paper that was mentioned earlier into an article and a theory. In the footnote, recall, Tarski indicated that just as one can, to use Sellars's phrase, make "the truth move" from "'Fa' is true" to "Fa," one can, to speak the current jargon, "deflate" reference by going from "∂ refers to a" to "ß=a," where "∂" is what Tarski called a "structural descriptive name" of the sign "ß." What Horwich problematically does is attempt to remove the problem of "aboutness" or reference by transforming "'ß' refers to a" or "∂ refers to a" into "ß=a." What he fails to see is that three problems remain. (i) Either there is an illicit use involving the semantic quotes to avoid stating explicitly that he makes use of aboutness or reference, in that it is understood that "ß" refers to ß, if we use a sentence involving a quoted expression, such as "'ß' refers to a," in place of "∂ refers to a." Or, one illicitly uses the meta-linguistic connection, if we retain the latter. (ii) That we take terms like "a" to be interpreted terms of a schema and hence as representing or referring to what they are coordinated with. (iii) The status of the biconditional "∂ refers to a if and only if ß=a" that is used to deflate "refers to." Is the latter true by stipulation, thereby giving a stipulative definition of "refers to"? Is it a sociological report of usage? All Horwich does is transform Tarski's suggestion into a variant of a familiar neo-Wittgensteinian "ordinary language" move that removes reference by deflating it to identity, rather than dismissing the philosophical issues regarding reference in the more familiar way of emphasizing that the "use" provides the meaning of referring expressions.

Sellars sought to dispense with the notion of reference or aboutness by introducing what he called a "fragment of a neo-Fregean semantical theory" to connect "individual concepts" or "senses" to singular terms. The senses and concepts are the "roles," embodying the various rules governing the signs, that tokens of the linguistic items perform in the schema. Such linguistic roles, embodying normative rules that govern, and socio-psychological generalities that describe, the use of linguistic tokens, supposedly allow him to hold that when we take the occurrence of a token of "ß" to be used to refer to a, we understand it to belong to a class of tokens that are involved in appropriate responses to the object a. Thus there is no need to introduce a basic relation of *reference* or *representation* between a sign (token or type) and an object. To meet the obvious objection that among the appropriate rules are rules regarding the use of signs to refer to a, Sellars gives a two-fold response.

One is along the lines that Goodman has made well known in his treatment of meaning (1972). That avoids taking meaning as a relation between what it is that purportedly *means* and what is *meant* by transforming patterns like "'x' means y" into "'x' means the same as 'y'." Thus we avoid talking about entities that are represented or meant by talking only about expressions with the same meaning. This is what lies behind Sellars's notorious dot quote convention—whereby one can use such quotes to characterize various terms in diverse languages that play the same role, as being of the same "kind." One is thus not limited, as one is with ordinary quotation marks, to talking about a specific term, "red" say, of a specific language and its role. This aids Sellars to express his analysis of statements like "Red is a quality" as a statement about the kind of role played by the English term "red," and by its correlates in other languages, and not about a purported universal color quality (1967, 62-78). Thus, at his most explicit, Sellars declared that abstract entities—qualities (the color red), classes (the class of red things), etc.—are "linguistic":

> ...if the term "abstract individual" is ... restricted to qualities, relations, propositions, kinds, classes, and the like ...
> All abstract individuals are linguistic
> expresses a truth. (1967, 74)

The second aspect of his response involves the transposition of questions about meaning and reference into questions about appropriate behavioral responses to stimuli, in a manner Quine has made familiar. Thus, in Sellars's complex presentation, we hear about "language entry" moves and "language exit" moves that are "word-world" connections. To speak of "a" referring to a is to speak of "a" being a linguistic type belonging to a rule governed scheme, where participating in the use of such a scheme involves learning to use tokens of that type in certain contexts (the world-word moves). These include appropriate uses in the presence of extra-linguistic phenomena (the word-world moves) and in ways that connect the tokens with other tokens of other types within the scheme, according to the "intra-systematic" rules (the word-word moves). All this amounts to specifying the detailed complexities regarding when a token of "a" is and should be used by providing a sketch of the socio-psychological conditions and causes involved in language learning and use. But Sellars never came to terms with a basic problem, a problem that can be seen in his never abandoning the notion of a word-world connection and in his speaking of linguistic "pictures" (theories) being correct or not. Thus applying "F" to an object a is correct if a is an F. But, the move has to be held to be correct if "Fa" fits into the current scheme that, at its limit, is his "ideal Peircean conceptual scheme." The similarity to Dewey's instrumentalist version of idealism, the endless pursuit of "inquiry" that progresses towards an unattainable ideal limit, and to the earlier turn of the century Hegelian patterns of Bosanquet and Bradley, that involved a progressive filling out of the structure of the Absolute, via forms of holistic coherence theories of truth and meaning, is unmistakable. It was thus no accident that Sellars, like Dewey, came to focus on the "normative" and "social" aspects of linguistic use and the "rules" governing such use as embodied in the social structure of the "community" of language users. This seems to be an obvious move for the modern descendants of classical idealism to make in connection with the "linguistic turn," as can be seen in R. Brandom's recent book (1994).

3c. Truth: Davidson's Fast Track to the Meaning of "Meaning"

In recent years, Davidson has attempted to offer a theory of meaning in terms of truth conditions that is "deflationary" in the fashion of Sellars. As a critical part of his analysis of meaning that is involved in what contemporaries often refer to as his "project" (using, somewhat ironically, a term often associated with Sartre), Davidson claimed that "s means that p" can be rendered as "s is true if and only if p" (1967, 309). A person, S, is then taken to know or understand the meaning of "Fa" if S knows or understands that: "Fa" is true if and only if (iff) Fa—where the right side of the biconditional, here "Fa" itself, furnishes a statement of the truth condition for "Fa." Davidson attempts to avoid the acknowledgment of a correlated fact as a truth ground by producing a token of a Tarskian T-sentence. But to deal with the classical philosophical issues involved, one must probe into the role "Fa" (or "p") plays in such an analysis and face the problem of connecting a sentence or sentence token to a ground of truth. Doing that involves more than uttering a token of the sentence in question or a transcription of it. But that is all Davidson does to furnish a truth condition. Thus we hear the proverbial—"Snow is white" is true iff snow is white—or a variant employing a transcription in another language.

It is interesting to note how one avoids talking about what a truth condition is by talking about "giving a truth condition for" (as Geach (1971, 58 ff.), among others, avoids philosophical questions about what concepts are by talking about what it is to "possess" a concept). Davidson seeks to dispense with meanings, as useless entities, by appealing to truth conditions. In doing so he plays on the obvious fact that when one asks for the meaning of a sentence, in ordinary contexts, a satisfactory answer is provided by furnishing another sentence. Russell and Wittgenstein also sought to avoid classical propositions or content properties as intermediaries between judgments (or atomic sentences) and facts, taken as truth grounds for such sentences (judgments), by connecting atomic sentences directly to facts. Under Tarski's influence, Davidson alters the pattern of Russell and Wittgenstein, so that in place of "S knows that 'Fa' represents Fa" explicating "S knows the meaning of 'Fa'," we have "S knows that: 'Fa' is true iff Fa." While this copies the basic pattern of Russell and Wittgenstein, it leaves out its substance: the recognition of facts as truth grounds. For the question about the truth ground of "Fa" is never raised, except, as we will see, in an odd way.

To raise that question is to recognize the philosophical implications of the use, and not merely the mention, of the sentence "Fa" in the formula "S knows that 'Fa' is true iff Fa." For it is to account for "Fa" having a truth value. A truth ground is not provided by repeating or transcribing the sentence to which a truth predicate is ascribed—by "disquoting" it. The relevant question about the meaning of "Fa" becomes a problem about whatever one puts for "p" in "'Fa' is true iff p." Quine's view that Tarski has taught us that truth is disquotation expresses the idea that seeking a ground of truth is pointless in that to assert that a sentence is true is to do no more than to assert the sentence, which was Ramsey's old redundancy theory of truth (1931c, 1991). There are two points to Quine's view, though he would not put them so. (A) Given a definition of a truth predicate, we need not take such a predicate to stand for a property that is exemplified by truth bearers, whether the latter be sentences, beliefs, thoughts, propositions, etc. (B) If one imposes the Tarskian condition requiring that T-sentences be derived from a definition of a truth predicate, plus standard logic, in a certain type of schema, then for every statement ascribing a truth predicate to a sentence there is an "equivalent" sentence without such a predicate—the sentence to which truth is ascribed. But all this is misleading. Truth may be said to be mere disquotation in the sense captured by (A) and (B). But (A) and (B) have nothing to do with giving a theory of truth, as opposed to introducing a predicate into a schema. A theory of truth specifies what "things" constitute grounds of truth for sentences or thoughts and, perhaps, shows why such grounds are not needed in certain cases. Thus such a theory specifies what it is that is such that its existence suffices to ground the truth of basic sentences (propositions, thoughts) that are purported truth bearers. For such basic truth bearers, the statement that a certain truth ground exists will entail that a "corresponding" statement is true.

There are places where Davidson suggests that there are truth grounds—the objects or the Tarskian "sequences" that satisfy the predicates and open sentences (as well as sentences) of a schema. Put in simple terms what this amounts to, to use an example with a dyadic predicate, "R," and a sign for an ordered pair "<a, b>," is: <a, b> satisfies "R" $\equiv$ aRb. Thus, in place of facts as truth grounds, he has *satisfiers*—objects, pairs of objects, triples of objects, etc. (1969, 758) To avoid taking "F" to represent an attribute, and the sentence to represent a fact, Davidson talks in terms of "F," or "Fx," being satisfied by or, as Quine sometimes puts it, *true of* a. But these notions are so understood that to use them is to do one of two things. First, if one holds that to speak of a satisfying "F" is simply to say that a is F, one merely repeats or transcribes "Fa." Alternatively, one can treat satisfaction as a relation between a thing or sequence and a sign (predicate, open sentence) and take the truth maker as a dyadic fact that has a linguistic item, a predicate or open sentence, as a constituent. Thus we arrive at a variant of linguistic idealism, in that a linguistic item is involved in the truth maker, rather than merely the truth bearer. Goodman has explicitly developed the pattern and, consistent to the end, he speaks of making worlds from words and notes that "... the English language makes them white just by applying the term "white" to them ..." (1984, 49). Earlier we noted that Sartre and Lacan have continental versions of the pattern that explain much of their seemingly mysterious, if picturesque, language, such as Sartre talking of being responsible for your own birth ("birth" is our concept and we "choose" to use it) and Lacan's comment about his daughter not being his daughter without language—without there being the symbol and, thus, the language. In this vein, Goodman, precise, explicit and cryptic, poetically wrote of a world independent of conceptual schemes as a "world well lost" and of the role of language in "world making" (1976, 1978). Davidson's variant of this comes out in a remarkable statement about laws of nature: "But laws are linguistic; and so events can instantiate laws, and hence be explained or predicted in the light of laws ..." (1986, 215). Without language there would be no daughters and no laws of nature. The American novelist James T. Farrell seemed to have a better grip on reality when he wrote *A World I Never Made*, for he was not talking about language at all.

Aside from linguistic items, predicates, open sentences, etc., Davidson only recognizes objects (we can ignore events here) or sequences of them, in connection with sentences like "Fa" and "aRb." Yet an object cannot be the ground of truth, though it is a "satisfier" for Davidson (1969, 758). For an object a can satisfy the primitive predicates "F" and "G," but "Fa" and "Ga" cannot be said to have the same ground of truth, unless one takes such truths to be necessary—as grounded by the "nature" of the object (for a detailed argument on this point see Hochberg, 1967). In fact it is almost astounding to read in a recent, basically appreciative, book on Davidson by S. Evnine:

> By contrast, on his approach, the only things that correspond to sentences are the objects which satisfy them. If, however, the only relations

between sentences and things in the world are of this sort, such relations cease to explain the truth of sentences. Dolores and Dagmar both correspond to (i.e. satisfy) the sentences "Dolores loves Dagmar" and "Dolores is next to Dagmar," yet the two sentences, if true, are clearly true for different reasons. The first is true because Dolores loves Dagmar; the second because she is next to him. The very fact that what is supposed to "correspond" to the sentence does not include the relations that apply to the objects makes this sense of correspondence too tenuous to justify the idea that we have an explanation of truth in terms of correspondence.

In a recent retrospection of his work on truth, Davidson has recognized this: ....(1991, 136-37)

It is most amazing that one has to still say what Evnine sensibly says and for Davidson to "recognize this" in 1987 (ignoring the fact that Peter and Paul also satisfy the sentence if Dolores loves Dagmar, due to a trivial, if odd sounding, feature of Tarski's semantic conception of truth). But we must not be misled here. Davidson has not really recognized what seems obvious. What he actually recognized is that he should not have said, in 1983, that he held a kind of "correspondence theory." All that he has come to realize is that his belief that putting words in relation to objects would suffice to "give some grip for the idea of correspondence" appears to have been "a mistake." He is still committed to a "Tarski-style" theory:

The mistake is in a way only a misnomer, but terminological infelicities have a way of breeding conceptual confusion, and so it is here. Correspondence theories have always been conceived as providing an explanation or analysis of truth, and this a Tarski-style theory of truth certainly does not do. (2001, 154-55)

The answer to his problem is simply to note that "truth" is indefinable, though a general claim about it can be made: "the truth of an utterance depends on just two things: what the words as spoken mean, and how the world is arranged." But, again, one should not be misled, as all he means by speaking of "how the world is arranged" is that the Tarskian T-sentences are enough to ensure the "domain of application" of "truth." Thus, nothing has been realized, and one should recall that Tarski noted it made no difference whether one defined a truth predicate or "introduced" it as a primitive term (governed by postulates) so long as it satisfied the constraints of the semantic conception of truth, such as Convention-T.

For one concerned with the fundamental issues of philosophy there is clearly a problem for those, like Davidson, Quine and Sellars, and their recent offspring, like Horwich, who seek to avoid recognizing facts as truth grounds by the technique of "deflation" that employs Tarskian style biconditionals and loose talk about "truth conditions." However, one should note that Davidson, like Tarski, is not really concerned with the philosophical problems posed by truth—they are simply dismissed. He is concerned with giving a "theory of truth for a speaker or group of speakers ..." (2001, 156), as part of the task of "interpreting" someone's or some group's speech. And Horwich essentially uses Tarski as a substitute for the later Wittgenstein to buttress an essentially ordinary language dismissal of the issues by "deflating" them. The heart of the philosophical problem has always been to specify, in general, what it is for atomic relational and subject-predicate sentences to be true. Limit the case to a monadic atomic sentence. The correspondence theory of truth, simply put, holds that such a sentence is true if and only if there is a fact formed from a term represented by the subject sign and an attribute represented by the predicate sign.

Davidson and Quine, not recognizing facts, reject this. But, since we consider the general case, and they are thus not furnished with a specific sentence that is purportedly true, they are forced into the pattern of a coherence theory of truth. We can easily see why. Suppose one were to propose, in the spirit of Tarski, something like "(p)(ß)[ß names p ⊃ (ß is true ≡ p)]," to specify a general "truth condition" for such sentences, where "ß" is a variable, taking names of subject-predicate sentences as substitution instances, and "p" a variable taking subject-predicate sentences as substitution instances. This will obviously not do. For, consider a sentential instance of "p," say "Fa." It is used as a sentence after the occurrence of "≡," but not as a sentence after the occurrence of "names" in "'Fa' names Fa," for a specific instance like: "Fa" names Fa ⊃ ("Fa" is true ≡ Fa). Thus a question arises about what the sentence "Fa" represents as it occurs after "names." It is one thing to hold that: the expression "'Fa'" names the sentence "Fa." It is quite another thing to hold that: the sentence "Fa" names Fa. But it is the latter claim that is relevant, and it is not at all clear just what it is that the sentence is then said to "name."

Consider a context like "'ß' names ß." Here there is no problem, since we take the sign within the inner quotes to be the name of the sign "ß," and the latter to name some object. To treat sentences along such lines abandons the kind of move Davidson makes and returns us to the problem we discussed in connection with a Meinongian-style semantics. It is also why Sellars attempts to convince us that the perspicuous way of rendering such statements is to transform them into metalingusitic statements by the use of his "dot" quoting device. Thus the problematic sentence becomes: any instance of "Fa" is an instance of •Fa•—or "Fa"s are •Fa•s—on his attempt to dispense with any connection between sentences and facts by semantically ascending. Sellars's special quoting device plays the role of forming expressions, from an expression in one language, that are used as signs that apply to expressions in various languages that play corresponding roles in those languages. Thus, "red" and "röd" are both •red•s or, alternatively, both •röd•s. But, recognizing that he must still specify the basis for taking an assertion as "correct" no matter how he handles the term "true," Sellars will be led into a coherence account of truth and speak of "correctness" (i. e. truth in the normal sense) in terms of the sentence being "semantically assertible"—which means belonging to his ideal conceptual scheme (Peircean ideal scheme).

An alternative might appear to be found in holding that a subject-predicate sentence is true if and only if the predicate is satisfied by (is true of) the object. This, as we noted earlier, involves taking Tarskian "satisfaction" as a basic relation, between an object (or sequence) and a predicate sign, and, hence, it takes a linguistic sign to be part of the truth ground. The point is simple. One cannot replace "is satisfied by" in the familiar way Davidson typically employs in the examples he uses, since no specific sentence is provided as the purported truth bearer. That is, one cannot play the familiar deflationary move of semantic descent—what Sellars calls "the truth move," by employing a biconditional, as in: a satisfies "F" ≡ Fa. If one could one would eliminate the use of "satisfies," via a Tarskian T-sentence, by offering an *equivalent* sentence that employs neither the term "satisfies" nor a semantical device for referring to a sentence. Since one cannot do that, one does not then avoid facts. Rather one recognizes esoteric facts, involving an object being related to a sign, as a truth ground.

One can also raise a question about the implied use of a relation of satisfaction (and hence a relational fact). On the analysis in question that is understood in terms of the ordered pair of the predicate and the object satisfying the relational predicate "is satisfied by." The obvious regress then ensues if one attempts to treat that use of the relational predicate "is satisfied by" on the pattern employed. For on that pattern one dispenses with properties and relations by appealing to the satisfaction of predicates. This might be thought to be similar to an attempt to raise a Bradley-style regress for the correspondence theory by questioning whether it is, in turn, a fact that there is a fact grounding the truth of "Fa." But for a carefully stated correspondence theory no regress begins, since to state that the described fact is a fact is simply to state that it exists. The problem arises for the "disquotational" or deflationist account because its adherents deny the existence of any fact to cut off the regress, while trying to avoid recognizing satisfaction as a relation by purporting to analyze, and thereby eliminate, the use of the relational predicate "satisfies." As this is hopeless, one may then, as a kind of last resort, attempt to employ a substitutional account of quantification, as Sellars once sketched in a rather esoteric form that is too involved (and needlessly so) for us to go into. In a simple, straightforward substitutional account one would hold: For any x and any Φ, a subject-predicate sentence with Φ as predicate and x as subject is true if and only if Φx.

On such an account the quantifiers are understood to range over subject signs and predicate signs, as substitutional quantifiers, and not over objects and properties, respectively. One now appears to specify a general condition for the truth of subject-predicate sentences at the price of giving up quantification over objects (and properties). But it is mere appearance, devoid of any reality or real content. For an unanswerable question arises about the reading of the occurrence of "Φx" after the biconditional with the use of substitutional quantifiers. The only sensible way of understanding that occurrence of "Φx" is as elliptical for "'Φx' is true," which obviously gets us nowhere. That is, what is really said, if one thinks about it, is: "For any singular term x and any predicate Φ, a subject-predicate sentence with x as subject term and Φ as predicate is true if and only if ...." But "..." must be replaced by a sentence, and there are only two choices. One can use the statement that the object represented by the singular term has the property represented by the predicate; or the statement that the sentence formed from the subject and predicate terms *is true*. Either alternative is clearly hopeless. The simple point is that with the use of bound variables after the biconditional interpreted substitutionally, the expression is gibberish. One easily sees that by considering "$(\exists x)(\exists \Phi)\Phi x$." To read this "substitutionally" is to read it in terms of "There is a singular term and there is a predicate such that the subject-predicate sentence formed from them is true." And such a reading, involved in the substitutional account, is transparently useless in the present context. That the substitutional account is, in itself, hopeless is another matter that we need not pursue. We need only note that it requires a true generalization to the effect that *for every object* there is a sign for it in the language—and thus it must employ a quantifier ranging over objects, not signs.

Deflationism, if thought out, as Sellars consciously did, but neither Davidson nor Horwich do, forces one into holding a variant of: For any singular term and any predicate sign, a subject-predicate sentence composed of those signs is true if and only if it is a theorem of, or linked in some appropriate way to, a conceptual scheme S. This amounts to Carnap's "internalism" that leads to the dismissal of so-called "external" questions or to some form of "internal realism" or anti-realism or holism, and is the basic pattern of Bradley's and Bosanquet's coherence theory of truth and identification of reality with "knowledge" ("truth," "thought"—Bradley, 1944a, 112-14; 1897, 172-73). As such, it is not a semantical account of truth, though it is also the pattern that Quine ends up with in the form of a "web of belief" and the respective depths of the various beliefs "in" the conceptual scheme that, like for Bradley and Bosanquet, replaces an independent and objective reality that correct "thought" corresponds to.

> Hence it is meaningless, I suggest, to inquire into the absolute correctness of a conceptual scheme as a mirror of reality. Our standard of appraising basic changes of conceptual scheme must be, not a realistic standard of correspondence to reality, but a pragmatic standard. (Quine, 1953, 79)

Such a pragmatic-coherence theory is also one Davidson once thought to advocate, though none of these more contemporary figures proposed to "analyze" truth or define "is true" in terms of some form of coherence.

Davidson, reaffirming his commitment to Tarski's semantic conception of truth, and taking truth to be a primitive notion, regretted "having called my view a 'coherence theory'" (2001, 155), since he simply meant "that all that counts as evidence or justification for a belief must come from the same totality of belief to which it belongs" (2001, 155). But that amounts to little, virtually nothing, if it is innocently taken as the view that coherence is the *criterion* for *verifying* or justifying a claim as to what "the facts are." It is neither innocent nor innocuous if taken as holding that there are no facts that ground the truth of a claim, irrespective of the way of verifying or justifying the claim. The latter, simply put, is the coherence theory. Irrespective of his regrets, Davidson seems to hold a coherence theory. (I say "seems," since he does not distinguish between specifying a ground of truth from the way of verifying or justifying that something is true.) He also clearly holds a holistic-coherence style "theory" of meaning. But neither his holism nor his *principle of charity* of interpretation, employed in developing his theory of meaning, are of any relevance to the classical philosophical problems. They simply amount to a variant of the familiar "naturalizing" move, more clearly seen in Quine's writings, that treats philosophical problems as problems of the kind that concern psychologists, social-psychologists, anthropologists and linguists interpreting the linguistic behavior of the subjects they study—much as linguists and psychologists study the apparent linguistic behavior of chimpanzees. The principle of charity simply prescribes not ascribing unreasonable beliefs, intentions, etc. to speakers—always give them the benefit of the doubt and take them to speak the truth, in so far as you can—when you interpret what they mean by their uses of language.

Davidson sees himself as providing a theory of meaning by dealing with how to determine "the meaning" of a speaker's words so that an interpreter can derive a correct interpretation. After all, "words" can only be taken in such a context as utterances of tokens used in a certain setting; and "meaning" must be understood in terms of providing other sentences purportedly explicating such uses, along the lines of: "When he said 'Jones is a red' he meant 'Jones is a communist' and not 'Jones is a red trope'." Like Goodman, Davidson finds "meanings" to be "useless" entities for explanatory purposes—aside from their being "intensional" entities, and therefore unacceptable to one who holds an "extensionalist" view of language. Regarding "intensional" entities, like propositions, "meanings" and properties, there are, supposedly, no clear cut criteria of identity. They thus crucially differ from individual things, classes and ordered pairs, for example. He does not find meanings to be unacceptable as "abstract" entities, but as "useless," since they lack explanatory power. Of course one has to ask, "Useful for explaining what?" In particular, are they useful to resolve the classical philosophical issues? Or, are we being told, in roundabout fashion, that such issues are "useless"? In any case, the dismissal of "meanings" is ambiguous. Russell, recall, dismissed meanings—Fregean senses and propositions, Meinongian contents, non-subsistent objectives and his own earlier "denoting complexes." But for logically proper names and primitive predicates he took meaning as reference. What Davidson does, in passing so to speak, is dismiss the classical problems posed by universals, reference, predication and truth grounds in dismissing "meanings" and facts as useless, and argues:

> The real objection to correspondence theories is simpler; it is that there is nothing for true sentences to correspond to. The point was made long ago by C. I. Lewis; he challenged the correspondence theorist to *locate* the fact or part of reality, or of the world, to which a true sentence corresponded. ... Following out this line of thought led Lewis to conclude that if true sentences correspond to anything at all, it must be the

universe as a whole; thus all true sentences correspond to the same thing. Frege, as we know, independently reached the same conclusion through a similar course of reasoning. Frege's argument, if Alonzo Church is right, can be formalized .... (2001, 183)

One is puzzled to see the point. Of course one does not locate facts, as one locates particulars. Some, like Armstrong, think of facts as particulars (though higher order facts with a basic causal relation pose a problem for him), but, generally, nobody would think of a fact as being at a place. The cat is in the room, the mat is in the room, but the cat's being on the mat is hardly taken to be "in the room," surely not next to the cat or the mat or between them, though one might say, in response to a question, "The cat is on the mat in the next room." Why this should lead one down the trail Davidson takes, in Lewis's tracks, is difficult to understand, unless one has the simple view that all existents are "locatable" in space (but then Davidson's ordered pairs and sequences surely are not). One would think, in this century, that it is rather obvious that one is presented with facts just as one is presented with things, in the sense in which Russell and Moore spoke of apprehension and acquaintance. After all, I see that the cat is on the mat just as I see the cat—or even that the object on the mat is a cat. What Davidson has not digested is that facts are simply different sorts of things than physical objects. In a way this is not surprising. Facts were clearly recognized quite late in philosophical discussions and only emphasized at the end of the nineteenth and early in the twentieth century. Russell, for example, spoke of "complex unities," virtually as complex objects, in the early years of the twentieth century, though Stumpf was then writing about "states of affairs," and gradually shifted to talking of facts (though Russell still spoke of "complexes," as well as facts, when Wittgenstein was at Cambridge). It was Moore's papers and 1910-11 lectures that became *Some Main Problems of Philosophy* as well as Wittgenstein's *Tractatus* that emphasized the notions of "state of affairs," "situation" and "fact" and made them central to philosophical discussions about truth and truth grounds. Nevertheless, the relatively unknown Swedish philosopher Ivar Segelberg was far more aware than Davidson of a distinction between facts and events, though Davidson is well known for his writings on events, in pointing out an obvious difference:

> One cannot imagine two exactly similar facts, because a fact, obviously, is not localized in either space or time. A fact can contain properties of spatial and temporal localization, but it does not itself have such properties. The fact, for example, that King Gustavus Adolphus II fell in

battle at Lützen on November 6, 1632, is not localized either in Lützen or on November 6, 1632. By contrast, the event, which constitutes Gustavus Adophus II's death, is localized in time and space. (1999, 159)

It is worth noting how Davidson's materialism plays a role in his rejection of facts. Consider a visual field (or auditory field, etc.) and the percepts and sense data of Moore and Russell. Depending on how one construes such fields, one may or may not take the question of their location to be sensible though one can speak of location within such a field. As Russell once put it, the space of the visual field is "absolute." But a phenomenal flash of color or a sound will not have a location in physical space, unless one identifies (or replaces) phenomenal entities, via some form of materialism, with (by) physical ones. Space aside, that a flash of red color preceded a flash of blue will be a fact (hardly requiring location) and quite different from what would be the case if a flash of blue preceded a flash of red. (Davidson's events, which he recognizes as particulars, do not help as, granting such entities, there will be facts involving them.) Davidson's argument against facts is without substance or, perhaps, even content. Be that as it may, the above quotation leads Davidson into one of his many presentations of the Great Fact argument against facts, which I will briefly consider since many still discuss what is clearly a pointless argument and it has recently been revived in a lengthy reconsideration and defense of it.

Let "S" and "T" be any two true sentences. We will use Carnap's "designates" to state the argument. Given the familiar designation rules we have as premises:

(GF) 1. S
2. T
3. "S" designates S (the fact that-S—I simply use "S" without quotes to represent the fact).

We then supposedly can derive "'S' designates T" thus showing that any true sentence designates the same fact as any other true sentence, since "S" and "T" are any two true sentences. The argument assumes, first, (P) that we may substitute logically equivalent sentences and, second, (P*) we may substitute "coextensive" singular terms. It then proceeds as follows:

4. $(\iota x)(x = \text{Socrates} \,\&\, S) = (\iota x)(x = \text{Socrates})$
5. $(\iota x)(x = \text{Socrates} \,\&\, T) = (\iota x)(x = \text{Socrates})$

6. $(\iota x)(x = \text{Socrates} \& S) = (\iota x)(x = \text{Socrates} \& T)$
7. "S" is logically equivalent to "$(\iota x)(x = \text{Socrates} \& S) = (\iota x)(x = \text{Socrates})$"
8. "S" designates $(\iota x)(x = \text{Socrates} \& S) = (\iota x)(x = \text{Socrates})$
9. "S" designates $(\iota x)(x = \text{Socrates} \& T) = (\iota x)(x = \text{Socrates})$
10. "T" is logically equivalent to "$(\iota x)(x = \text{Socrates} \& T) = (\iota x)(x = \text{Socrates})$"
11. "S" designates T.

We assume, it should be noted, that "Socrates" is a name of something and hence that "Socrates = $(\iota x)(x = \text{Socrates})$" is true. Each step then supposedly follows from applying either (P) or (P*) and standard logic. If descriptive phrases of the form "$(\iota x)(\Phi x)$" are treated like proper names, as basic patterns, in an extensional system, where one takes expressions like "x = Socrates & S" as predicates with extensions, then it is not worth discussing, as the rules governing them come into question. If descriptions are treated along the lines of Russell's theory of definite descriptions, then the descriptive phrases are contextually defined signs. Therefore, we should expand them to examine the argument. If we attempt to do so an immediate problem arises about the scope of descriptions in contexts like (8) and (9). Putting that aside, we take the scope(s) as "secondary," just governing the sentential expression after the occurrence of "designates." If one expands the definite descriptions in (4)-(8) it becomes immediately obvious that there is no way to get to (9) unless one is allowed to replace an occurrence of "S" by an occurrence of "T." In fact (P*) becomes totally irrelevant, since the definite descriptions have "disappeared" (for the details see Hochberg, 1975). Gödel had pointed out quite early that one cannot simply reason along lines Davidson employs (which as Davidson notes he derived from Church), if one employs a definite descriptive operator as a contextually defined sign in Russell's manner and not as a primitive sign pattern. Church had noted something similar in his use of a lambda operator in place of a definite description operator. [It recalls Russell's well known discussion of the case of the expressions "Scott" and "the author of *Waverley*" and what George IV wished to know in "On Denoting." Russell pointed out that if the scope of the description was taken to be secondary in the sentence "George IV wished to know whether Scott was the author of *Waverley*," one could not validly conclude that George IV wished to know whether "Scott = Scott," given the true identity "Scott=the author of *Waverley*." Thus such a context was one where scope makes a difference even when the description is fulfilled. See Hochberg, 2001b, 49-51, for the details.] But to replace an occurrence of "S" by an occurrence of "T" is to use a different rule, one concerning sentences that merely have the same truth value but are not "logically equivalent" sentences. Thus, with 1*, 2* and 3* as premises, we can simply argue,

(Dav) 1*. S
     2*. T
     3*. "S" designates S, therefore
     4*. "S" designates T.

This, of course, is absurd. But it no more absurd than Davidson's argument, which, following Church, supposedly employs a principle of replacement based on logical equivalence (which Gödel was not concerned with). Some are deluded by the use of class abstracts like "$\{x \mid x = x \ \& \ S\}$" in place of definite descriptions in some of the many presentations of the argument. But, then one must ask about the rules for such abstracts and the built in conditions for existence claims. On Russell's *Principia* account, class abstracts are not treated in a significantly different way than definite descriptions in this kind of context. I ignore treating the descriptions in (8) and (9) as having primary scope, as all of Davidson's manipulations involve only what occurs on the right hand side of "designates." We should keep in mind that on Russell's theory of descriptions scope differences cancel out in extensional contexts when the description is fulfilled. But in (GF) primary scope will still not enable one to derive Davidson's conclusion, though it does allow for an odd derivation and presents an opportunity to point to further problems with the argument (Hochberg, 1975; 1978b, 213-20). Nor can one treat Davidson's argument along the lines of some arguments, as we noted in Chapter 2 (section 2b), where there is a corresponding valid argument for arguments employing a description in an "apparent" identity statement.

S. Neale, in a recent book (2001) of some 250 pages, repeats an earlier attempt to justify "the Great Fact" argument of Davidson (and Quine) that he presented in an overly long article in *Mind* (1995). In a way the book and the article, like Davidson's writings and Hale and Wright's "neo-Fregeanim," are illustrations of what analytic philosophy has become. Against a background discussion of the history of the great fact argument and expositions of Russell's analysis of descriptive expressions in "extensional" and "nonextensional" contexts, the point of Neale's book—or at least the "philosophical" point—is found on one page. It is an apparent defense of the line of reasoning in Davidson's argument. But all it amounts too is a complex presentation of (Dav) that is disguised by the use of "inference" principles previously, and purportedly innocently, introduced amidst a mass of symbols. What results is a pattern that is a complex variant of (GF). [The complexity is due, in part, to the use of a variant of descriptions like "$(\iota x)(x = \text{Socrates} \& S)$" to guarantee that the description will be fulfilled, whether "S" is true or not. That need not concern us, though I will indicate what is involved below.] Neale gives two versions of the argument (170-74)—the reasons for the differences also need not concern us. What is astounding is that, at the crucial place in both of them, one simply replaces "S" by "T," which is based on "$S \equiv T$"— taken as a premise, along with what plays the role of 3* in one version of Neale's variant. On the other version the premises are those of (GF), again with his version of (3). I will simply deal with the second argument which he calls a "complete connective proof." With the sign "©" in front of a sentence to indicate a context for the sentence—a context like " 'S' designates ..." or "the fact that-p = the fact that-..." and "Φ" and "Ψ" as sentential expression variables, we have:

1N. $\Phi \equiv \Psi$ premise
2N. ©Φ premise
3N. ©$(a = (\iota x)((x = a \& \Phi) \vee (x = b \& \neg \Phi)))$

(3N) comes from (2N) with the use of the principle of the substitution of logical equivalences. The more complex definite description simply allows for taking the definite description to be uniquely satisfied whether "Φ" is true or false and has no real bearing on the point at issue. It is also understood that the descriptive phrase in the context is just shorthand for the expanded Russellian version that results in the apparent identity sentence being an existential statement. That existential statement is logically equivalent to "Φ". So, thus far there is no problem. Then we get to step (4N):

4N. $(\iota x)((x = a \& \Phi) \vee (x = b \& \neg \Phi)) =$
$(\iota x)((x = a \& \Psi) \vee (x = b \& \neg \Psi))$.

(4N) comes from (1N) and the use of the Russellian contextual definition for definite descriptions. Thus (4N) is shorthand for:

$(\exists x)[(y)(((y=a \& \Phi) \vee (y=b \& \neg\Phi)) \equiv y=x) \& (\exists z)((w)(((w=a \& \Psi) \vee (w=b \& \neg\Psi)) \equiv w=z) \& x=z)]$.

The next step is the crucial one. It takes us from (4N) and (3N) to

5N. $©(a = (\iota x)((x = a \ \& \ \Psi) \lor (x = b \ \& \ \neg \Psi)))$,

from which one goes directly, via the principle of substitution of logical equivalences, to

6N. $©\Psi$

Thus concludes this latest, most complex, version of the Great Fact argument, (173-74).

Let us return to (5N), which follows by a "principle of substitution" that Neale employs—aping Davidson's and Quine's use of such a principle. Neale, however, gives an extended justification of the use of the principle. The justification purportedly shows that the objection that was raised above to the move to step (9) in (GF) is not viable. For it is supposedly the case that the move to step (9) that Davidson employs is mirrored by a sequence of steps employing expansions of the definite descriptions along Russellian lines. But when we look at the principle of substitution Neale employs and the claim that it is justified by there being a corresponding sequence of steps using expansions of the descriptions (160-61), we find that he appeals to the expansion of "$(\iota x)(x = $ Socrates $\& \ S) = (\iota x)(x = $ Socrates$)$" in (8) being an "extensional sentence." Its being so allows for the replacement of any sentence by one materially equivalent to it. That means, simply put, that the expansion of "$(\iota x)(x = $ Socrates $\& \ S) = (\iota x)(x = $ Socrates$)$" can be replaced by the expansion of "$(\iota x)(x = $ Socrates $\& \ T) = (\iota x)(x = $ Socrates$)$"—for they are materially equivalent given that "S" and "T" are. Thus, all we have is a version of (Dav). What takes up so much writing is Neale's reiterating the familiar points that Russell and Whitehead took the contexts of *Principia* to be truth functional. (That is, of course, basically true and, in fact, was one reason for Russell's developing his multiple relation analysis of intentional verbs after apparently employing a more Fregean style analysis of intentional contexts in "On Denoting.")[7] Neale seems to think that not understanding this feature of *Principia* is what lies behind the objection to (GF) based on the move from step

---

[7]There is a qualification to be made regarding the "extensionality" of the first edition of *Principia Mathematica*. Given the use of functions and the taking of diverse functions of different order to have identical extensions, there is a sense in which *Principia's* functions are not extensional and a sense in which they are, as the term "extensional" is used. See Hochberg, 1987 on this matter and its connection to the notorious "axiom of reducibility."

(8) to (9). What he fails to understand is that the objection is based on the appeal to extensional contexts that amounts to allowing the move from (3*) to (4*) in (Dav). For no one would pay attention to (Dav) as an argument against facts. All that happens in Davidson's argument, and Neale's lengthy exposition, is making the move from (3*) to (4*) in (Dav) and disguising it in the dress of Russellian definite descriptions and the purported substitution of singular terms.

A further question arises about taking expressions like "x = Socrates & S" as predicates (representing properties?) that are "satisfied by" objects like Socrates and as terms that have an individual, Socrates in this case, as an "extension." This leads to taking Socrates to be the extension of "(ι x)(x = Socrates & S)," thus compressing the difference between a name and a description. In part it all results from ignoring properties and thinking in terms of objects satisfying predicates (Hochberg, 1978, 217-19). This tendency to think, informally, in terms of sentential contexts with free variables expressing properties is one of the causes behind disputes focusing on modal operators. Thus "□(x = x)," with "□" transcribed as "necessarily" or "necessary that," is taken as a predicate expression that is satisfied by Socrates. Socrates is then said to be "necessarily" self-identical and identity is taken to be such that "□ a=b" is true if "a=b" is. All this is connected to the recent discussions of purported "analytic *a posteriori* statements" like "a=a" and "a=b" (recall the earlier discussion in section (2f); also see section (4b) below). This leads to other "properties" being taken to be had necessarily, if had at all, and hence to the reintroduction of the traditional "essential" attributes of objects, as well as problems about "quantifying into" modal contexts (Quine, 1976, 1-18, 68-76).

Note that nothing has been said in the present discussion of the Great Fact argument about the use of "designates" involving a context that is non-extensional, or one where such substitution of descriptions is not allowed or about the principle of substitution of logically equivalent sentences. The question has solely been about the use of a principle that allows for the interchange of materially equivalent statements—which traditionally provides one sense of the term "extensional." So, in that sense, if one does not allow the replacement of one materially equivalent statement for another in certain contexts one does not deal with extensional contexts. And, clearly, acknowledging facts in a setting that makes use of a Carnapian-style semantical rule along the lines of "'S' designates the state of affairs that-S" will employ a context with "designates" that is "non-extensional." This is one factor involved in Carnap's developing his account of "intensional isomorphism" in *Meaning and Necessity*. Obviously any viable theory of facts (states of affairs) involving such a concept will not acknowledge that "Socrates is wise" designates purported disjunctive and conjunctive facts, such as (Socrates is wise or Socrates is wise) and (Socrates is wise and Socrates is wise)—though the disjunctive and conjunctive sentences are logically equivalent to "Socrates is wise." That one might well hold that the fact that Socrates is wise is the truth ground for such a disjunction and conjunction (or what makes them true) is another matter that we will consider later.

It is interesting to see just how trivial Davidson's argument is when you consider it in the context of the way facts are "denoted" by definite descriptions on the view expressed in this book. There is no denotation or designation relation involving definite descriptions, as there is a reference or designation relation for primitive predicates and logically proper names. What we then have, in place of (3) and (4), are the familiar three part biconditionals as semantic rules. So, consider two true atomic sentences, "Fa" and "Gb." We can take as premises, aping the Great Fact argument:

(1) Fa
(2) Gb
(3R) "Fa" is true $\equiv$ Fa $\equiv$ the fact having a as a term, F as attribute and Φx as form exists
(4R) "Gb" is true $\equiv$ Gb $\equiv$ the fact having b as a term, G as attribute and Φx as form exists

with (3R) and (4R) as semantical rules. We arrive very quickly at

(5) "Fa" is true $\equiv$ Gb $\equiv$ the fact having b as a term, G as attribute and Φx as form exists,

since we have (1) and (2), and hence "Fa $\equiv$ Gb." But that is completely harmless and trivial. We do not, and cannot, arrive at the conclusion that (5) is a semantical rule giving the truth ground for "Fa" or that "the fact having b as a term, G as attribute and Φx as form = the fact having a as a term, F as attribute and Φx as form." (There is a question about the use of "=" with descriptions of facts that we will take up in Chapter 4.) That can be seen as the way the non-extensionality of the earlier contexts involving "designates," linking sentences and names of sentences, is paralleled. Introducing descriptions like "$(\imath x)(x = \text{Socrates})$" will not lead anywhere.

Davidson fails to address the basic issues about truth grounds. And if his account of truth is philosophically deficient, his attempt to develop a theory of meaning based on it is problematic from the outset. In his way, Davidson, like his mentor Quine, follows the path of Carnap and the logical positivists— attempting to resolve issues by a focus on schematic formalisms and the logical categories of formal languages. Thus Davidson's philosophy of language, based on a variant of Frege's principle of compositionality, involves him in talk of "logical form," "derivations," and the construction of "axiomatic theories." It involves the postulating of semantic axioms and rules providing "meaning" for primitive terms, for basic combinations of them and for the meaning of non-primitive terms of a linguistic structure, as well as for the consequent derivation, as theorems, of the meaning of further non-primitive terms and complex linguistic patterns. In a way it amounts to the application of the techniques of "formal semantics," in Carnap's sense, as embodied in *Introduction to Semantics* and *Meaning and Necessity*, to ordinary language. Davidson's focus on sentence meaning also reflects his following Frege's early emphasis on the meaning of a term being dependent on the context of the sentence in which it occurs, which obviously jars with a principle of compositionality that takes the meaning of a sentence to depend on the meaning and the arrangement of the terms of which it is composed.

Davidson appears struck by a simple fact of language. Any ordinary language or standard formal symbolism that one considers contains an infinite number of sentences or "well-formed formulae." Just consider that given a sentence one can negate it. Then one can negate the negation and so on *ad infinitum*. This sort of thing is what struck Descartes in his consideration of the natural numbers and the idea of infinity. For Descartes, one could not simply, as Hume would later suggest, get the idea of infinity from the notion that one can go on to the next one without end in such an omega series. For that, as Descartes saw it, presupposes that one already has the idea of infinity—one just disguises the appeal to it by speaking of "without end." This led Descartes to hold that we could not get such an idea from experience or by composing it from other ideas (defining the term "infinite") and hence it was presumed to be an "innate" idea. Davidson is struck by a different feature of such examples. We have the ability to understand and employ an infinite number of sentences based on a finite number of ultimate components—in the above case we start, in a way, with just two (forgetting the constituents of the sentence), the sentence and negation—just as one can start, in a manner of speaking, from zero and the notion of "successor of" and arrive at any natural number, on a familiar pattern. Thus Davidson thinks in terms of starting from a finite number of axioms specifying the semantic roles of the terms of a language, which we can call "L," and the various ways they can combine into complex expressions, including sentences. This finite set of axioms yields an infinite number of theorems. This is no more complicated than what you do in the most elementary of logic classes when you note that if you take any tautology you obtain a further tautology by double negation, or by any of a variety of procedures, and can continue to do so "without end." Davidson takes this to indicate an important feature—that a language is not "learnable" if the axiomatic theory giving the "semantics" of the schema does not embody the feature that the "meaning of each sentence" is "a function of a finite number of features of the sentence." What this means is that L is characterized as "learnable" provided that there are only a finite number of axioms governing the meaning of the words of L and their ways of combination, though these will yield infinitely many theorems. But this has nothing to do with characterizing a theory for a language that would enable us to understand the language. For it is not, as Davidson notes, an account of actual language acquisition or use nor of ordinary linguistic use and practice. Since, as we will now see, it has no bearing on the classical philosophical issues of intentionality, reference, predication and truth, it is hard to see the point of Davidson's "project."

The "axioms" and resultant theorems of a theory of meaning supposedly give the "semantic properties" of the words and sentences of L, as Carnap's L-rules and postulates do. But in Carnap's case it is clear what these semantic properties are, as he has designation rules involving a designation relation and, hence, the linking of linguistic items, the terms and sentences of L, to objects, properties, relations, states of affairs, etc. For all the talk of axioms, theorems, being finite, learnability, etc., Davidson's story is amazingly simple. Given Frege's context principle, we begin with sentences—in fact that seems to be the point of bringing in the context principle in the first place. Next, we distinguish, in Carnap's and Tarski's fashion, between an object language, L say, which is the language for which we have a theory of meaning, and a metalanguage for L, L*, in which we state the theory about L. The axioms and theorems of the theory thus belong to L* and provide the "semantics" of L—giving "the meaning" of the sentences of L. But, in giving the meaning of those sentences, we cannot appeal to notions like "means," "expresses," "denotes," "refers to" or "designates" as Carnap, Moore and Russell do in statements like:

> The proposition that the sun is larger than the moon designates the fact (state of affairs) that the sun is larger than the moon.

We cannot do so for a number of reasons. Davidson, following Quine, is a nominalist who does not recognize properties and relations—merely the relevant "predicates." (Davidson objects to being called a "nominalist" since, influenced by Quine's notion of "Platonism," he accepts abstract objects like ordered pairs.) Moreover, like Quine, he is an "extensionalist," while a sentence like that above is "non-extensional"—recall the Great Fact argument. For example, one cannot replace the first occurrence of "the sun is larger than the moon" in the above sentence by "Jupiter is larger than Mars," though both, being true, have the "same extension"—the same truth value. We must have a theory where replacing co-extensive expressions in sentences results in sentences having the same truth values as the original sentences. As terms like "means," "designates," etc. appear to occur in non-extensional contexts, they cannot straightforwardly be employed in a satisfactory semantic theory. There is a point to note here.

Suppose, for example, one did not allow the replacement of the predicate "large" in "'L' refers to the property of being large" by a co-extensive predicate (one applying to the same objects), but insisted on it being replaced by a predicate that referred to the same property—and in that sense could be said to have the same extension, the same "entity" as its referent. Such a move will not do since it introduces a kind of entity Davidson, again following Quine, rejects—properties. Thus, it is not a simple question of dealing with the "extension," as that notion is ambiguous here. In any case we are confined to recognize only particulars—individual objects, events—though we also recognize the "abstract" entities, ordered pairs and, generally, sequences, that are needed for Davidson's Tarski-style use of the semantic conception of truth. Moreover, predicates are, in effect, interpreted in terms of classes of particulars. For Davidson takes singular terms and predicates to have "extensions"—objects in the first case (which, so to speak, carry sequences of objects along with them), and classes of such things that "satisfy" predicates, in the second. Thus, in the manner of Carnap's method of "intension-extension" in *Meaning and Necessity*, terms and predicates are "connected to" particulars and classes, respectively—much as one does in logic classes. And for all the seemingly formal talk about axioms, theorems, semantics and so forth, what a "theory," in Davidson's terms, amounts to is setting down statements on the order of "My utterance of 'Wagener died happy' is true iff Wagener died happy" (2001, 13), "(x) (x satisfies 'is white' if and only if x is white)," "(x)(y)(<x, y> satisfies 'loves' if and only if x loves y" and so on (or, if one wants to make it look more impressively formal, one can employ sequences in place of objects and pairs). It is interesting that the first example reflects that a speaker "cannot improve" on that "sort of statement" to say what his words mean, while an interpreter "... has no reason to assume that will be his best way of stating the truth conditions of the speaker's utterance" (2001, 13). That supposedly resolves the issue of "first person authority" as regards intentional states—

propositional attitudes—and the asymmetry between self-ascriptions and ascriptions to others. Just how it purportedly does so is neither clear nor spelled out. For the obvious question regards why the speaker "cannot improve" on that sort of statement. Can it be because he knows what he means, or, in another kind of case, what he thinks, feels or experiences? But then, much of what Davidson has to say is pointless.

Abstract entities, like ordered pairs and sequences generally, do not bear the liability Quine sees as infecting propositions, properties and facts—for while the latter purportedly do not have clear cut identity conditions, ordered pairs and sequences do, particularly if they are construed along the standard Wiener-Kuratowski lines as classes. Davidson never seems to note the similarity of ordered pairs to facts. Both are "complex," as contrasted with their "elements," and both, if one is concerned with philosophical issues and not merely with words, involve an "ordering" that has to be accounted for. The set-theoretical treatment of ordered pairs, via a Wiener-Kuratowski type construction, will not do as an analysis of "order" (Hochberg, 1981). That aside, classes are identical if and only if they have the same elements—the familiar extensionality axiom of standard class or set theories. Properties and facts purportedly have no such clear cut criteria for identity—as properties, for example, can be co-extensive but diverse. While Davidson focuses on the uselessness of such entities, rather than on their lack of clear-cut identity criteria (1967, 309), he clearly shares Quine's motives. In any case, it is worth taking a slight detour, given the stress on "identity criteria" by Quine, Goodman, Sellars, Davidson and others, to note a slight paradox in their common approach.

Ordered pairs (sequences generally) are acknowledged by Davidson since, like classes, they can be construed as being identical or different in terms of their "ordered" elements being so. But consider the basic question that arises about the "identity criteria" for the elements themselves. For, if we have "clear-cut" identity criteria for classes, ordered pairs and sequences that depend on the identity of the "constituent" elements, then such criteria are only as good as our criteria for the identity of the elements. Ironically this is not only a classic philosophical problem, but a classic attempt to resolve it involves appealing to "Leibniz's Law," which we may put, for our purposes, as "a=b ≡ (f)(fa ≡ fb)"—"a is identical with b if and only if for any property it is a property of a if and only if it is a property of b." This not only brings properties back into the discussion but points to a distinction that must be made. (One should here note that, given the "criterion" for class identity, it will hardly do to read Leibniz's law in terms of things being identical if and only if they belong to the same classes.) The distinction is that between the nebulous notion of giving a "criterion of identity" and specifying a definition of "identity." One can take Leibniz's Law to provide a definition of identity for particulars (or even for properties if one suitably "raises the types" or takes it as "type-ambiguous"). That provides a perfectly clear "sense" for the notion of identity, whether viable or not, but it does not provide for a "criterion" to apply in order to decide when two objects have the same properties.

Davidson, like Quine, could of course talk in terms of satisfying all the same predicates—rather than in terms of having the same properties. But, as has been often noted, to talk of the "same" predicates or "same word" involves us in the so-called type-token distinction, which is simply another way of calling attention to the classic problem of universals and the appeal to properties. For tokens of the "same" word are particulars that are of the "same kind." Moreover, we are back to the problem we already noted in Davidson's account of truth—the problem raised by the appeal to "satisfies" or "is true of" in order to avoid properties, relations and facts. Be that as it may, Davidson's "solution" to the problem of meaning turns out to be something we also noted earlier. It is quickly and simply put.

> The theory will have done its work if it provides, for every sentence s in the language under study, a matching sentence (to replace "p") [in "s means that p"] that, in some way yet to be made clear, "gives the meaning" of s. One obvious candidate for the matching sentence is just s itself, if the object language is contained in the metalanguage; otherwise a translation of s in the metalanguage. As a final bold step, let us try treating the position occupied by "p" extensionally: to implement this, sweep away the obscure "means that," provide the sentence that replaces "p" with a proper sentential connective, and supply the description that replaces "s" with its own predicate. (1967, 310)

The "bold step" and the "sweeping away" give us the key to the problem:

(DT) s is true $\equiv p$.

Thus "means that" is replaced by a combination of "is true" and "$\equiv$" and meaning is thus deflated to truth. For we not only have the proverbial "'Snow is white' is true if and only if snow is white," but we use it to unlock the secret to the meaning of "means that." There is a bit more. Since one cannot take truth conditions to be "meanings" (as there are no "meanings"), though by giving the truth conditions of a sentence we supposedly do *give* its meaning, there is more to be said, first, to clarify that claim and, second, since we take for granted that "p" is a meaningful sentence in the meta-language. This takes us to the giant step to holism.

As Davidson's road from meaning to truth is quick and simple, once the mechanics of Tarski's semantic conception of truth are brought into play, so is his move to a kind of linguistic holism to resolve two basic problems he faces. Take an obvious problem due to his extensionalism. Consider (DT) above and the familiar instance of a case of a T-sentence:

(DT*) "Snow is white" is true ≡ snow is white.

For Tarski's purposes no harm is done if we replace the right side of the biconditional by another true sentence, say "Davidson is a philosopher," and thus arrive at:

(DT**) "Snow is white" is true ≡ Davidson is a philosopher.

For that, by the standard use of the biconditional, will be true, given that both sides have the same truth value. But it will hardly do if we are using such patterns to explicate

(DT***) "Snow is white" means that snow is white.

So, what are we to do? Well, first, we take into account the whole linguistic framework embodying our knowledge and beliefs regarding snow, Davidson, being white, being a philosopher and so forth. In short, given what we know about snow, a sentence like "Snow is white" has certain links to sentences like "Snow is cold" and "Snow is wet" but not to philosophers or Davidson. Such links will serve as "constraints" on our extensionalism so that we can differentiate going from (DT*) to

"Snow is white" is true ≡ snow is cold

as opposed to going to (DT**).

We can do so since, to stretch the notion of a "law" a bit, to keep to the example, one of the biconditionals reflects empirical laws or generalities about snow, such as it being both white and cold in its "natural" condition. We operate within a whole framework of knowledge and belief. Moreover, we cannot consider the meanings of sentences in isolation, for knowing the rules about sentences that yield the appropriate T-sentences involving terms like "snow," "cold," etc. involves knowing a great deal about the terms and other sentences they enter into, yielding additional T-sentences. The word "snow" is satisfied by the sort of thing of which one can sensibly say that it is cold and falls in flakes, while the expression "is a philosopher" can be satisfied by something that is cold but that cannot sensibly be said to fall in flakes, and the phrase "is a prime number" is not sensibly spoken of as "applying" to things that are cold or fall in flakes. To know how to interpret specific sentences is to know how the words in them function in numerous other sentences. Moreover, interpreting involves knowledge and belief, and given any belief we have a network, "a pattern of beliefs" which determines "what the belief is about" (1975, 168). But there is more. For even such patterns do not provide sufficient constraints on "extensional substitution." Thus we must employ Davidson's "principle of charity" and take note of the "indeterminacy of meaning" to avoid both "'Snow is white' means that Davidson is a philosopher" and "'Snow is white' means that snow is cold." One must, as it were, treat Davidson's view involving charity charitably.

Quine has written much on the indeterminacy of translation, from which Davidson's talk of indeterminacy derives. What it all goes back to is a problem of interpreting behavior, especially linguistic behavior and other forms of communication, where the possibility of alternative interpretations are ever present. Wittgenstein made use of a well-known example. Suppose you point to a chair and say "That is a table." You might be using the term "table" like most of us use "chair." But you might also be using an odd pointing convention, so that what you are indicating is not what you point at but something in some relation to what you point at—something just behind what you point at, for example. This sort of thing has led to all kinds of complicated examples and claims about the indeterminacy of "reference" or ambiguity of the notion of reference, sometimes employing esoteric variations of Carnap's argument against the "name relation" as ambiguous, in *Meaning and Necessity* (Hochberg, 2001a, 362-64), which led him to introduce his method of "extensions and intensions" to replace it.

Davidson's holism and his introduction of indeterminacy and charity present a more schematic version of Sellars's long story (itself quite "sketchy" and programmatic) about "intra-linguistic" or "language-language" moves employed in connection with "world-word" and "word-world" moves that focused on behavioral, including linguistic, responses to appropriate stimuli in formulating an ideal Peircean conceptual framework that would express the "scientific image" as opposed to the everyday "manifest image." In Davidson's case such a holistic framework supposedly resolves the issues raised about presupposing the meaning of the sentences employed as the right sides of the familiar biconditionals, the unquoted sentences, and the need for appropriate constraints on extensional substitutions. Such sentences are meaningful in that they belong to, and have a role in, a holistic linguistic framework that also furnishes the "constraints" on substitution.

Still, just what is it that comprises giving a theory of meaning for a language—the setting down of axioms and deriving of theorems? Imagine you are an anthropologist studying an Inuk society in Canada who reads Davidson and is impressed by Davidson's axiomatic approach to matters. What you do is set down axioms, such as: (1) The expression "ak" is satisfied by women over the age of thirty; (2) the expression "Rk" is satisfied by an ordered pair where the first element eats the second; (3) the expression "uk" is satisfied by seals; (4) where x is an expression of the $\emptyset$-kind, Y an expression of the Ω-kind and z an expression of the $\sum$-kind, then the complex pattern "x-Y-z" (indicating a written concatenation pattern or a sequence of utterances) is true if and only if xYz; (5) "ak" is of the $\emptyset$-kind, "Rk" is of the Ω-kind and "sk" is of the $\sum$-kind. Thus, we can deduce Theorem 1: "ak-Rk-sk" is true if and only if women over thirty eat seals. But in sketching out what is required for such a theory, as I just did, I cannot be said to be doing linguistics or anthropology (from the armchair). For we must distinguish between what the anthropologist in Canada is doing and the setting out of what it is for such research to result in the formulation of a theory of meaning for the language of the Inuk society. The latter is what is done by giving a theory of meaning—and hence embodying a philosophy of language. An anthropologist giving such a theory of meaning, assuming the language of the Inuk society is unknown to the investigator, will face problems of translation, for Quine, and of interpretation, for Davidson. Guiding the translation of utterances from one language to another, Quine employed a principle of charity in terms of which one would, basically, not employ translations giving inconsistent beliefs (characterized behavioristically) to the subjects studied. Davidson's version is more generous, not attributing irrational beliefs to the language users. But, as some see it, Davidson is free to employ mentalistic terms, while Quine is supposedly not, given Quine's physicalistic reductionism as regards the mental and the physical. Actually Quine is too (recall the discussion in Chapter 1 of his "rechristening" physical entities), as Davidson notes (2001, 72-73) but as commentators who do not read Quine carefully enough often overlook. The coherence of Quine's view is another matter (Hochberg, 1959). Be that as it may, Davidson is supposedly free to employ a mentalistic idiom since his "anomalous monism" is nonreductive in virtue of the "definitional and nomological irreducibility of the propositional attitudes" (2001, 72). What anomalous monism amounts to is quite simple.

There are classic problems the materialist faces regarding the identification of mental states, events and entities to physical ones. So, for example, in recognizing that a space alien or an octopus could be hungry or angry while having a quite different neuro-physiological state than a person (residing on our planet), some were led to speak of the same "role" or "function" played by the different kinds of neuro-physiological states. Davidson's version is simpler. Each mental state is identical with some particular physical state, but there is not an identity of "kind" and hence neither definitions nor psycho-physical laws linking "kinds" (1986, 214). Hence, a *type* of mental state is not identical with some *kind* of physical state, though each particular mental state or episode is identical with a particular physical state. Thus the materialism (since not every physical state is identical with a mental state), or monism, is anomalous. A consequence is that one can supposedly freely use the mental idioms to characterize people regarding beliefs, attitudes, desires, actions, intentions, etc. And the attribution of such notions is to be governed by the principle of charity in developing a theory applying such concepts to people. Just what to call such an approach is puzzling, since all the philosophical issues are simply ignored or dismissed and no arguments are given to support the materialism involved in "anomalous monism." In fact anomalous monism can be seen as simply a variant of Quine's dropping reference to mental entities by the device of employing a mental phrase to explain what physical state it is identified with, as described in Chapter 1, though Quine is presupposing, and, really, simply postulating laws between "types," while Davidson is denying that there are such and settling for identifying "tokens."

3d. Dummett's Anti-Realism: Meaning as Use and Truth as Proof

Following the later Wittgenstein, Dummett has taken "use," as the key to meaning, and joined it to his version of Frege's context principle to hold that to know the meaning of a term is to know how it contributes to knowing the "truth conditions" of the sentences in which it can occur and, thus, knowing when to use it. Out of this he has developed a form of anti-realism that connects his finitism and "intuitionism" in the philosophy of mathematics, with a general view about truth and language. Taken all together his view is a version of the familiar theme from the heyday of logical positivism: the verification theory of meaning.

Per Lindström has argued against such a view in the philosophy of mathematics as well as against Carnap's "internalism," a notion Dummett employs in setting out his own philosophy of mathematics. In Carnap's case that grew out of his distinction between "external" and "internal" questions and the resultant dismissal of the philosophical problems about mathematical objects as pseudo-problems— problems to be replaced by syntactical and semantical questions about linguistic schemata and reasons for choosing one such schema rather than another. Carnap dismissed questions like "Do natural numbers really exist?" as external pseudo-questions without cognitive content, as opposed to internal questions like "Is 2 the only even prime?" For, the latter, unlike the former, is not only answered within the context of the appropriate system but can be answered simply and "trivially," as the answer follows from the "rules." Thus, for Carnap, the answers to such questions were "analytic," or "L-true," and thus trivial. By contrast, an external or "metaphysical question" about the reality of the number 2 is not a "real" question, since it cannot be answered in such a normal or canonical way. The problem Carnap faced in dismissing "metaphysical" questions in general and philosophical questions about logic itself was the problem faced by the positivists generally in connection with their statement of a verification criterion of meaning—and one we earlier noticed Dummett faces in linking Frege's context principle determining meaning to determining truth conditions. Just as the verification criterion is problematic as applying to itself and Dummett's view faces the problem of applying to the statement of his version of "the principle," Carnap has to appeal to, or take for granted, familiar logical concepts and some system of logic.

Carnap takes the answers to the internal questions about arithmetic to be answered by logical analysis based on the rules governing the expressions. Lindström raises a question about the status of such rules, as they appear to amount to a set of axioms and rules of inference that comprise a formal theory. He argues that if the formal theory could be a complete formal theory for the system of natural numbers, Carnap's view "might have been tenable." But, by Gödel's theorem, it cannot be such a theory. Moreover, there is a second problem. Like Russell many years before and Frege in arguing against "formalism" in mathematics, Lindström points out that a philosophy of arithmetic (classical first order number theory) must recognize that we have to assign the right truth value to each arithmetical statement. But, on Carnap's approach, there is no reason to accept the answers yielded by the system of rules as assigning the right truth values—as being "correct."

> What are these "rules"? The answer seems to be: axioms and rules of inference, in other words, a formal theory. But, the concepts required to define a linguistic framework (formal system) suffice to define an ω-sequence and so Carnap's ideas, at least in the case of first order arith-

metic, represent no conceptual gain, or reduction, at all. Furthermore, by Gödel's theorem, there is no formal theory that answers correctly all (first order) internal questions about the natural numbers. Finally, it is not clear why we should accept the answers given by the "rules for the new expressions" as correct; these answers may even be inconsistent. It follows that Carnap's idea (taken as an account of mathematics as it is ordinarily understood and applied) is untenable. (2000, 135-136)

As Lindström notes, his line of argument is found earlier, and in greater detail, in Gödel's unpublished "Is Mathematics Syntax of Language?" (now published in Gödel, 1986 /1995) that was originally intended as his contribution to the Carnap volume in the Library of Living Philosophers.

In his paper Gödel set out two arguments relevant to the present discussion. Though Lindström's argument only explicitly reiterates the line of reasoning of the second of them, the last sentence of the above quoted passage echoes Gödel's first argument.

Moreover a rule about the truth of sentences can be called *syntactical* only if it is clear from its formulation, or if it somehow can be known beforehand, that it does not imply the truth or falsehood of any "factual" sentence (i. e., one whose truth, owing to the semantical rules of the language, depends on extralinguistic facts). This requirement not only follows from the concept of a convention about the use of symbols, but also from the fact that it is the lack of content of mathematics upon which its a priori admissibility in spite of strict empiricism is to be based. The requirement under discussion implies that the rules of syntax must be demonstrably consistent, since from an inconsistency *every* proposition follows, all factual propositions included. (1986/1995, 339)

The point behind the argument appears to be that by Gödel's Second Incompleteness Theorem one will have to justify the rules by making use of mathematics that is beyond the scope of the rules in question (by characterizing the syntax of the system, notions like well-formed formula of the system, proof in the system and, thereby, that if it is consistent it is incomplete, etc.). [I say "appears to be" since Gödel might be requiring that Carnap prove the consistency of the rules of syntax.] Thus Carnap's claim that "mathematics" can be taken to be embodied in such rules cannot be true. The argument is elegantly simple. If the formal system, embodying the rules of the language, cannot be characterized in a certain way, then it cannot be sensibly claimed that factual sentences (Carnap's F-Truths or F-Falsehoods) do not follow from such rules. But then the rules cannot be claimed to be formal (syntactical) rules without employing a suitable amount of mathematics in the characterization. Since the rules of the system in question cannot be shown to be consistent, if they are, it must be clear from the very formulation of the rules that they embody no factual content.

The second argument, like Lindström's, depends on the First Incompleteness Theorem, since, by it, Carnap's notion of something being a consequence of the axioms of the system cannot be taken in terms of it being derivable within the system from the axioms and rules, as not all relevant truths are derivable in any such deductive system. One is forced to take the notion of a "consequence" in terms of a meta-linguistic semantical concept that makes use of a suitably rich mathematical framework.

> ... in order not to substitute for intuitive mathematics a "syntax" as unacceptable for empiricists as intuitive mathematics itself ...it will have to be required that: (1) not only in the rules of syntax, but also in the derivation of the mathematical axioms from them and in the proof of their consistency only syntactical concepts ... be used ... and (2) only procedures of proof which cannot be rejected by anyone who knows how to apply these concepts at all.
>
> The necessity of the first requirement should be beyond dispute. For, if mathematical intuition and the assumption of mathematical objects or facts is to be dispensed with by means of syntax, it certainly will be ... based on considerations about finite combinations of symbols. If, instead, in the formulation of the syntactical rules some of the very same abstract or transfinite concepts are being used—or in the consistency proof, some of the axioms usually assumed about them—then the whole program completely changes its meaning and is turned into its downright opposite: instead of clarifying the meanings of the non-finitary mathematical terms by explaining them in terms of syntactical rules, non-finitary terms are [used] in order to formulate the syntactical rules; and, instead of justifying the mathematical axioms by reducing them to syntactical rules, these axioms (or at least some of them) are necessary in order to justify the syntactical rules (as consistent). (1986/1995, 341-42)

Lindström carefully restricts his criticism of Carnap to the issues posed by (first order) arithmetic. But there is a more fundamental point involved that applies to any use of Carnap's distinction between internal and external questions to reject philosophical problems, and especially philosophical issues raised by logic itself. This raises the basic issue of whether Carnap's positivism arbitrarily dismisses, and does not resolve, the classic philosophical issues by labeling them *pseudo-issues*. The basic and simple point that emerges from Lindström's and Gödel's attacks on Carnap is that what is an external question, whether about the nature of the "objects" or about what kinds of truths the arithmetical truths are, and hence not a question answerable within a formal system of arithmetic itself, is an internal question within another framework, where we ask and seek to resolve philosophical questions about arithmetic and about such a formal system of arithmetic. Admittedly the procedures are not those of the mathematician or logician. They are not, in Carnap's terms, "scientific." But all this means is that they are not resolved within the context of a formal system that derives such answers by formal rules from "axioms." Such a context would hardly help resolve philosophical issues, however one might help clarify presuppositions various philosophical positions depend on, by attempting to axiomatize philosophical "systems" along the lines A. Wedberg employed in setting out the views of various philosophers in his *Filosofins Historia*. But such historical analyses aside, there is no canonical method of deciding philosophical issues in the sense that there are assumed to be such methods for deriving standard arithmetical theorems, and even theorems like Gödel's celebrated incompleteness results. But the basic point is that the arguments against Carnap's approach to the questions about arithmetical truth make a more fundamental objection to any use of Carnap's use of the distinction between internal and external questions to reject, in the fashion of the logical positivists, all philosophical problems, and especially the issues raised by "truth" and "logical truth." For, in general, external questions about some subject matter are internal questions within a framework where we ask and seek to resolve philosophical questions about that subject matter. This is illustrated, as noted earlier, by Dummett's tying of meaning to the determining of truth conditions, since that simply amounts to either the dismissal of classical philosophical issues or their trivialization. Recall Dummett's argument that there obviously are abstract objects since we can determine whether we have crossed the Equator and his also noting that we constantly refer to such objects in talking about air pollution, gas emission and so forth.

Sellars, following Carnap's "internalist" pattern, long ago walked the same path Dummett did and noted the problem Gödel's results raised:

> In the case of arithmetic, for example, the concept of truth (S-assertibility) coincides with that of provability. It follows, of course, from Goedel's results that, with respect to the conceptual structure (in

> the sense of axiomatics) to which it belongs, not every arithmetical proposition is either true or false. It also follows that not every arithmetical proposition which is in some sense true is true in the absolute sense, i. e. with respect to our current conceptual structure, if this is taken to be an axiomatics. (1968, 135)

But while Sellars paid careful attention to the philosophical tradition in attempting to fit his analyses to that history, Dummett and Carnap systematically ignore the rich "dialectical" history that provides a context of questions, arguments and counter-arguments for the "internality" of philosophical questions and answers—though hardly a formal system of axioms and rules or a "canonical" method of resolving such questions. If that were not so, how could we even discuss Carnap's approach or Gödel's criticisms of it? For that matter, how could Carnap even argue for his view, as opposed to simply stipulating it? Moreover, one can acknowledge that all questions and answers are posed within some context, so long as one notes that the context for questions *in* mathematics is not the same as the context for philosophical questions *about* mathematics. At places the boundary between questions in the philosophy of mathematics and mathematics proper is blurred, as happens in other areas of philosophy, such as the philosophy of logic. One has only to think of the various issues about acceptable proof procedures, the "actual" infinite, classes as one and classes as many, the distinction between classes and sets, the history of the axiom of choice, the questions about the connection between the "meaning" of the logical functors and quantifiers and the "rules" governing them, the particular problems posed by negation that have persisted from the time of the Greeks, etc. Some of these even appear to motivate Dummett's philosophy of language as he thinks in terms of applying intuitionist and constructivist views in the philosophy of mathematics to questions of meaning, truth and language in general. This we will shortly consider. But, in any case, the fact that philosophical questions about mathematics and logic, as distinct from mathematical and logical problems, raise issues of different kinds and require answers supported in different ways hardly shows that only the one set of questions consists of real questions. Nor does it show that there is not a coherent context for the raising of philosophical questions.

Dummett's philosophy of mathematics and language, like Sellars's, clearly follows the pattern of Carnap's. "internalism," which leads into his "anti-realism." In his well known paper "Truth," Dummett reiterated the point behind his construal of Frege's context principle without mentioning that principle:

> The conception pervades the thought of Frege that the general form of explanation of the sense of a statement consists in laying down the conditions under which it is true and those under which it is false ... this same conception is expressed in the *Tractatus* in the words, 'In order to be able to say that "p" is true (or false), I must have determined under what conditions I call "p" true, and this is how I determine the sense of the sentence.' (4.063) (1978, 7)

He goes on to endorse the cardinal principle of the later Wittgenstein.

> This shows how it is possible to hold that the intuitionist substitution of an account of the *use* of a statement for an account of its truth-conditions as the general form of explanation of meaning should be applied to all realms of discourse without thinking that we create the world; we can abandon realism without falling into subjective idealism. .... Of course the doctrine that meaning is to be explained in terms of use is the cardinal doctrine of the later Wittgenstein; but I do not think the point of this doctrine has so far been generally understood. (1978, 18-19)

What Dummett has in mind in his general defense of intuitionism in mathematics, and its subsequent carrying over into philosophy, is really two-fold, and the points involved can be seen in very simple contexts. Consider the purported explications of the meaning of the logical signs, stemming from statements in Wittgenstein's *Tractatus* and in line with Dummett's adaptations of those views, in terms of introduction rules or elimination rules or both. On such a pattern, the meanings of "&" and "¬" are supposedly given by the introduction rules "p & q ⊣ p, q" and "¬ ¬ p ⊣ p" and/or the elimination rules "p ⊣ p & q" and "p ⊣ ¬¬ p."[8] But while such rules may be said to codify the use or meaning of the signs "&" and "¬" in a way somewhat like the truth tables may be said to codify their use as the signs for conjunction and negation, they do not even do what the truth tables do. For their acceptance clearly relies on the truth tables to justify such rules. Moreover, even the truth table for

---

[8] The use of "⊣" (derived from) here and the earlier use of "⊨" (entails) embody the familiar distinction between a proof as a matter of formal (syntactical) rules and entailment (validity) as involving the conclusion being true in every model in which the premises are.

negation, for example, neither tells us the meaning of "¬" nor resolves the problems about negative facts and questions regarding an ontological correlate of the negation sign. That such rules, by themselves or in connection with truth tables or tableaux, are indispensable in the teaching or learning of elementary logic is not the point, anymore than the way I learn what or who a proper name refers to suffices to yield a satisfactory analysis of what it is to refer to something. What the standard truth table shows us is (i) that "¬" is taken as the sign for negation, (ii) that every sentence of the schema is taken to be true or false, and (iii) that "or" in (ii) is taken in the exclusive sense in that a sentence is not both true and false. (ii) and (iii) are reflected in our placing one and only one of the pair ("T," "F") on each line of a truth table. The use of true and false, in the context of a bivalent logic (without gaps) embodies, but does not explicate, *negation*. For one makes use of negation, as well as of truth and falsity in the very construction of a truth table. In a way this can be taken to show that there is a point to the old idea that the laws of non-contradiction and excluded middle are basic "laws" of logic—in spite of the fact that all tautologies are "equivalent." Equally, there is a point to Frege's claim that Truth is a basic notion. But what we can recognize is the difference between acknowledging that and the problems posed by specifying grounds of truth that are addressed by those who propose correspondence or coherence theories of truth. One no more defines "truth" or formulates a theory of truth by introducing a truth predicate into a schema than one defines negation by giving a truth table—one employs them, as well as the laws of logic, in the very use of the truth tables. The earlier use of (T) makes that poignantly clear, as one simply introduces a semantic rule involving a three part biconditional and not a designation rule or a definition. Even in the case of a Tarski-style definition the obvious question arises—Why transcribe the predicate that is defined by the term "truth"? That is obviously only based on our normally taking both a statement S and the statement that S is true to have the same truth value. And even that, as we know, cannot be taken generally (unrestrictedly) in a Tarski-style schema, given the semantic paradoxes. Hence we have theories involving types, gaps, etc.

Given Dummett's views about abstract entities and his rejection of "nominalism," he has to hold, in this context, that there are truth functions, truth values, quantifiers, states of affairs and so on. And here one is distinguishing, as Frege did, the functions, etc. from the "signs" for them—that denote them. After all we know how to distinguish & from ¬ (not just "&" from "¬") and decide the truth value of a negation of a proposition, given the truth value of the proposition, just as we distinguish the Equator from the North Pole and know how to determine if we have crossed the Equator. But this will not do as a philosophical analysis, for all it does, more or less, is accept what we talk about in ordinary contexts as objects—whether abstract or concrete. (Is the river Jordan an abstract or concrete object? The center of the solar system?) The point becomes poignant when we recognize what Dummett has in mind in the above quotation about "not falling into subjective idealism." For, on his view of things, we bring entities into existence by our "investigations" as "we probe." Thus he leads into the above quotation by writing:

> ...we could have instead the picture of a mathematical reality not already in existence but as it were coming into being as we probe. Our investigations bring into existence what was not there before, but what they bring into existence is not of our own making. Whether this picture is right or wrong for mathematics, it is available for other regions of reality as an alternative to the realist conception of the world. This shows how ... the general form of explanation of meaning should be applied to all realms of discourse without thinking that we create the world; we can abandon realism without falling into subjective idealism. .... (1978, 18-19)

Aside from it not being clear what it means to bring objects into existence without them being of "our own making," we can focus on the phrase "subjective idealism"—for that is what we supposedly avoid, along with realism. The question, however, is not whether we avoid "subjective" idealism but whether we avoid "idealism," what we might call "social idealism," as language and proof procedures are aspects of social or "communal" reality and not personal or subjective. (It is not a coincidence that one hears much about the creation of "social reality" today, and the role that language plays in that, from philosophers like Searle.) He can hardly mean, after all, that our investigations and probing simply reveal objects that we do not "make," for that is what realism amounts to. Our probing and investigating cannot merely be essential to our discovering what is there. If his statements are at all clear or meant in a literal sense, the probing and investigating is somehow a condition for the existence of what is thereby brought "into existence." Perhaps he thinks that this is not idealism since it does not follow that they would not exist if we did not exist, for they could be brought into existence is some other way. Thus we who probe and investigate are in fact instrumental, but not essential, to the existence of the objects investigated. Or, perhaps, it is simply another variation on the theme that leads Sartre to claim that we are responsible for our own births. Sartre, too, claims that he is not an idealist as there is Being, uncharacterized as it were, besides Nothingness (consciousness).

Dummett's philosophy of mathematics is so closely tied to his philosophy of language that it provides a test case for the latter, as certain problems in his philosophy of mathematics become problems for his philosophy of language. [In what follows I make use of Lindström's critique of Dummett's view (Lindström, 2000; and the text of a lecture given in Stockholm, spring 2002).][9] Dummett holds that any justification for adopting one logic rather than another as "the logic for mathematics must turn on questions of meaning" (1978, 215). In adhering to the later Wittgenstein's thesis that meaning is determined by use, Dummett holds that "use" must be public, as opposed to private, since "...the meaning of a statement consists solely in its role as an instrument of communication between individuals ... . an individual cannot communicate what he cannot be observed to communicate" (1978, 216). Lindström dismisses such premises of Dummett's argument as "almost certainly false" in that if you cannot communicate what you cannot be observed to communicate "then you cannot communicate anything at all" (2000, 146). The point is cryptically put, but I think essentially right. What one observes is manifest behavior, including linguistic utterances (of "words," not the mere making of noises). Even in Dummett's own terms, when I observe someone communicating with me what I observe is the behavior, the words written or uttered, etc., and, if fortunate, understand the "sense" of the message. I do not, cannot in fact, given Dummett's own use of the notion of "sense," observe "the sense" of what is said, though I can understand what it is. I can observe someone using a knife and fork, even observe the proper use of such instruments, but not the rules of etiquette, though I can read about them. And, though I can observe someone communicating by saying "It is going to rain," even observe, though odd to put it this way if I am not an anthropologist, that one is communicating that it is going to rain, I can hardly observe the meaning, what is communicated, as I obviously cannot observe "the role" that the words and statements play in communication. Even granting Dummett's point of view about meaning, I may discover that role by observing utterances and the behavioral reactions of people to such utterances, but I do not observe the role that words or statements play in language though I can, of course, observe indications of, or what I take to be evidence for, their playing a certain role.

---

[9]Lindström's paper was presented at a symposium honoring the Swedish logician P. Martin-Löf, who has defended ideas similar to Dummett's about the meaning of logical concepts (Martin-Löf, 1996). However, the section on Dummett was omitted from the lecture.

And, in any case, not accepting Dummett's approach and recalling the discussion of Sellars, it seems obvious that a key role of the statement "It is raining" is to communicate (or describe) to someone the fact that it is raining. What can it mean to speak of observing that role? A role that the word "Dummett" plays is its use to refer to Dummett. But the reader of the above paragraphs, to whom I hope to communicate some things, is surely not "observing" the role, or the reference made, not the "referent" (whatever one's theory of reference is), or the contribution the term "Dummett" is making to the senses of the statements in which it occurs. What one can be said to observe are neither senses nor roles but people uttering or writing words (not noises or marks), in isolation or in patterns, which, hopefully, are understood. Russell put a related point quite concisely in replying to Strawson:

> Unless fundamental words in the individual's vocabulary had this kind of direct relation to fact, language in general would have no such relation. I defy Mr. Strawson to give the usual meaning to the word 'red' unless there is something which the word designates. (1973, 123)

Influenced by his neo-Wittgensteinian view of Frege's context principle, Dummett proceeds to infer from his views about meaning that to understand a statement is to have the ability to recognize "what counts as verifying the statement, i. e. as conclusively establishing it as true" (1978, 227). This is intimately linked to his views of understanding mathematical statements, and is, in effect, taken as a generalization of it, generally replacing *truth* by *verification*, as it is replaced by *proof* in mathematical contexts:

> ...a grasp of the meaning of a statement consists in a capacity to recognize a proof of it when one is presented to us, and a grasp of the meaning of any expression smaller than a sentence must consist in the knowledge of the way in which its presence in a sentence contributes to determining what is to count as a proof of that sentence. (1978, 225-26)

Here "proof" plays the role "truth" played in our earlier discussion of his version of the context principle as "the notion of truth" has been replaced as "the central notion of the theory of meaning for mathematical statements, by the notion of *proof* ...." (1978, 225). One thing that immediately strikes one is the obvious question as to how one can understand the way in which a term's "presence in a sentence contributes to" determining what is to count as a proof of the sentence, or to knowing how to determine the truth of a sentence in a non-mathematical context, unless one understands the term. It doesn't really help to claim that that is what it is to understand the term. I know how the term "Scott" contributes to the truth of the sentence "Scott is dead" by knowing (not in Russell's sense of "being acquainted with") who Scott was—to whom the name referred, *and* the "grammar" of the term, as Wittgenstein insisted in the *Tractatus*. Moreover, I must know that on that particular occasion the uttered, or inscribed, token of "Scott" is used to refer to a certain individual and not to my neighbor's dog, also named "Scott." But all this was taken up earlier in the discussion of Strawson's attack on Russell's views. What was said there directly bears on and critically applies to Dummett's views about knowing the meaning of expressions.

Our understanding of a mathematical statement supposedly consists in our ability to recognize what counts as a proof (disproof) of it—establishing it as true (false). Understanding a mathematical statement, say S, requires our being able to distinguish proofs of S from non-proofs. But this ability to distinguish proofs from non-proofs cannot then depend on our understanding of S. The classification of potential proofs of S into proofs and non-proofs cannot be based on the meaning of S, as S has no meaning or truth value prior to establishing such a classification, which thus appears to be arbitrary. In what sense then is S a statement? And in what sense can one speak of such a "proof" or "disproof" of S as establishing it to be true or false? Lindström notes that in the above quote Dummett shifts to the term "sentence" rather than "statement" and, taking a sentence to be a "string of symbols," argues that one does not prove (or even assert) sentences, in the ordinary sense of "prove," and thus establish "strings of symbols" as true. Thus proofs in Dummett's sense "are not proofs in the ordinary sense; indeed, they have almost nothing in common with proofs in the ordinary sense" (2000, 134). I think Dummett simply uses the terms interchangeably, but then, if it is a statement, I must clearly know what it means to grasp that a sequence of other statements provides a proof of it. Lindström's remark is, and is possibly meant to be, ironic, given Dummett's "ordinary language" perspective. More important is that there is no basis, aside from having chosen them, for adopting one set of rules of logic as opposed to another, especially the rules of classical logic. This has the consequence, on Dummett's view, that the meanings of the statements change if the rules of inference differ, so, for example, the meaning of arithmetical statements in terms of a system of classical logic is different from that given to them in a system employing intuitionist logic. But this poses a problem for Dummett's view, as it would seem to follow that with respect to a system of classical logic we have, in Carnap's terms, a purely internal question regarding whether they "establish their conclusions as true" and hence the answer is trivially "yes." For that follows from the "meaning" of those conclusions. But Dummett takes the answer to be "no." (How else could he, unlike Carnap, reject one system as incorrect and accept another as correct—thus employing "external" criteria and making "pseudo-statements"—instead of merely proposing the adoption of one linguistic framework, rather than another, on pragmatic grounds?) Lindström concludes that Dummett must then accept that "these conclusion have a meaning independent of what is regarded as (defined to be) a 'proof'" (2000, 135). This leads him to argue that Dummett's view is not only implausible but incoherent.

Dummett has recognized this type of problem with his view and attempts to respond to it. Lindström simply dismisses the response as "unsuccessful" (2000, 146). But it is worth taking a closer, if brief, look at it. Dummett claims, in effect, that the problem only arises if one adopts a holistic view of language, a view like Davidson's. I say "in effect" since he simply shifts the discussion from the problem he faces to the issue of a holistic theory of meaning and rejects the latter:

> An existing practice in the use of a certain fragment of language is capable of being subjected to criticism if it is impossible to systematize it, that is, to frame a model whereby each sentence carries a determinate content which can, in turn, be explained in terms of the use of that sentence. What makes it possible that such a practice may prove to be incoherent and therefore in need of revision is that there are different aspects to the use of a sentence; if the whole practice is to be capable of systematization in the present sense, there must be a certain harmony between these different aspects. (1978, 220)

But this will not do at all, especially when one is seeking to reject classical logic. For, of course, systematic presentations with rules for classical logic, intuitionist logic, relevance logic, para-consistent logic, etc. can be and have been given. Moreover, how is "systematize" to be understood in the above passage? Its use raises the very problem at issue, especially given the use of "incoherent" in the next sentence, along with the more innocuous "harmony." Clearly, "to systematize" is being understood in terms of a "coherent (logically coherent)" framework. But this is precisely what raises the issue and the problem.

Moore made a line of argument famous, or infamous, depending on one's perspective, that, simply put, goes as follows. Hume's philosophy, for example, entails that I don't know that physical objects exist. Thus, either Hume's philosophy is wrong or my belief that I know that physical objects exist is wrong. But I do know that physical objects exist (strictly speaking, according to Moore, I know that I know that physical objects exist). Hence, Hume's philosophy must be wrong. This led eventually to the well known defense of common sense involving "This is a hand; a hand is a physical object: therefore physical objects exist." In a way, Moore's techniques of argument gave rise to an aspect of the linguistic turn—the focus on conceptual and, eventually, linguistic analysis—that played a role alongside Wittgenstein's influence. There is always a question as to when the Moorean line is appropriate. But Dummett's views on the natural numbers as an infinite totality seem to provide an appropriate occasion, given his views about meaning and truth and his linking them to his views in the philosophy of mathematics. He has argued against our having a clear concept of an infinite totality, and hence of the natural numbers, taken as an infinite collection. Interestingly his line of argument has changed over time in such a way as to suggest that he has a view in search of an argument. He started out holding that where you have an "indefinitely extensible" concept it is ambiguous. Take the Russell class of those classes that are not members of themselves. If you think that there is such a class and that it is a definite totality, T, then T cannot belong to itself without paradox, so we have to recognize that T is not a member of itself and think of an extended class, consisting of all the elements of T and T, T*. But then we can "extend" that to a new class and so on. Thus the concept involved is "indefinitely extensible" and, being so, is "inherently vague"—not having a determinate extension. What Dummett has in mind is a notion Bernays had employed much earlier in a 1935 paper purporting to refute Platonism in mathematics:

> The essential importance of these antinomies is to bring out the impossibility of combining the following two things: the idea of the totality of all mathematical objects and the general concepts of set and function; for the totality itself would form a domain of elements for sets, and arguments and values for functions. (1964, 277)

[Thus Dummett did not "introduce" the notion in 1963 (Hale and Wright, 2002, 294)—though it is right, in a sense, to say, as they do, that it "...ultimately derives from Russell." Dummett may well have introduced the phrase.] In an early paper Dummett noted that the concept of natural number was not indefinitely extensible, since the class of natural numbers is not itself a natural number. So he sought another ground for holding it to be "indeterminate" or "inherently vague" (1978, 197). He supposedly found it in the fact that the natural numbers form a totality to which mathematical induction applies. For that involves an "impredicative" use of quantifiers and the idea that induction holds for any well-defined property, where the concept of a well-defined property is itself indefinitely extensible. It does so since a well-defined property is one expressible with the linguistic apparatus of a precisely specified language. We can then define, "by reference to the expressions of this language" another property "which we also recognize as well-defined, but which we cannot express in the language" (1978, 198).

One problem this raises concerns talking about properties as being language dependent in this way and of "properties," not predicates, as "defined," though logicians generally do speak of a class being "well-defined" or not. There is also a serious question we cannot take up here regarding the notion that properties (or functions), rather than predicates, are "impredicative." It bears on the early disputes among Russell, Ramsey and Wittgenstein regarding Russell's "Axiom of Reducibility" and Quine's later comments on it (Hochberg, 1987). That aside, what is relevant here is Dummett's failure to find a common feature linking the concept of natural number to "inherently vague" concepts like that of class of classes that are not members of themselves. Not doing so, he stretches for an argument by bringing in the second-order "impredicative" version of mathematical induction and, implicitly, the Frege-Russell logistic construal of "natural number." For without the latter construal of the concept, the principle of induction is simply a truth about natural numbers and not a part of the explication of the concept. But Dummett himself obviously felt the inadequacies of his argument, for he later sought to strengthen it by holding that the concept of natural number really was indefinitely extensible.

The first step is to argue that the concept of real number is indefinitely extensible, given the acceptance of Cantor's diagonal argument for there being non-denumerably many real numbers. Dummett sees that argument as having "... precisely the form of a principle of extension for an indefinitely extensible concept: given any denumerable totality of real numbers, we can define, in terms of that totality, a real number that does not belong to it" (2002, 27). Of course shifting to speaking of "precisely the form" is somewhat slippery, since we do not talk about the totality of real numbers but merely of any denumerable totality of real numbers—it is any of those that can be "extended" by the addition of a real number not in the totality. But, since Cantor's argument takes there to be a determinate totality of real numbers "the alternative is to regard the concept real number as an indefinitely extensible one" (27). This is not an argument. It is not even clear that he is saying anything at all. But it is on such a weak basis that Dummett rests his argument that the concept of a real number is "indefinitely extensible." Moreover, he does not stop there. He notes that the totality of natural numbers is also not a natural number, i. e. is not a finite cardinal, where we "... assume we have a grasp of the totality of natural numbers..." and asks "... but do we?" (28) Well how do we decide this? For Dummett "... a conception of the totality of the natural numbers is supposed to be conveyed to one as yet unaware of any but finite totalities, but all that he is given is a principle ... for passing from any finite totality to a larger one" (28). Thus "The fact is that a concept determining an intrinsically infinite totality ... simply *is* an indefinitely extensible one" (28). But that is hardly a fact, given the shift in the meaning of "indefinitely extensible" from the earlier paper. He simply stipulates something and declares the result he seeks. It is an amazing performance. Perhaps what he does is based on his thinking that one requires an axiom of infinity in standard set theory, yielding an inductive class—one cannot simply postulate the existence of the null class and introduce a notion of successor in terms of class union. Similarly for what Peano does, he needs the fifth postulate— mathematical induction (whether in a first or second order version is not relevant at this point as the issue of impredicativity is no longer relevant). Recalling Dummett's earlier argument that "natural number" is inherently vague, though not indefinitely extensible, it seems as if Dummett writes in the shadow of Descartes' innate ideas. For it is almost as if it is assumed that we can viably speak of the successor of a natural number, since we have some anchor on concepts like *three cups* and of having "one more than," just as we do of *red* in terms of noting something being red or not. Yet that doesn't get us to a satisfactory concept of "infinitely" many without induction and the notion of an inductive collection (even though the first four Peano postulates suffice for having infinitely many natural numbers). Whether or not that is what lies behind his thinking, Dummett holds that we must show that we can "convey" the concept of a natural number to one who does not already have it (i. e. that such a one can "learn" it). This, Dummett's philosophy of language simply declares, cannot be done, just as we cannot prove there is an infinite class without a suitable infinity axiom. But it seems that we do have a quite definite concept of a natural number, which has been conveyed to us in some way, and which we convey to others, unless we continuously invent and reinvent it or, in Cartesian fashion, have it innately. (This is not to say we have a philosophically satisfactory concept without considerably more being said. But that applies to object, property, fact, etc.) The Moorean choice seems to indicate that there is something wrong with Dummett's philosophy of language and mathematics.

3e. Quine's Attack on Dogma: Analyticity and Meaning

In "Two Dogmas of Empiricism," Quine distinguished, following Carnap, three types of purported analytic statements: (1) the tautologies of propositional logic; (2) the valid formulae of first order predicate logic; (3) the truths of meaning that Carnap had attempted to characterize as L-True. But while Quine did not direct his early attack against either (1) or (2), he pounced on an error Carnap had made regarding the sameness of meaning of "Human" and "Rational Animal" and the transparent circularity of Carnap's attempt to explicate and justify the L-Truths "of meaning." Inexplicably, Carnap shifted between the clearly stipulational character of meaning postulates for an artificial linguistic schema and the supposed significant "real definitions," grounded in sociological and historical facts, concerning the linguistic roles of terms of ordinary languages. Carnap's transparent error occurs when, after introducing "'Hx'—x is human (a human being)" and "'Rx'—x is a rational animal" among the rules of designation for predicates, he explains that: "The English words here used are supposed to be understood in such a way that 'human being' and 'rational animal' mean the same" (1956, 4). This is a puzzling mistake, given that Carnap is supposedly analyzing the concept of meaning in terms of his designation rules and the concept of L-True. One avoids it by simply recognizing that interpretation or semantic rules are simply stipulations. That makes pointless the attempt to arrive at any further explication of "analyticity" or account of "real definitions" for cases that are supposedly "true by the meaning of the terms," such as "All bachelors are unmarried."

Subsequently, Quine generalized his attack on the synthetic-analytic distinction by holding that it presupposed a basic distinction between the logical and non-logical terms of a linguistic schema that could only be made in an arbitrary or relative manner. (He had, in his early paper, already noted that the two dogmas are "at root identical" (1953a, 41). In this vein he suggested that with appropriate rules any predicate terms, say "green" and "red," could be taken as logical terms, along with the connectives, variables and quantifiers. This followed his characterization, in his logic text *Mathematical Logic*, of the logical truths as those truths in which only the logical terms occurred "non-vacuously." Thus, for example, in "Fa $\vee \neg$ Fa" while any sign of the same syntactical kind could uniformly replace either "F" or "a" without affecting the truth value of the statement, changing "$\vee$" to "&" would alter the truth value. Thus "$\vee$" occurred non-vacuously while "F" and "a" both occurred vacuously.

This showed both the link between the notions of logical truth and logical sign and the dependency of the former on the latter. Thus, in dealing with propositional logic in an elementary logic class, one can easily introduce the notion of a logical connective in terms of truth tables, then the notions of propositional tautology and contradiction in terms of such tables and, finally, explicate the notion of logically valid in terms of logical truth (or logical contradiction). What Quine later did was question the non-arbitrary nature of the standard logical signs. Actually, this later attack was already involved in his earlier paper's attack on a second purported dogma of empiricism—the reductionist dogma requiring the analysis of the meaning of the non-logical signs of the language in terms of what is "given" in experience. So, in a sense, the early paper contains his later comprehensive attack on the synthetic-analytic distinction.

Quine's later explicit argument is two-fold. First, there is the classic issue of the synthetic *a priori*. Thus statements like "Whatever is green is extended" are problematic in that they are not analytic, as they do not fall under any of the three types of analytic statements we characterized above. Yet they appear to be as "necessary" as analytic statements. If one is not inclined to introduce the recent vocabulary of "metaphysical necessity" that Quine and Carnap would have jointly dismissed out of hand, the sentence poses a problem. That does not mean there is not the obvious and seemingly unproblematic difference between statements like "It is raining or it is not raining" and "It is raining" that can be taken to illustrate the difference between an analytic and a synthetic statement. This leads to the second thread of Quine's later argument. It can be illustrated by the claim that terms like "green," "red" and "extended" can be added to the logical terms of a schema, given the addition of accompanying rules or axioms, such as "Everything that is green is extended" and "Something is green (all over at a time) if and only if it is not red." With such an extended list of axioms and (or) rules, "green," "red" and "extended" would occur non-vacuously in appropriate sentences. Hence, such sentences would supposedly become analytic truths in the same sense that "All red apples are red" is. As this can then be done for any predicates, the distinction between logical and non-logical signs becomes arbitrary. But Quine's argument is clearly problematic. For it overlooks the simple fact that one is adding constant predicates (as opposed to predicate variables) like "red" and "green" to such a list, while retaining the syntactical distinctions between connectives, quantifiers, variables, etc. and such constant terms. Thus we still have a non-arbitrary distinction between "extended" and "green," on the one hand, and the connectives, quantifiers and variables, on the other. Of course part of the problem is about the ambiguity of a term like "arbitrary." Clearly one can give reasons, and not merely indicate a whim, by separating the traditional logical signs from the non-logical signs. One takes a sign like "red" to indicate a color; we do not take variables in such a manner nor do we respond to questions about what the weather is like with statements like "It is raining or it is not raining." Yet there remain the familiar problems of the apparent "necessity" of truths like "Whatever is colored is extended" and "Nothing is both red and blue all over at the same time." It may well be that Wittgenstein's dissatisfaction with his attempted solutions of the problems posed by the apparent logical necessity of statements like those of color incompatibility led to his extending the notion of "logic" to the general conception of the "logic" of language in his later views, where grasping the logic of a term or concept involved understanding its role or use in the language (language game). Thus to say of something that it was both red and green all over was to reveal a failure to understand the use of such terms, as one would fail to understand the use of "not" by saying that it was raining and not raining. Pushing such an approach to its extreme can also lead to denying an "absolute" difference between analytic and synthetic statements in favor of taking such differences to be matters of degree. In Quine's case, that line of thought resulted in such "degrees" being a matter of the strength of our reluctance to abandon different beliefs. Those we might be most reluctant to abandon, for example the formulae of standard (first order) logic and a significant portion of mathematics, would lie at the core of *our* "web of belief." Of course that will vary with who "we" are. Sts. Augustine, Anselm and Aquinas, unlike Quine, might find "God exists" to be more firmly entrenched than "God exists or does not exist."

Quine's notion of a web of belief and truths lying at the core is part of his attack on the second purported dogma of empiricism—the empiricist attempt to reduce the meaning of non-logical expressions of a language or conceptual scheme to the referential connection of basic terms and sentences to sense experience. His alternative picture, one that has become widely known and cited, is that of a conceptual structure of interrelated terms and sentences that makes contact with "experience" by means of elements at its "periphery" that anchor it to "experience" (1953a, 42-46; Quine & Ullian, 1970, 28). But the picture that he paints is either incoherent or simply circular, given his "naturalizing" of epistemology and his behaviorist reconstruction of "the mental." His talk of "experience" and "stimulus meaning" has to be taken in the context of his overall view that "stimuli" and "experience" are understood in terms of a combined behaviorist and physiological psychology of perception. Thus experiences and stimuli are understood in terms of scientific theories about perception. But such theories themselves belong to the conceptual structure. So how can one, without circularity, claim to anchor the entire conceptual structure to *experience*? For experience itself, as "naturalized," is understood in terms of scientific theories, as "electrons" are in physics, that are part of the conceptual structure to be anchored. As the distinguished physicist J. Wheeler has said in another context: "The dragon eats its tail." (Quine is quite prepared to accept the circularity involved, 1953, 78-79.) That makes a fitting epitaph for contextualist, coherence theories of meaning and truth.

CHAPTER 4

FACTS, INTENTIONS AND ABSTRACTION

4a. Facts: Problems and Solutions

As noted in Chapter 1, Bradley and Bosanquet (1948, 135) believed, as Plato once had, that negative concepts were problematic. They sought to avoid them by treating negated predicates in terms of incompatibility. Thus "¬ Fξ" became "($\exists \Phi$)($\Phi\xi$ & Φ is incompatible with F)." We also noted that R. Demos (1917) sought to avoid negative facts by taking "¬ p" in terms of "($\exists$q)(q is true & q is incompatible with (in opposition to) p),"with "p" and "q" ranging over propositions. [He used a descriptive phrase to specify the "negative" proposition as "the thing (at least one thing), such that that thing is a proposition that stands in the relation of opposition to proposition p."] In the logical atomism essays Russell argued that such views simply employ another form of negative fact—incompatibility facts. A year later he took Demos's view to generate an unending series by considering how to state "p and q are not both true" (1956, 288-289). Russell's point was that Demos must hold that propositions in "opposition" could not both be true, but yet he could not take that as an explication of "opposition," since it involved using "not." Hence, Demos must apply his analysis, in terms of "opposition," to that use of "not."

Though Russell argued for negative facts in 1918 and 1919, in the second edition of *Principia* he proposed an alternative.

> Given all true atomic propositions, together with the fact that they are all, every other true proposition can theoretically be deduced by logical methods. That is to say, the apparatus of crude fact required in proofs can all be condensed into true propositions together with the fact that every true atomic proposition is one of the following: (here the list

should follow). If used this method would presumably involve an infinite enumeration.... (1925, xv)

Taking this in a context where atomic facts are the truth grounds for atomic propositions, one can take him to claim that "a is not-F" is true since no atomic fact is the fact that a is F. But Russell does not attempt to "define" negation or replace negations by universal generalizations: he employs a basic (Scheffer) stroke function in the second edition. Rather, what he says can be understood as an attempt to avoid molecular facts, including negative facts, by appeal to atomic facts and a general fact that the atomic facts are all the atomic facts, even though he speaks of a general fact about a set (list) of all true atomic propositions. For he had taken atomic facts to ground the truth of true atomic propositions and negative facts to ground the truth of true negations of atomic propositions in 1918 and 1919. This can also be inferred from what is said in the first edition, (1925, 43), and from other works at the time (1973d, 223). But Russell's move, as it stands and has been repeated by others in recent times, is problematic. Before turning to that, it is interesting to note that Russell had earlier defined "negation" in *Principles of Mathematics*:

> Hence we proceed to the definition of negation: not-p is equivalent to the assertion that p implies all propositions, i.e. that "r implies r" implies "p implies r" whatever r may be. (1956, 18)

A footnote makes it clear that he is using "implies" for the "material" conditional. Thus, as he says, he could as easily have used "(q)(p $\supset$ q)," reminiscent of the current use of "p $\supset$ f." This raises issues about his use of the quantifier in propositional logic, the use of "T" and "F" in the truth tables for the conditional and the connection of the conditional to the other connectives. It is especially worth noting what Russell goes on to say, regarding the equivalence used in the definition being a "significant proposition" and "... not mere indications of the way in which symbols are going to be used."

> Such an objection is, I think, well-founded, if the above account is advocated as giving the true philosophic analysis of the matter. But where a purely formal purpose is to be served, any equivalence in which a certain notion appears on one side but not on the other will do for a definition. (1956, 18)

This is interesting, given the date, 1903, as the remark about "a purely formal purpose" is a suitable comment on Tarski's subsequent semantic conception of truth and its consequent "philosophic" employment by Davidson.

One issue that arises is whether negated atomic statements like "$\neg$ Fa" can be taken to be true in virtue of the "list" of atomic facts together with the general claim that they are all the atomic facts—if the negative statement can be derived from statements not involving a negation. A second issue that arises concerns what is to count as a negation. A third issue is whether true negative atomic statements require a "ground of truth" at all or whether they can be held to be true in virtue of the absence or non-existence of "positive" facts.

Consider the claim that "$\neg$ Fa" is "made true," to use Russell's phrase, by the fact (p)(p $\neq$ a's being F), with "p" as a variable over existent (atomic) facts—the fact that no atomic fact is a-being-F. Let us limit discussion to a small world or "model" with two atomic facts, Ga and Fb (using the atomic sentences to represent the facts). Russell's notion of a list of atomic facts comprising the totality of all atomic facts can then be expressed by the universal generalization "(p)(p =Ga $\vee$ p=Fb)." Such a generalization reveals an obvious problem.

The claim that there are only two particulars can be stated as "($\exists$x)($\exists$y)(x$\neq$y & (z)(z=x $\vee$ z=y))," just as the claim that a and b are the only particulars can be expressed by "(x)(x=a $\vee$ x=b)." The latter statement entails, with an additional name "c": ($\exists$x)(x=c) $\vDash$ c=a $\vee$ c=b. But as "(x)(x=a $\vee$ x=b)" does not entail "$\neg$ ($\exists$x)(x=c)," neither does "(p)(p=Ga $\vee$ p= Fb)" entail either "$\neg$ ($\exists$p)(p=Fa)" or that "$\neg$ Fa" is true. All, of relevance, that follows is: ($\exists$p)(p=Fa) $\vDash$ Fa =Ga $\vee$ Fa =Fb. But this amounts to: Fa $\neq$ Ga, Fa $\neq$ Fb $\vDash \neg$ ($\exists$p)(p=Fa)—if we assume, in both cases, that we can instantiate to "Fa," as we assumed about "c" above. Thus, stating that the truth ground for "$\neg$ Fa" is the non-existence of the fact that a is F can be seen as involving the two claims expressed by "Fa $\neq$ Ga" and "Fa $\neq$ Fb." But that means that we face the odd situation of claiming that the fact that a is F is diverse from the facts that a is G and b is F, while recognizing that the fact that a is F does not exist. One thus apparently avoids negative facts by accepting not only facts of diversity but by allowing for denoting expressions for non-existent facts.

There is an issue about whether the truth grounds or truth makers for true statements of difference can simply be the diverse terms, without there being a relation of difference and facts of diversity. To claim they can is problematic, as Plato knew long ago when he took difference as a basic form. For it is the existence of a and of b, where the "and" carries the sense that a is diverse from b. "a≠b" does not follow from "(∃x)(x =a) & (∃y)(y=b)" without an additional premise or interpretation rule that rules out "a=b." To speak of a and b being the truth grounds for "a≠b" assumes their diversity, which can be expressed by "(∃x)(∃y)(x =a & y =b & x≠y)," or by presupposing that diverse names name diverse things.

The problem of stating what "Fa ≠ Ga" purportedly states, without recognizing the non-existent fact that a is F, is resolved by the pattern that makes use of Russell's theory of descriptions and the formal relations T, A and IN to "denote" purported atomic facts. To express the truth ground for a negated atomic sentence, "¬ Fa," we can simply use "¬ E ! (ɩ p)(T(a, p) & A(F, p) & IN(Φx, p))"—the fact having a as a term and F as its attribute and is of the form Φx does not exist. From this point on I will simply use, for brevity, the expression "(ɩ p)Ø (a, F, p)" to abbreviate the definite description of the fact—(ɩ p)(T(a, p) & A(F, p) & IN(Φx, p))—and dispense with quotation marks when what is intended is clear.

The crucial question that arises is whether claiming that the described fact does not belong to the totality of atomic facts gets us anywhere. For using such a definite description makes clear that such a claim simply repeats the negated existential claim "¬Fa" that merely abbreviates "¬ E! (ɩ p)Ø (a, F, p)"! We can easily see that if we consider the generality to be expressed as:

(N) (q)(q ≠ (ɩ p)Ø (a, F, p)).

Where the variables "q" and "p" range over (existent) atomic facts, this serves the same purpose as a "list" or a corresponding disjunction, and avoids obvious questions about the "infinite enumeration" of true atomic propositions that Russell speaks of. If "≠" is a primitive sign in (N), as diversity (as opposed to identity) is taken by some as phenomenologically basic, then (N) becomes:

(∃$_u$p)(Ø (a, F, p) & (q)(q≠p)),

using the subscripted "u" for simplicity to indicate "uniqueness" in place of a uniqueness clause. This will obviously not do as an expression of the truth ground for "¬ Fa," since there must then be the fact a-being-F that is diverse from every fact, which is absurd. Rejecting diversity as basic and taking "≠" in terms of "¬" and "=," (N) becomes (q)¬ (q= (ɩ p)∅ (a, F, p))

or

¬ (∃q)(q= (ɩ p)∅ (a, F, p)).

Thus we are back to the problematic use of an explicit or embedded negated existential claim in stating that no fact is the fact that a is F. But there are alternative ways of attempting to specify a truth ground for "¬ Fa."

Limiting the discussion to monadic atomic facts, we can specify the truth ground for "¬ Fa" by

(TN) "¬ Fa" is true ≡ ¬ Fa ≡ ¬ E! (ɩ p)∅ (a, F, p).

Assume a general fact about monadic atomic facts, stating that no monadic atomic fact is such that F is its attribute and a is its term:

(G) $(x)(\Phi)(q)[(T(x, q) \& A(\Phi, q)) \supset (\Phi \neq F \vee x \neq a)]$.

That allows for a simple derivation of "¬ Fa." Assume "Fa," i. e. "E! (ɩ p)∅ (a, F, p)." We can then instantiate "q" in (G) to "(ɩ p)∅ (a, F, p)" and the "x" and "Φ" to "a" and "F," respectively, as we also take F and a to be existents. Thus we get a conditional statement where the left side is:

T(a, (ɩ p)∅ (a, F, p)) & A (F, (ɩ p)∅ (a, F, p)),

which is logically equivalent to the assumption "Fa." Hence, we arrive at the right side, the contradiction "F≠F ∨ a≠a." Consequently, we derive the negation of the assumption, the required negation "¬ Fa." The only negation-like sentences that occur in the argument are (i) the claim that every property and term of a fact are such that the property is different from F or the term is different from a; and (ii) the use of "≠" in "F≠F ∨ a≠a." But (G) is quite unlike the Russellian idea of a general list, since a statement like (G) is required for each negation—though it avoids the problem of speaking of, and providing, an "infinite list" of atomic sentences, if there are infinitely many atomic facts.

The appeal to "difference" is more explicit in the following argument, with "p" and "q" ranging over monadic (first order) atomic facts but employing a premise more on the order of a finite Russellian list:

1. a≠b
2. F≠G
3. (p)(p = Fb ∨ p = Ga)
4. Monadic first order atomic facts are the same if and only if their terms and attributes are the same.[10] ⊢ ¬ Fa.

With "Fb" and "Ga" understood as abbreviating the appropriate descriptions of facts as used earlier, it is a valid argument. For, assuming "E! Fa" and using the description that "Fa" abbreviates, we can instantiate (3) to (5) "Fa=Fb ∨ Fa =Ga." By (1), (2) and (4), we get the negation of (5), so we arrive at the denial of the assumption, which is "¬ Fa." We have then "grounded" the truth of "¬ Fa" without appealing to a negative fact—that-a is not F. But the focus is now on (1) and (2)—the facts of difference. Are they "negative" facts? Are there really such facts, or do the diverse entities suffice as truth grounds? We thus raise an issue as to whether a ≠b or ¬ (a=b), if taken as a fact, is a negative fact, as well as questions about whether ≠ (diversity) is a basic relation, and not to be understood simply in terms of the denial of an identity. Finally, there is a question as to whether the truth grounds for true statements of difference are simply the diverse entities or if the fact that they are diverse is required. As noted, corresponding questions arise about the first argument. Interestingly, though, (G), unlike the premises of the second argument, does not entail that diverse facts must differ in a term or attribute.[11] But, as noted, though using (G) does not run into a problem about Russell's "infinite lists," every negation requires its own general fact. Finally, by appealing to general facts employing the conditional, one raises a question about the significance of the logical equivalences involving conditionals, negations, disjunctions, etc. While not raising the same problems of circularity that were criticized earlier, this does raise questions about the logical form of general facts, especially those we have appealed to. We will briefly return to that below.

If "≠" is construed in terms of "¬" and "=," then it is also clear that facts of diversity are negative facts. But one need not argue about that. Such facts are not facts like ¬ Fa would seem to be. Thus the proponents and opponents of negative facts each have a point. If, however, ≠ (difference) is a

[10] Or, in symbols: (p)(q)[{(x)(y)(Φ)(Ψ)((x=y) & (Φ=Ψ) & T(x, p) & A(Φ, p) & T(y, q) & A(Ψ, q))} ≡ p=q].

[11] I am obliged to Per Lindström for suggesting (G) in place of the original "(q){E! q ⊃ . (x)(Φ)[(T(x, q) & A(Φ, q)) ⊃ (Φ ≠ F ∨ x≠a)]}" and for calling my attention to the fact that (G) allows diverse facts with the same terms and attributes.

basic relation, there is a clear sense in which we avoid negative facts altogether and, hence, a sense in which Plato was right to attempt to construe negation in terms of difference. It is clear, phenomenologically speaking, that diversity, not identity, is basic (Russell, 1973, 40; Segelberg, 1999, 39). One is presented with or directly aware of such facts of diversity, but never with the fact that something is self-identical. Yet, if diversity is taken as basic "≠" should be a primitive sign used to define "=." But this appears to create problems for the use of definite descriptions.

Consider "(q)(q ≠ (ɿ p)∅ (a, F, p))." One can, with "≠" as primitive, only expand the description so that we have an existential claim—either explicitly or embedded, depending on whether we take the scope to include the universal quantifier or not—which is hardly what is intended. Since we consider atomic sentences as abbreviations for existential claims that a definitely described fact exists, we do not have "(p)p" as a well formed formula, but, instead, "(p)E! p," which poses two problems. One concerns the sentence's truth value—that we will take up below: the other requires modifying the rules regarding contexts for "E!" so that they differ from Russell's use of that sign in *Principia*.

For Russell, "E!" could only be combined with certain kinds of abstracts, definite descriptions and class abstracts, for example, and was contextually defined differently for such different cases. "E!" could not be combined with a variable so that one had "E!x" or "(x)E!x" as well formed expressions. Thus "E!" is not here used in conformity with Russell's use of that sign, but the difference causes no problems. Like Russell, we are not allowing instantiation to definite descriptions of purported facts from *all* contexts of the form "(p)(...p...)," including "(p)E!p," without the familiar additional existential assumption. It is allowed only in the case of restricted contexts, as in (1) and (2) below, expressing obvious logical truths. [Whether this poses a problem will be taken up shortly.] Recognizing that difference and allowing for the use of "E!" with sentential variables ranging over atomic facts, the standard "laws of logic," as applied to such facts, become the logically equivalent:

(1) excluded middle— (p)(E! p ∨ ¬ E! p)
(2) non-contradiction— (p)¬ (E! p & ¬ E! p).

We must keep in mind that while "p" ranges over the atomic facts, the signs that one instantiates to, which are the signs of the category for which "p" is a variable, are definite descriptions—not atomic sentences or names of facts. They are not constants in the sense in which signs like "a" and "F" are. Thus, in place of a standard law of identity, (p)(p=p), we require something along the lines of a familiar *Principia* theorem for definite descriptions:

(3) identity— (p)(E! p ≡ p=p).

(In (1), (2) and (3), "(∃q)(q=p)" will obviously do in place of "E!p".) But, the matter is complicated by a different notion of identity being involved in the case of monadic atomic facts, where identity of facts depends on the identity of terms and properties, than the notion applicable to the terms and properties (relations) of such facts.

Among the atomic facts we include basic facts of diversity for particulars and properties: a≠b, F≠G, etc. Identity for such entities is simply the negate of diversity: "x=y =df ¬ x≠y." Identity for atomic facts is not so defined. We will continue to confine the discussion to first level monadic facts, for simplicity and to avoid the complications of dealing with order in the case of relational facts, so that "p" and "q" still range only over (first order) monadic atomic facts. We can take identity for them, indicated by "=$_M$," as:

q=$_M$ p =df (∃x)(∃y)(∃Φ)(∃Ψ)[Ø(x, Φ, p) & Ø(y, Ψ, q) & x=y & Φ=Ψ],

where we adjust the shorthand notation "Ø(a, F, p)" in an obvious way to accommodate the use of variables like "x" and "Φ". If we allow "(p)E!p" as well formed, then we must choose whether or not we require an appropriate existential premise in order to instantiate to a definite description of a purported fact. We did so above and used the corresponding pattern in the case of universal instantiation:

(p)E!p & E! (ι p)Ø (a, F, p) ⊢ E! (ι p)Ø (a, F, p),

This renders it trivially acceptable, as in the case of "(x)Ψx & E!(ι y)(Φy) . ⊃ Ψ(ι y) (Φy)" being a theorem of *Principia*, where "E!(ι y)(Φy) ≡ Φ(ι y)(Φy)" is also a theorem. As noted above, this use of "E!" with a sentential variable differs from the use of "E!" in *Principia* since "(x)E!x" is not well-formed—which reflects that "E!" is not a predicate transcribing "exists." That reinforces the notion that "existence" is not a property, but is perspicuously represented, in so far as it is represented by a sign, by the existential quantifier.

Since we only recognize existent atomic facts "p" ranges over such atomic facts, and not possibilities. Hence, there are cases where we obviously want a universal generalization to be true, such as "(p)(∃q)(p $=_M$ q)." But without the existential restriction on universal instantiation to definite descriptions of purported facts, we would then run into the familiar problem of deriving a false sentence from a true one since we have "non-denoting" definite description. Thus one is forced to recognize the restriction on universal instantiation—following Russell's familiar treatment—which permits "(p)E!p" to be true, as it should be and as "(x)(∃y)(x=y)" is. That poses no problem, as "(x)(x=x)" poses no problem in *Principia*. Yet the standard laws of logic discussed earlier might appear to. For it would seem that we should be able to instantiate the bound variable in such laws to any description of a fact, whether there is such a fact or not. That is, universal instantiation should be allowable from them without the added existential premise that Russell's theory of descriptions requires. And it turns out that they can be so instantiated, as we can see from the following case.

Confined to (first order) monadic atomic cases, and thinking in terms of logical entailment, rather than derivation, instantiating the law of excluded middle yields:

(p)(E! p ∨ ¬ E! p) & E! (ɿ p)∅ (a, F, p) ⊨ E! (ɿ p)∅ (a, F, p) ∨ ¬ E! (ɿ p)∅ (a, F, p).

This is, trivially, logically equivalent to

(p)(E! p ∨ ¬ E! p) ⊨ E! (ɿ p)∅ (a, F, p) ∨ ¬ E! (ɿ p)∅ (a, F, p),

since the consequent is a logical truth. Thus the restriction on universal instantiation may be said to "disappear" in the case of this logical law. The same triviality obviously holds for non-contradiction, and, recall, "identity" was altered, at the outset, to fit the use of Russellian definite descriptions.

A second problem concerns taking ≠ as a basic relation between particulars and properties, and not defining "≠" in terms of "¬" and "=." The problem is then stating that (ɿ p)∅ (a, F, p) does not exist by (i) "(q)(q≠ (ɿ p) ∅ (a, F, p))" or by (ii) "¬ E! (ɿ p)∅ (a, F, p)." The two should be equivalent. But if "≠" is basic, there is no room for a difference of scope, so (i) must be transcribed, using "u" to express uniqueness, as "(∃up)(∅(a, F, p) & (q)(q≠p))," which is false whether the fact exists or does not exist. But the problem is only apparent. Given the definition of "$=_M$" we have not taken "≠" as basic for facts. Hence, (i) must be construed in terms of "(q)¬ (q $=_M$ (ɿp)∅(a, F, p))," and not in terms of " ≠." Taking the scope for such contexts in the appropriate way, we have "(q)¬ (∃up)(∅(a, F, p) & q =$_M$ p)," which is true, since there is no monadic atomic fact with a as its term and F as its attribute, and hence any description of an existent atomic fact that "q" can be instantiated to will denote a fact that does not contain both a and F.

If we acknowledge domains of facts, of particulars, and of properties, we can attempt to treat quantified statements in a similar reductive manner as in the case of the connectives. But again, this is one of those matters of detail that, while important for the present view, cannot be gone into here. In the logical atomism essays Russell not only argued for negative facts but, as he saw no way to avoid a universally general fact, he argued that at least one such general fact must be acknowledged. It is simpler to deal with Russell's argument in terms of particulars, rather than facts. Suppose we have only two particulars, a and b. Then we have "(x)(x =a ∨ x=b)" or, what amounts to the same thing, the class {a, b} being the domain. (Russell's corresponding assumption in the case of facts is a disjunction like that considered in the discussion of negative facts.) From "Fa," "Fb" and "(x)(x =a ∨ x=b)" we easily derive "(x)Fx." But that statement is not derivable from "Fa & Fb" This, in essence, is Russell's simple argument for the need to recognize general facts, since the supposition that a and b are the only particulars is expressed by stating "they are all" and not, as Wittgenstein suggests, simply given by the list "a, b." (It is worth comparing Russell's view on a and b being all with the claim that a and b suffice to ground the truth of "a≠b.") Infinite domains pose other problems, as they do in the case of negative facts, but we are not dealing with a precisely specified formal system, simply a sketch of a schema. Yet we can note that in the case of having an infinite domain of monadic atomic facts, (G) will do for handling the issue of negative facts, aside from questions about its equivalence to a disjunction involving an embedded negation, though we would have to employ some condition to specify the elements of an infinite domain of objects. In any case, the basic point is simply Russell's claim that we do require at least one general fact, (x)(x =a ∨ x=b), in the present simple case. Recognizing such a universal fact, a "domain" fact," means that we recognize the logical form of universal generality, (x)Φx— a "quantifier." If we also recognize the form ¬Φx, irrespective of any question about recognizing negative facts aside from facts involving "diversity," we then also have the forms (x)¬Φx and ¬(x) Φx, whether or not we have facts of such a form. Recognizing such forms will clearly play a role in assessing the significance of the logical equivalences of patterns involving negation to generalizations like (G).

4b. Truth and Modality

One question about modal facts is raised by taking atomic sentences like "Fa" to be interpreted in terms of representing states of affairs. We have avoided representing non-existent states of affairs by using Russell's pattern employing definite descriptions. Wittgenstein did not avoid such entities by his cryptic statement in *Tractatus* 4. 022 taking an atomic statement, or a thought expressed by one, to represent a situation in that it *shows* its sense, whether or not it is true, and *states* that what is shown obtains. Showing or representing was a relation between a statement or thought, on the one hand, and a possible state of affairs on the other. That relation obtained whether or not the represented situation did, as it later did for Searle (section 1h). This was reflected in Searle's talk of the relation being intrinsic, as others spoke of it being logical (Bergmann) or internal (Armstrong, Segelberg). We saw how Searle thought he avoided the problem, but actually just ignored it. Armstrong overlooks the problem by shifting his discussion of "possibilities" to the issue of whether an actualist combinatorial account of possibility, along what he takes to be Wittgenstein's *Tractarian* lines, can avoid possible facts, and the possible worlds of D. Lewis (1986), while accounting for the truth that it is possible that a is F—the truth of the modal claim "◊Fa" when "¬ Fa" is true (1997, 165-66). What he overlooks is the more basic problem involved in the very use of the atomic sentence embedded in the modal sentence: the issue raised by the use of the juxtaposition of the subject and predicate terms to express a possible state of affairs. Thus Armstrong collapses two questions into one by taking the sentential juxtaposition of a subject and a predicate, as in "Fa," to represent a possible situation, without acknowledging that he does so, and focusing on the question raised about the "truth maker" for "◊Fa." In answering the latter, he presupposes he has answered the former. The mereological sums of the objects and properties involved, F+a and a+R+b, respectively, do not ground either the truths of "◊Fa" and "◊aRb" ("◊bRa"), or furnish the basis for "Fa" and "aRb" expressing "possibilities." For Wittgenstein, the relevant objects and properties (relations) could ground "Fa" and "aRb" being well formed sentences since their natures or essential (internal) properties or "forms" carried the possibilities of combination and determined the possible facts. He thus packed possible facts (situations) into the natures of properties and particulars, which were then said to determine the possibilities of combination.

Armstrong later proposed a revised solution to the ontological problem posed by modalities by suggesting that the contingency of the fact that a is F suffices to ground a modal truth like "$\Diamond\neg$ Fa" (2000, 155-59). But his revised view still faces the basic problem of his the earlier view. We see that immediately if, instead of simply dealing with the modal sentence, we again ask what grounds "Fa" being well formed—i. e. expressing a possibility, in an obvious sense of that term. Armstrong continues to avoid the question by focusing on the explicit modal sentence "$\Diamond\neg$ Fa" and simply assuming that "Fa" represents a possible state of affairs. That aside, his later use of "contingent" remains vague. If the modal sentence is to be true because the atomic sentence is contingently true, then he either takes atomic facts to embody a basic modality of contingency or he simply means that since a can combine with F, both "Fa" and "¬Fa" express contingent truths. The later does not help, while taking the fact that a is F to embody a modality of contingency, as Armstrong appears to do, compounds the problem. For not only does one introduce a basic modality, as a mode of facts, but he now requires a ground for the connection between facts being contingent and truths about possibilities and necessities. For one commonly understands "p is contingent" in terms of necessity and/or possibility, as Carnap once noted: "... 'p' is contingent means 'p' is neither necessary nor impossible ..." (1956, 175). There is another problem with taking atomic facts to embody a basic mode of contingency, since if the atomic sentence is false, there is no fact to embody anything on Armstrong's view, as he does not recognize negative facts.

Let "C" express "being contingent" and be a modal sign that combines with sentences, so that we have "C (Fa)" as a well-formed pattern. We must now either introduce axioms or rules, so that we have "C (Fa) $\rightarrow$ $\Diamond\neg$ Fa," or problematically seek to define the other modal concepts in terms of "C" and "¬." Armstrong may not note that he must do such things as he takes all facts to be contingent, and, as he denies that there are any necessary facts, he speaks of Fa being a fact as amounting to characterizing it as contingent. But if he introduces a new basic modality of contingency, he must then either make the modality of contingency an internal or necessary property of facts or take it as a basic mode that does not form a further contingent fact, one consisting of the fact that a is F instantiating the mode of contingency. Oddly, if C is an internal or necessary property, then, by Armstrong's notion of an internal property, it *supervenes*, and that means that the truth maker for "C

(Fa)" simply becomes the fact that a is F, since what is supervenient is not an "addition to being." This use of "supervenient" follows his use of it in holding that diversity "supervenes" since a and b suffice as truth makers for "a≠b." Thus there really is not a relation of diversity, just the sign used in sentences to express that a is diverse from b, for example. Thus, oddly, he ends up having to simply declare that since the fact that a is F is the truth maker for "C (Fa)," and there is no further state of affairs involved, that fact suffices as the truth maker for "◊¬ Fa." It does so since the latter sentence is true in virtue of the contingency of the fact that a is F. As this consequence is obviously absurd, he must take the modal fact— C(Fa)—to be a further fact, and one that is necessary, since he leans towards accepting the modality C as basic and holding that "C (Fa)" is a necessary truth. He does not avoid such a necessity by holding that necessary truths have, as truth makers, "the possibility of the existence of their terms" (2000, 158). Hence, the (possibility of the) existence of C and of the fact that a is F ground the truth of "C (Fa)"—while the latter possibility was formerly based on the existence of F and of a. Such a use of "necessary truth" remains, of course, puzzling, while his use of "possibility" is unexplicated and circular. For he not only faces the problems about possibility we noted earlier, but he now uses that notion to explicate "C (Fa)" being a necessary truth. Yet the latter is used to explicate "◊" in "◊¬ Fa." It is a tangled web he weaves.

Some necessary truths are obviously based on entities being of certain logical kinds. Thus that a and F are, respectively, a particular and a property are such truths. To speak of categorial properties "supervening," and thus not really existing, does not clarify anything. Rather, it is reasonable to begin by taking such categorial truths to be logical truths in the sense that they are reflected by the very categories and the formation rules of a schema. Thus we might say that taking "a" to combine with "F" to form an atomic sentence reflects a more basic logical truth than the tautological sentence "Fa ∨ ¬ Fa," as the former is expressed by the rules for the schema rather than by a sentence of the schema. Moreover, the standard logical truths presuppose such truths of logic—for every logical schema requires formation rules as well as logical inference, or transformation, rules. Even if one were to introduce predicates for such categorial properties or natures, such as being a particular, P, and being a universal, U, the categorically true statement "Pa" would already "show" that a is a particular by the type of sign used to represent it—or at least reflect that the sign is coordinated to a particular in the semantical rule that provides an interpretation for it.

Given a domain of two objects, a and b, the reason that it is possible that there is a further object is that "$(\exists x)(\exists y)(z)(x \neq y\ \&\ (z=x \vee z=y))$" is not a logical truth. If there is an ontological ground or truth maker for such a possibility, it is furnished by whatever is taken to ground statements being or not being logical truths. However one deals with such problems about standard logic, it is clear that the structural categories of a *Principia* type schema, embodying a standard system of logic, have nothing to do with modal logics, and thus sentences of a modal calculus containing "$\Diamond$" are irrelevant to the philosophical issue. Moreover, we must recognize the categorial distinctions that are employed by attempts to use modal axioms about purported modal operators in functional modal logics—such as the subject-predicate distinction. Such categorial distinctions are obviously not explicated by axioms about modal operators in such systems. We thus need not talk literally about possible facts and possible worlds. Yet we can provide sufficient grounds for the truth that "Fa" expresses a possibility, which, while similar sounding, is not to be confused with "$\Diamond Fa$," by explicitly recognizing logical forms and categorial relations, such as is a term in, is the attribute in and is the form of. Particulars are then taken to be entities that can be terms of atomic facts but cannot be attributes (relations). They are not predicables, to put it in a way that is a variant of a medieval and Aristotelian pattern. Qualities and relations, by contrast, are predicables—they are what can be attributes in facts (as well as terms of higher order facts, general facts, etc.). This admittedly involves one or more further and unexplicated modal concepts of possibility and (or) necessity, expressed by the uses of "can" and "cannot" in the previous sentences. But such uses of modal terms have nothing to do with modal logic and notions expressed by signs like "$\Diamond$," since (functional) modal logics already incorporate the subject-predicate distinction—and even sentential modal logics incorporate the distinction between modal operators, truth functions and propositions (or whatever sentences are taken to represent or express).

We deal here with logical categories at the very foundations of our logical concepts and distinctions. In doing so we have avoided introducing possible facts, though we have recognized basic logical forms, like Φx, in grounding linguistic predicative juxtaposition, and $(x)\ \Phi x$, in acknowledging general facts. This neither "defines" the relevant sign patterns nor explains what they "mean" in an ordinary sense of "mean," anymore than acknowledging numbers as abstract objects or classes helps a child learn either the meaning of "7" or arithmetic. But that is not what is involved in philosophical issues, which is why some take them to be "useless." But a question can still be raised about the ontological ground for such necessities and possibilities that I have taken to reflect "logical categories," a question that MacBride (2003) has pointedly raised. For I have claimed that it is a matter of logical necessity that universals are predicables, as well as terms for facts, while particulars can only be terms, i. e. are necessarily only terms. To put it another way, entities, including facts, are necessarily of the logical kinds they embody. But what this comes down to is that it is a matter of logic, and logical truth, that particulars, predicables and forms are of the categorial kinds that they are. The issue then amounts to one thread of the question regarding what grounds logical truths being logical truths. Another thread is seen in the question of whether it is a matter of logical necessity that standard logical truths are logical truths, for, clearly, that "p ∨ ¬ p" is a sentential tautology is not itself such a logical truth. Are there then senses of "possible" and "necessary" in terms of which one can sensibly raise questions about "standard" logics themselves? (Hochberg, 1955) That aspect of the question I will leave. But there is another aspect of the question about logic that seems to have a clear answer. For it is reasonable to acknowledge that in so far as we have logical truths expressed by the sentential and functional "tautologies" of logical schemata, the formation rules of such schemata also express or reflect logical truths.

What has just been claimed is not a matter of simply declaring that certain things cannot be said or thought in Wittgensteinian fashion. That gets one nowhere—though it is true that certain things are more appropriately said about a schema than viably said within it. Whether one then speaks, somewhat poetically, of the logical categories and truths, reflected by the formation rules of an idealized schema, as well as of the standard logical truths themselves, being ultimately grounded by the "world's logical form," or acknowledges that there is a sense in which it is a matter of fact that the logic of things is the way it is, or that we simply start from such a logical framework or that we have raised a question that still requires an answer is something I leave open here. But it is worth noting the difference between such "necessities" that are taken to be logical, in being presupposed by logical schemata, and the current widely used, but inherently vague and problematic, phrase "metaphysical necessity" (Kripke, 1980, 36). The necessities we are concerned with deal, first, with the logical categories reflected by basic linguistic categories—subject terms, predicates, quantifiers and sentences—categories made use of and required in the development of logical systems themselves; and, second, are about logical systems themselves. We are not concerned with a particular kind of object, like a human being, and whether it could have been a donkey or not. The latter sort of possibility is dealt with in standard science fiction and has been considered in classical literature (recall *The Golden Ass* of Apuleius). Noting the difference between talking of the possibility of one kind of thing becoming another kind of thing and the possibility supposedly expressed by the phrase "could have been" is of no consequence and simply leads to absurd, if amusing, examples.

> How could a person originating from different parents, from a totally different sperm and egg, be *this very woman*? One can imagine, *given* the woman that various things in her life could have changed....
> ...we can imagine making a table out of another block of wood or even from ice...this is *not* to imagine *this* table ... but rather it is to imagine another table....(Kripke, 1980, 113-14).

What seems obvious, if anything involved in such talk about what we can or cannot imagine can be obvious, is that it all depends on what you mean by "this woman," "that table" and "that sperm." We are not asking for a vote on what we would ordinarily say—if ordinary language has anything "to say" about such things. Aside from the vagueness introduced by talk about what we "can" and "cannot" imagine, it seems reasonably clear that to speak of such metaphysical necessities with the assurance that x could not have been y, or that something of (natural) kind F could not have been of (natural) kind G, is to be forced back to the classical issues surrounding the notions of bare substrata and individuation, essential properties and natures and the ontological analysis of "things." Do we get down to the atoms, electrons, etc. of an egg and a sperm? Perhaps even their "bare particulars"? Or is it just clear what "the same sperm" is? Possibly it is so "by definition," to recall Kripke's discourse about tables, cited in Chapter 2. Perhaps it would be best to simply go back to the "identity" of the familiar ships and stockings that are redone plank by plank and thread by thread, and forget the paraphernalia of possible worlds and the verbiage about them. In its way, Kripke's talk of sperm, eggs and "this woman" is as irrelevant to the philosophical issues about necessity as Hale and Wright's talk about distinguishing tigers from trees and Caesar from numbers is to the philosophy of arithmetic. In the one case, Kripke's, one relies on ordinary language philosophy to dismiss the philosophical problems posed by individuation; in the other, one dodges the problems created by appealing to "implicit definitions" as providing analyses. One might also wonder about the use of "totally different" in the above quotation—won't "different" do here? But these are precisely the issues we earlier saw that Kripke, who readily deals with purported metaphysical necessities, shirks by shifting to the seemingly safe haven of ordinary language. Recall, there are certain questions we just "Don't ask!"

The modal notion of *necessity* has been used in a recent paper by B. Smith to attempt to arrive at a definition of "x makes p true" and a theory of "truth makers":

> Necessitation is to be conceived as a real tie spanning the divide between ontology and logic. We define:
> DN $xNp := E! x \,\&\, (E! x \rightarrow p)$,
> where $p \rightarrow q$ abbreviates $\neg \Diamond (p \,\&\, \neg q)$, and where p, q, ..., are schematic letters standing in for particular judgments ...and other candidate bearers of truth. (1999, 276)

It is easy to see where a problem lies that is related to our earlier discussion of negation and diversity. For to take the existence of a and b to necessitate "a≠b," as both Smith and Armstrong do, is to take "a exists and b exists" to be true along with "((a exists & b exists) → a≠b)." Clearly if "→" is read in terms of "(a exists & b exists) ⊃ a≠b" being a logical truth, i. e. in terms of "⊨," the claim is false, unless one presupposes "a≠b," which is hardly enlightening. It is also problematic, since he speaks of a *necessitation* relation while "necessitates" is a defined predicate, thus seemingly assuming that defined predicates stand for properties and relations. That aside, Smith obviously does not think in terms of the above conditional being a standard logical truth, as he uses a primitive modal notion throughout the paper—thus employing a notion of necessitation that is never explicated. To speak of an implicit definition of the modal concepts, recalling Hale and Wright on "number," is clearly pointless, especially given the variety of modal systems. Taking a version of a modal calculus (perhaps modified in certain ways) to govern the use of modal signs is not to provide either a philosophical explication of modal terms or an ontological analysis of modality. Moreover, as his use of "entails" is not that of "logically entails," Smith's introductory abstract is quite misleading:

> On the one hand is the relation of necessitation, which holds between an object x and a judgment p when the existence of x entails the truth of p.

One expects standard logic. One gets principles of necessitation and the use of a primitive modal operator. Moreover, even treating $\rightarrow$ as a primitive necessary connection (ignoring his taking "$\Diamond$" rather than "$\square$" as his primitive modal sign), he must still assume that a is diverse from b. One gets absolutely nowhere with the claim that it is simply a and b that furnish the truth ground for "a$\neq$b." Armstrong's claim, shared by Smith, that it is the mereological sum a+b that suffices, does not help. For one must presuppose that a is a proper part of the sum or, to put it differently, that a+b is diverse from a (and thus a is diverse from b). There is no escaping the need to appeal to diversity.

There is another problem. Taking "E!x $\rightarrow$ p" to be true in the relevant case, using some modal term (be it "$\Diamond$" or "$\square$") in an unexplicated sense, raises the issue of whether such truths require truth makers. If not, what is the reason they are true? If so, we would have a modal truth based on the relation between x's existence (that x exists) and p, where p is a truth bearer of some kind—a sentence, judgment, proposition, etc. Thus there will be a primitive modality involved in connecting the two terms of the relation. This raises a question as to whether we have modal facts grounding such true necessitations (perhaps necessary facts) involving a "real tie spanning the divide" between ontology and logic. Without such facts one can only invoke stipulative definitions and appeal to logical entailment, which does not work. Smith is satisfied by a set of axioms governing his use of "necessitates" that follows the lines of some modal calculus with axioms about "$\Diamond$." But this neither explicates his use of "necessitates" nor avoids introducing a basic modality. Thus, no real explication is offered, in spite of the long chain of definitions he introduces linking "necessitates" with "makes true." Much of that tedious chain is irrelevant, as the key move is already involved in using "necessitates," with the definition given in the above quotation, in the definition of "x makes p true." This points to a further problem.

In some cases the truth maker that necessitates a judgment (proposition, statement) being true will be a fact. Thus the appropriate sign replacing the variable "x" in "E!x & E!x → p" will be a sign for a fact. Smith is forced to use a definite description of a fact or introduce purported names of facts and the possibilities that go along with them, as on Carnap's early 1940s discussion. What sort of definite description is open to him? Consider the case of "Fa." However he takes the definite description which, assume, is "∂," it must be such that "E!∂ → p" holds. Thus, even with an unexplicated modal notion, so that he does not have to show that "E! ∂" entails "Fa" (which is reason enough to reject his view), he must at least make it plausible that he can speak of a conditional being a necessary truth. This will force him to make a claim that plays the role of (T), on the view presented earlier in the present book, and that will connect ∂ to "p." But, then, for atomic sentences, and their negations, his discussion of "makes true" and "necessitation" is irrelevant. (T) along with our earlier discussion of negation and a straightforward concept of logical entailment will capture what is viably involved in talk of truth makers and necessitation for true atomic sentences or true negations of such. Giving corresponding truth rules for complex propositions (statements, judgments) will do the same in those cases. Questions about whether objects, like a, are also truth makers—for existential claims—are of no real import, as "(∃x)(x=a)" will either be used to define "E!," as it is used with names, or the latter will be taken as a primitive predicate of existence. The problems involved in the latter I ignore, for, in either case, the statements will be trivially true in a perspicuous schema where all primitive predicates and logically proper names (primitive zero level signs of the schema—"F," "a," etc.) will refer to or name properties (relations) and particulars, respectively. Moreover, "p" will then simply be an existential statement like "E! a" or "(∃x)(x=a)." So the entailment will hold, and a will necessitate "p" since the existential statement will be trivially true, being a consequence of the interpretation rules of the schema. Whether one then says that it is a or a's existing that is the relevant ground of truth, to shift from talk of truth makers and necessitation, is of no import. But, one can note how Smith's and Armstrong's loose notions of necessitation permit them to speak of the existence of a and of b necessitating the truth of "a≠b" without "$(\exists x)(x=a)$ & $(\exists x)(x=b)$" entailing "a≠b." What that means here is that "$(\exists x)(x=a)$ & $(\exists x)(x=b)$" will necessitate, but not entail, "a≠b." Such a claim is clearly vacuous, but it is a simple example of a current trend in analytic metaphysics.

The shift from Russell's early theme of facts making (certain) sentences true to the recent phrasing that focuses on "truth makers" and, especially, "things" as truth makers has led to various claims regarding the sorts of truths particular entities make true. In the recent revival of interest in the original metaphysical issues—issues that dominated the early years of the founding of the analytic tradition—the appeal to the "truth making" roles of particulars has become the basic ground for defending the appeal to "individual properties" (the traditional medieval "accidents") that supposedly allow one to avoid the recognition of universal qualities and relations—and, in the case of some philosophers (Smith and K. Mulligan for example) to avoid relations altogether by appealing to "fundaments" internal to objects. The trend is nicely exhibited in a recent book that defends the replacement of universal qualities by "tropes," the currently popular term for such "particularized" properties.

Tropes are introduced to avoid both extreme nominalism, which takes predicates to simply apply to ordinary particulars and not represent properties and relations, and the form of realism that takes predicates to represent universal properties and relations that can be common to numerous terms and pairs, triples, etc. of terms. Another motive for trope theories is the belief that tropes allow one to avoid bare particulars or substrata that are the bearers of properties and, with properties, combine, in some manner, to form ordinary objects or facts or both. Tropes supposedly allow one to answer classical questions about common properties, individuation and truth grounds for the ascription of predicates. They are taken to be able to do this by being characterized as particular, abstract and simple and such that "we must never lose sight of the fact that these traits are postulated, and that they are, in this sense, part of the basic set of assumptions from which the present work departs" (Maurin, 2002, 11). Of course one cannot offer arguments for everything—one must start somewhere. But to postulate or assume something does not mean that such postulates can merely be repeated in response to objections—especially objections arguing that tropes are employed in ways that reveal that they are not so simple. One cannot arbitrarily respond to the charge that tropes are complex, in that they are taken to be entities that have a nature and therefore involve a distinction between what has the nature and the nature itself, by merely declaring that the trope and its nature are one and the same—the trope is its nature, because it is simple, and being simple we cannot distinguish the nature from the trope. What is especially interesting about this recent defense of "individual properties" is that it clearly and concisely summarizes the views of a host of recent trope theorists and lays bare unquestioned postulates employed by such theories. In doing so it transparently, if unintentionally, reveals the problems of the view.

Tropes being, by assumption, simple account, like the bare or thin particulars of other philosophers, for the diversity of complex entities, but require no further account of their own diversity—they just differ. Arguing that the problem of individuation only arises if we refuse "to accept that two different basic facts may be true of one and the same simple entity," she seems to mean that those who argue that tropes are complex, because one must account for the diversity of two tropes and for the two tropes being of one and the same kind, refuse to accept the basic assumption of the theory. Some critics of tropes claim that tropes simply duplicate the classical problems that lead some to universals and substrata. This is not just a matter of "refusing to accept that two different basic facts may be true of one and the same entity," or, as Maurin would have it, simply a matter that is settled by holding that those who raise an objection are against the "very possibility of the entire trope-theoretical enterprise" and is of "no interest ... here (where the possible existence of tropes is assumed)." (19) This takes us to one of those points where argument ceases, but what is of interest is just what the trope theorist is driven to say in defense of tropes.

Suppose we forget about individuation and simply ask how is it that a trope is identical with its nature? Actually, here, only one aspect of its nature is relevant, for the natures are quite rich. We have two red tropes, say, that are both such that we can say we have cases of "being red"—they are red tropes as opposed to blue tropes. Thus, unlike bare particulars or substrata they have a nature (aside from being tropes or particulars) that they *are* (identified with). If the nature is distinct from the trope we have a trope and a red nature, or red making nature, or whatever one here says—that is what grounds the trope being red, and not the trope itself. If they are one and the same, as is now commonly asserted by trope theorists, then the nature (as the trope) is diverse from the nature of the other red trope—which is identified with that trope.

How then are they of the same kind? Maurin wants to say they just are and that is that. But even if one gives the trope theorist diversity, whether as a basic notion or as the negation of identity, the trope and its nature are taken to be the same—yet not exactly one and the same—not really identical—for diverse tropes are of the same kind, red tropes. Thus, unlike the case of simple diversity, a question arises about the use of "same," since we really mean one and the same kind. And then the obvious question arises: What is involved in the appeal to a "kind"? Maurin would have us accept, as simply accepting the hypothesis of trope theory, that that question is taken care of by tropes being the kind of simples that they are—end of discussion! But this takes us nowhere. In short, grant the assumption that diverse tropes are simply different; one must still explain how diverse tropes are of the same kind, if they are said to "be their natures." But if they are not said to be so—what are their natures? And if there are no natures at all—then they are bare particulars, or at least things about which the question of how they come to belong to the same similarity circle arises. Red tropes are said to be similar because they are red tropes, and not red because they are similar. Fair enough, as an opening move—but not good enough for a solid defense that blunts criticism. What K. Campbell, from whom Maurin borrows this approach, doesn't seem to see, let alone appreciate, is why a deeper trope theorist like Meinong turned to exact similarity and, consistent to the end, took such a relation in terms of tropes themselves. For Maurin the two tropes suffice as the truth ground for "red_1 is exactly similar to red_2." Thus exact similarity is a "pseudo-addition" (109) to a tropist ontology.

The final term of the triumvirate of *simple, particular,* and *abstract* that Maurin focuses on is "abstract." Due to the wide influence of Quine, philosophers have tended to lump together "things" like sets, numbers, properties, concepts, propositions, functions and so forth as "abstract" entities. The tendency has been, as in the case of talk of "particulars," to contrast concrete spatio-temporal objects with non-localizable abstract entities. It has been further aided by the familiar tendency, influenced by Carnap and others, to treat predicates, taken in extension, as standing for classes while, taken in "intension," as standing for properties or concepts. But, clearly, classes, normally construed, are not predicable of anything. Then there is the old tradition of taking properties to be separated in thought from the objects that instantiate them. Thus one is said to "abstract" or remove them in thought. Maurin is simply concerned to justify her use of the phrase "abstract particular" to apply to tropes and takes the phrase to suggest that tropes are qualities or relations but not universals.

The most interesting part of her defense of tropes is her attempt to deal with a version of the Bradley regress the trope theorist might be thought to face. For, since she recognizes relational compresence tropes, she rightly feels obliged to show such a regress cannot be raised against her view. She claims that it is a "brute fact about relations" that no further additional connection is needed. This, of course, is the familiar Frege-Russell response, but it is not an answer to Bradley without a further story, and she attempts to supply a story in terms of the special features of a "compresence" relation. As the relation of exact resemblance holds "necessarily," since what the related tropes are "is intimately connected to the relation in which they stand" she claims that though the connection is not as apparent in the case of the compresence relation (compresence relational tropes), something along similar lines can be argued. Actually in the case of *exact similarity*, a relation traditional trope theories recognized, she holds that there really is no such relation, and hence no need for relational tropes of exact similarity. Exact similarity, like other relations, is a "pseudo-addition" to be explained away via "fundaments" internal to objects. But *compresence* is a "real" relation and not such a pseudo-entity. Thus, it must be taken in terms of tropes, as Meinong took relations, and, as for any other trope, its being what it is exhausts the being of a compresence trope, since tropes are identified with their natures.

Such a relation cannot be dismissed in terms of fundaments internal to the thing, but must be taken as external to the entities it relates. For, as Maurin sees it, if one does not recognize compresence as "real" the constituent tropes of a trope bundle would necessarily go together, if they exist, being the ground for such a bundle. Since the existence of such bundles is obviously contingent, a compresence relation must be recognized. Moreover, it must, on a comprehensive trope theory, be taken in terms of tropes, as qualities are, and not as a universal relation. A compresence trope differs from other tropes, however, in being a relation-trope and being such that it must relate exactly the tropes that it does in fact relate. It is "specifically dependent" on them, and this dependency is "one way" or "one sided." It is external to the tropes, in that they can exist without being in that specific trope relation, hence the contingency of ordinary objects, construed as trope bundles, is saved, but the "bundled" tropes are "internal" to their compresence trope in that it cannot exist without relating precisely the tropes it relates. Its doing so is "its nature" and shows that a compresence trope that unifies ordinary tropes into complexes is a categorially different kind of trope. A compresence trope's "dependency" supposedly resolves any purported Bradley-type problem.

One question that then arises is the one that can be raised in connection with "similarity circles" of tropes, red tropes say, if they are taken to be entities like G. F. Stout's distributive unities. Given that you have a compresence trope tying a variety of tropes, do you also have a subset of those unified tropes also unified by another compresence trope of a smaller adicity? Whatever you say, unless you stipulate that all complexes of tropes are of the same adicity, you will have compresence tropes of different adicities. Do they all form a similarity circle of compresence tropes? Or do only those of the same adicity do so? Or are compresence trope relations what Quine calls "multi-grade," as Russell's compresence relation among qualities was in 1940 and 1948 (Hochberg, 2002b, 97-124). Moreover, and most crucially, given that diverse compresence tropes will be internally dependent on the different ordinary tropes that they combine—by their very nature—doesn't that mean that they are essentially different in that respect? Hence, how can they then be exactly similar? Recall that red tropes don't need to combine with the tropes they combine with to form objects. So how can compresence tropes be tropes of the same kind—since each must essentially differ from every other compresence trope via its essential connection to the terms it combines?

Trope theorists face other problems when they deal with time and space? Take the issue at its simplest—assuming places in space and moments of time. Two obvious problems arise (and variants of them will arise whatever your treatment of space and time is). How can one treat moments and places (say points in space) as tropes? Even with such points and moments one does not avoid spatial and temporal relations, as trope theorists seem to think you do in the familiar trope style of employing "foundations" (fundaments) within the terms. Suppose the natural numbers are objects. You require a relation like > to serially order them. One cannot simply say "9>7" is made true by 9 and 7. Does one really want to say it is "part" of the nature of 9 ("founded in" 9) to be greater than 7 (>6, etc., etc.) or that > is a relation but a "non-entity" relation or merely a "formal relation"? Serial order involves relations of certain logical kinds. Are not objects *at* places and "occurrences" taking place *prior to* others? Are not *being at* and *occupying* relations? And if you try to construe, as I think you can't anyway, things occurring prior to others in terms of their occurring at moments, questions about relations among the temporally ordered moments arise, similar to those about the numbers. Moreover, even if you do maintain that moments and places "found" the relations by their natures—are not their natures then sufficiently different so that the tropes that are identical with those natures are of different kinds, and hence not exactly similar? So how can we have a similarity circle of moments or one of places—without separating diverse aspects of such moments and places—and thus acknowledging they are complex? Or does one just stipulate that they can be exactly similar, yet essentially different in kind?

Smith's view of truth making, taking individuals as truth makers for relational statements, is tailor made for trope theories and makes explicit the problems of such theories as well as recent talk of a relation of "truth making." His analysis faces further problems, as he requires an existential conjunct so that in cases where existential statements like "E!∂" are false, but we nevertheless have "E!∂ $\rightarrow$ p" as true, we will not be able to conclude that ∂ necessitates p, a condition for taking ∂ as a truth maker. Yet, while he uses "p" as a schematic letter standing in for a particular judgment, the appropriate expressions it stands in for are not of the sort illustrated by "the judgment that a is F." Rather, they are simply sentences like "Fa." If it were otherwise, the modal apparatus, applicable to sentence-type expressions, would be inappropriate. But then it seems we deal more with Fregean-style propositions than with judgments, where the latter are judgments made by someone—Smith's judgment that a is diverse from b. But surely, the existence of a and of b (or even of the diversity, a≠b) is not such that the statement that they exist (or that the fact exists) stands in $\rightarrow$ to Smith's judgment that a is diverse from b. If the latter is a term of the $\rightarrow$ relation, it would seem to follow that Smith made such a judgment, while the existence of a and b (or of the fact of a being diverse from b) do not and should not entail that he did. The same point arises if one thinks in terms of propositions, rather than of judgments that were made. For, however one uses "necessary," since "E!a" trivially follows from itself, the conditional holding between "them" does so necessarily. Thus given the existence of a, on Smith's analysis "the judgment" that a exists is necessitated by the existence of a. But then "the judgment" must exist, whether anyone has explicitly made such a judgment or not. So what one should have is something on the order of a description of what will play the role of a truth maker and another description of what will play the role of a truth bearer. In short, given *both* an entity, (ι ß)(Ψß), and a truth, (ι †)(Ø†), we can take (ι ß)(Ψß) to be the truth maker for (ι †)(Ø†) by:

(TM) E!(ι ß)(Ψß) & (ι †)(Ø†) is true . ⊃ : (ι ß)(Ψß) makes (ι †)(Ø†) true ≡ . E! (ι ß)(Ψß) ⊨ (ι †)(Ø†) is true.

Such a statement simply specifies or stipulates the use of the phrase "... makes ___true" in context, given a suitable truth predicate. Smith defines such a relational predicate in a far more complex way, using the notion of necessitates, but (TM) captures, simply and less problematically, the idea involved by employing the standard use of "⊨" rather than "necessitates" and modal concepts. That not only avoids problematic uses of "necessitation" but the need to recognize propositional entities that are never apprehended, or judgments that are never made, as correlates of facts. For one can only speak of something making something else true if we have both "things" to start with—whether the truth bearers are sentences, propositions, thoughts or judgments. The simple point is that if "necessitates" is to have the force the term should have, the existence of something, along with an appropriate conditional statement being a necessary truth, will necessitate the existence of something else—an appropriate truth bearer. Smith speaks of judgments in connection with the variable "p" in "x necessitates p," but he clearly requires a sentence to represent a "specific judgment." Otherwise the use of "→" is not straightforward. But then he uses "specific judgment" in the sense of "specific proposition," and not, as he apparently intends to use it, in the sense of a judgment actually made by someone. This is not the case with (TM), as there are various alternatives open for the construal of "(ι †) (Ø†)," and the pattern of (TM) does not force the acceptance of "E! (ι †)(Ø†)" given "E! (ι ß) (Ψß)," which is as it should be if one does not accept a propositional entity for every fact that is a potential truth maker. Moreover, in his use of variables like "p," that can be replaced by sentences like "Fa," Smith implicitly employs the same pattern Searle and Armstrong use, one that implicitly recognizes possibilities or situations. For he must connect "Fa" to *something*, where the latter's existence makes "Fa" (or the proposition or content of a judgment it expresses) true.

Smith dismisses the issues surrounding true negations, as he dismisses the relation of diversity. This has an odd consequence for him. Consider "$(\exists x)\neg Fx$." That is an existential claim, so one would think it is true in virtue of the existence of something, and that cannot be a negative fact, like a's not being F or a's *lacking* F, for there are no such things according to Smith. Yet, it cannot be simply a, or the existence of a or any other particular that is not F, that is such a truth maker. That will not do, unless the particular is essentially not F. So it must be the *lack* or absence of a truth maker for "$(x)Fx$" that is the *truth maker* for the negation "$\neg (x)Fx$."

4c. Meaning and Intentionality

Assume one thinks to oneself what John Adams apparently expressed in his last words, "Jefferson lives." What takes place? Russell once sought to answer that question by providing an analysis of the fact involved, the fact that one judges that Jefferson lives, in terms of his multiple-relation account of intentional contexts. Let us consider it in a more traditional way, as an episode characterized in terms of there being a mental state of a certain kind with a specific content. We may ignore other senses of "thinks that," important as they are, such as being disposed to behave in a certain way, including performing "speech acts," and simply consider the episode as a mental state involving inner speech. Following the familiar line that distinguishes generic from content properties (recall Searle's contents and modes of intentional states), we will take such a mental state to have a generic property in virtue of which it is a state of belief rather than doubt. The situation that takes place can then be characterized in terms of there being an occurrence of an inner auditory token of "Jefferson" standing in a certain relation (temporal) to an inner utterance of "lives," where the tokens are taken to refer to Jefferson and to the property of being alive, respectively.

As we are considering it, the mental state has the content expressed by the sentence "Jefferson lives" since it is a complex, in which the component elements occur as representing a person and a property, and their doing so along with their standing in a certain relation forms a fact that is *taken to be true* if and only if the represented object has the represented property. Our earlier account of specifying truth grounds for atomic sentences involved three claims: (i) "Jefferson" refers to Jefferson; (ii) "lives" refers to the property of being alive; (iii) "Jefferson lives" is true ≡ Jefferson lives ≡ the fact with Jefferson as term and being alive as attribute exists. We can now employ them to characterize the content of a mental state, construed as a fact, in a way that attempts to avoid classical propositional entities—or Fregean thoughts and Meinongian contents—while not inadvertently introducing the non-existent situations we avoided in specifying the truth grounds for atomic statements. The task is to avoid introducing any basic properties that characterize such mental states and which refer to the state of affairs, actual or merely possible, of Jefferson being alive—to succeed in doing what we saw Searle failed to do—and what Strawson also failed to do, if we take seriously his introduction of "assertions." If we do not take mental states to be complexes or facts, we could recognize simple content properties and facts consisting of a mental state, as an individual object rather than a fact, exemplifying such a "content" character. Such primitive properties, like classical propositions and Frege's thoughts, would then be bearers of truth or falsity.

We can try to avoid such basic content characters by thinking in terms of mental tokens of morphologically different kinds, say auditory or visual, or even allowing for Wittgenstein's "thought elements" that function like linguistic patterns, to play the role of "Jefferson" and "lives" in the simple situation involving (i), (ii) and (iii) above. What is required for our simple case is that there be, first, elements of the mental state that occur as referring to the property and object involved and, second, some relation or structure that obtains between those elements, such that the resulting complex or fact is a mental state that functions like the atomic sentence. Such a mental state can thus be taken to be true if and only if Jefferson is alive. Obviously more must be said about what is involved in the use of the phrases "occur as referring to" and "taken to be true." Before doing that we can note how taking such content properties in terms of structured complexes allows for the easy resolution of some familiar contemporary disputes dividing "analytic" philosophers.

Consider the familiar questions that arise regarding the substitution of singular terms and predicates into intentional contexts, "quantifying into" such contexts and the scope of quantifiers in such contexts. We can speak of the fact that a person is in or has a mental state to involve a relation obtaining between the person and a mental state, where the state is one of belief, thus having an appropriate generic property. Just how one construes a "person" and the relevant relation is the sort of thing that has preoccupied philosophers, as diverse as Russell, in *The Analysis of Mind*, and Sartre, in *The Transcendence of the Ego*. Such questions in the philosophy of mind are not of concern here. All that is of concern here is how to characterize a state as having the content it has. That we can do, in the simple case we are considering, since the components of the state represent the object and the property and stand in some relation, call it "R," such that the fact that the components stand in R is linked to the statement that an appropriate fact exists. We need not specify what the elements of the mental state are, as we did specify them above. They could, for example, be auditory or visual tokens of the signs "Jefferson" and "lives" ("is alive") and "R" could be a spatial or temporal relation. This is not a version of J. B. Watson's behaviorism, where one takes silent thought to be non-vocal speech exhibited in bodily activities, such as changes in the laryngeal system that resemble what takes place in overt speech. Nor is it a matter of employing some mysterious and special "language of thought."

We have actually construed the characteristic that a belief state has in virtue of which it will be a belief of that kind in two ways. In one way it is taken to be composed of elements that literally are, and not merely might be, tokens (visual or auditory, for example) of "Jefferson" and of "lives" and which stand in R, and are such that the fact that they stand in R is linked by an appropriate semantic rule to the statement that the fact that Jefferson is alive exists. To put it simply, we have learned how to use the terms so that that is the case. This characterization differs slightly, but crucially, from the second way the matter was put, where the components were simply specified as representing the object and property, respectively, and standing in some appropriate relation, functioning as R does. Thus, they need not literally be tokens (visual, auditory, etc.) of "Jefferson" and "lives" ("is alive"). Call this more general characterization (B) and the first (A).

Given that "President Jefferson = Jefferson" we can then derive, from (A) or (B), and (i), (ii), and (iii), any statement resulting from the replacement of an occurrence of "Jefferson" (outside of the quoted contexts in (i), (ii) and (iii)) by an occurrence of "President Jefferson." This does not mean that one can derive a sentence stating that one has a mental state containing a constituent that is a token of the expression-type "President Jefferson," and, hence, in that sense that one has a belief that President Jefferson lives. But, if we are dealing with the situation as expressed by (B), rather than by (A), we can conclude that, in that sense, one has a belief that President Jefferson lives. But this is how matters should be. For the fact that I have such a mental state, as characterized in (B), does not mean that I have a mental state described in terms of containing a token of "President Jefferson." In the familiar cases involving the use of two "names" of the same thing, the present view allows for a simple solution. The same intentional property may be said to be involved, in the simple sense that the same object is intended, but there is a crucial difference in the manner the object is intended or represented.

The present view is a variant of taking the difference involved to be a matter of the "way" something is intended or thought of. This is reminiscent of the medieval notion of a mode or manner of signification that recurs in some interpretations of Frege's notion of a "sense" as a "way or manner of denoting." But it is not clear just what is involved in taking a Fregean sense, in Dummett's fashion, as the way the *Bedeutung* is given to us. Here it is clear what is meant, as we speak of different "ways" in terms of morphologically different kinds of mental tokens in inner mental states or in explicitly verbalized states—thinkings-out-loud—as Sellars sometimes put it and as Adams supposedly provided an instance of as he died. This is not meant as an interpretation of Frege. The view, like a view Goodman set out, is simply that, in one sense of "meaning," two tokens have (or are used with) the same meaning only if they are tokens of the same type. Goodman's version is actually more radical. Seeking to give a theory of meaning that appeals only to the extensions of words and to maintain his commitment to nominalism, he made use of a simple theme.

Consider the terms "Pegasus" and "Zeus." They do not denote anything, so their "extension" is the same, as are the extensions of the predicates "is identical with Pegasus" and "is identical with Zeus." But it is only their *primary* extension that is the same. If we consider compound expressions that contain the terms, such as "Pegasus-picture" and "Zeus-picture," we have terms that do not have the same extension. Taking "meaning" in terms of the extended extension of the term—encompassing primary, secondary, tertiary, etc. extensions, we can even extend the idea to give an account of "metaphorical meaning" in terms of the use of an expression to cover the application of predicates to objects. Thus, when we speak of someone being Napoleon-like, we use the term "Napoleon" to indicate certain characteristics ("applicable predicates," not properties) that enter into an extended construal of the extension. That allows Goodman to give an account of the metaphorical meaning or use of a term, while speaking only of extensions, albeit not primary extensions (1976; 1984, 70-80). He concludes that as no two terms have the same extended extensions they do not have the same meaning. A variant of his argument is compelling in the context of the present view. For, if we think in terms of a language where we have various terms or phrases to represent the same thing, and it is, as any adequate schema will be, non-extensional (or even if it is "extensional" in Goodman's "extended" sense of that term), then there will be contexts not allowing for substitution of tokens of different types, no matter what they represent (or fail to), while preserving truth value.

The above discussion clearly focuses on a very simple case. Most thoughts are hardly of that kind, though some surely are. It was also mentioned that we can accommodate the claim that one can have a mental state, a belief say, that has a content expressed by "Jefferson lives," where the mental state is taken to consist of unspecified constituents representing, respectively, the property of being alive and Jefferson, and standing in an unspecified relation or structure. Instead of having an "inner" token of some kind, we simply take there to be some element of the state that represents Jefferson. If one also holds that a mental state can be taken to have a content expressed by a sentence like "Jefferson lives," but not be a complex composed of representing constituents, one must introduce a primitive predicate representing a property that characterizes such a state, which is to introduce basic properties of mental states that can be taken to be reminiscent of Meinong's "contents" and Searle's propositional characters. These properties clearly play the role of classical propositional entities. Except for acknowledging such entities, the main features of the present analysis are not affected. For one would then simply take such properties to be "true" if and only if the specified described fact exists. One would have no need to take them to represent "situations" or Searle's conditions of truth that may or may not exist. Perhaps one could avoid appealing to such properties by adopting a form of mentalist "anomalous monism," paralleling Davidson's non-reductive materialism. Thus when various people had the same thought, or one person did on various occasions, there would be no need to speak of a common content property. There would just be different particular mental states. This seems rather empty, but is Davidson's anomalous monism different in that respect? That is not being facetious. It points to the general question of what one does in providing a philosophical account. While some think of talk of properties, facts, etc. as empty or pointless, the point is that one attempts to state what in fact is the case when a person has a belief or thought—the belief that Jefferson lives, in the above simple example. Such issues are neither resolved by giving an elaborate account of when it is appropriate to say things like "Jones believes that...." nor by considering the logic of anthropological studies of actual or hypothetical tribes (or of chimpanzees) that in "idealized" extreme situations call for "radical" interpretation or translation.

It has not been claimed that having a belief is "linguistic" in the sense that being in or having a mental state of belief requires the use of a language. Thoughts have been taken as complexes with constituents in representative roles, irrespective of whether such constituents are linguistic tokens of a specific "language," and, as just indicated, one can take thoughts to have simple content properties without basically altering the analysis. It should also be clear that the present view does not involve the absurdity (that Davidson at times embraced) of denying that relevant senses of "believes," "thinks," etc. are applicable to animals, infants, etc., since the latter do not have a suitable grasp of a "language." But we must still deal with what is meant by the phrases "taken to be true" and "occur as referring to" that were employed.

Reference is taken as a basic relation that obtains between elements of mental states, on the one hand, and the objects, properties, and relations that they represent, on the other. The causal conditions for such cases of direct intentional reference occurring, or the criteria employed to determine when, in certain cases, a reference is made, are ignored as irrelevant—just as questions about how one learns a language or those raised in an anthropologist's study of a group's linguistic usage are not relevant. It is simply assumed that a representative token (or auditory or visual image) can occur as referring to or directly intending an object, and that the notion of direct reference or direct intention is basic and is understood, as is what it means "to occur as referring." To put it another way, one knows in some cases what one refers to or intends and that one is referring to the object or property in question, whether or not one is also simultaneously "aware of" so doing. It is assumed that we know what it is for a mental token to occur as referring to (intending) something, as we usually know what we refer to when we use a demonstrative or indexical term. That sometimes we do not or are not clear is irrelevant. More important is the fact that the use of "refers to" is not "metaphorical," as Searle speaks of "being directed at" being a metaphor. Reference is an intentional relation between a thought element and its intentional object.

Understanding basic subject-predicate sentences involves knowing that for such sentences to be true certain facts must exist. The sense of "must" is captured by the tripartite biconditional, (iii), stating a semantic rule, as we earlier considered such rules in the discussion of truth grounds for atomic sentences or the thoughts they express. This incorporates what is correct about the notion that to know the meaning is to know the "conditions of truth" while, given rules like (i), (ii) and (iii), one also acknowledges the point that knowing the conditions of truth presupposes knowing the meaning. Moreover, by means of (A) and (B), an explanation has been given of what it is to understand that (believe that, think that, etc.) what a sentence expresses is true if and only if a described fact exists. Given what is expressed in (A) and (B), one can say that we know what it is to take a content or a mental state (with a certain content) to be true, just as we know what it is to directly refer to an object or a property or a relation. What has been done, for terms and atomic sentences, is to unpack the notion of "content" while avoiding the problematic possible facts of other accounts. Put another way, this can also be seen as taking truth to be a basic concept, irrespective of using semantic rules like (iii). We must not be misled by the fact that one is not acquainted with some relation, expressed by "taking to be true" or "taking to exist," as one may claim to be acquainted with reference (designates) while taking the latter as the basic intentional relation between an occurring thought element (mental token) and its intentional object. For we can be said to directly apprehend mental states that are instances of "taking something to be true" in cases involving relatively simple contents, just as we directly apprehend mental states that are cases of referring to specific objects and properties. I know what it is to take something to be true if and only if a certain fact exists, as codified in the semantic rules. And that is all that is required. One might, as already indicated, put the claim by saying that with respect to basic terms and atomic sentences there is an obvious sense in which the notions of reference (meaning) and truth are basic. Dealing with complex contents whose truth amounts to other contents or statements being true, such as, in a relatively simple case, taking a conjunction to be true if both conjuncts are true (rather than if a certain fact exists) is a matter of spelling out the details, and the lines for doing that are fairly standard. As one knows what it is to take an atomic sentence as true, given that one knows the logical forms involved, one knows what it is to take conjunctions, disjunctions, etc. to be true. The familiar systems of logic reflect such matters, as (iii) correlates with our knowing what it is to take an atomic sentence to be true. That there is a learning process involved is of no more relevance to the philosophical issues than that there are causal explanations of the process.

The role of (iii) and facts is crucial in this account of intentionality. For it is clear that what is asserted is not the "content" of the mental state, when one judges that Jefferson lives, but that a specific fact, linked by rules like (iii) to the content, exists. An early criticism of Frege by Russell is relevant to this and, in fact, it anticipated the use of Davidson's Great Fact argument as derived from Frege:

> Moreover, if Frege's view were correct on this point, we should have to hold that in an asserted proposition, it is the meaning, not the indication, that is asserted, for otherwise all asserted propositions would assert the very same thing, namely the true (for false propositions are not asserted). (1956, 504)

The issue about "asserted" and "false propositions" aside, what is pointed to is Russell's notion that what a proposition asserts must indicate what its truth ground is. Frege's view does not comply with this, as neither Davidson's nor Dummett's do.

In his defense of Frege's dismissal of a correspondence theory, Dummett claims that "for Frege a fact is simply a true thought" (1973, 369). If taken seriously this claim simply makes a thought its own truth ground. Moreover, to give the view some real content, one would have to (i) take it in the style of Moore's 1898-99 view that took true propositions to differ internally from false propositions in virtue of a constituent truth making or false making relation that combined the concepts in the proposition, or (ii) introduce a basic property of truth that some propositions instantiate, or (iii) take there to be facts consisting of true propositions standing in the denotation relation to the True. The commonsense core of a correspondence theory is hard to avoid.

4d. Access to The Abstract

It is remarkable that first order logic can be seen to amount to simple truths of propositional logic and rules like *modus ponens*, substitution, simplification, etc., depending on the system, together with an appropriate selection from rules like universal instantiation, existential generalization, etc. and "obvious" formulae of predicate logic. Patterns of similar structure and additions of a similar nature can be taken to yield a higher order logic. This may have contributed to Gödel's speaking of "perceiving" and "intuiting," as well as reasoning about, "real objects"—what is spoken of as his Platonism concerning mathematics and set theory. In a similar fashion, Russell claimed to "directly apprehend" logical forms and logical relations among them. While such notions are admittedly problematic, the diametrically opposed conventionalist move in logic and mathematics has a transparently hollow ring, whether that move follows the French fashion that includes Sartre's talk of being responsible for your own birth and Lacan's speaking of his daughter not being his daughter without language; or the Anglo-American "analytic" alternatives that talk of "language games," "ways of life," "inference tickets," "language-language" moves; or the pragmatists' emphasis on "the normative aspect" and the "social context" that logic is purportedly relative to; or the Viennese variant that culminated in the verification theory of meaning and Carnap's distinction between external and internal questions that led to the dismissal of the former. For Carnap's "internalism" is, in the end, a variant of conventionalism, as are the various forms of "anti-realism" and "internal realism" that it spawned, including the radical conventionalism of Goodman's charmingly written *Ways of World Making*.

That one employs model theory in dealing with the semantics of logical systems does not change the basic issue, in spite of the familiar features and problems that lead some to seek safety in misguided prudence. Thus they believe they are forced to think in terms of logic resting on axiomatic systems that inherently contain problems that require various "arbitrary" and unintuitive moves to ward off paradoxes. But conventionalism will not do, as an old point remains as cogent as ever. In order to discuss these matters sensibly our background framework employs a logical system that is codified along the lines indicated just above. Even the familiar paradox that faces conventionalism depends on the claim that if conventionalism is true it is, on its own terms, not true, and therefore not true. The "paradox" clearly assumes standard logic. The simple point is that either we begin with the fundamental logical truths in considering such matters or we do not begin at all. As Moore put it, in a completely different context that, in its way, was part of the foundation of analytic philosophy, the task is not to prove that logical truths are true but to articulate what recognizing them to be so involves.

Consider the logical form of monadic (first order) facts, Φx, and the function $(\lambda \Phi)(\lambda x)\Phi x$ that is parasitic on, but distinct from, it. They are distinct, as Russell recognized, since while Φx is the common form of the facts Fa and Gb, the function, for arguments, say F and a, has such a fact as its value. In a similar way we distinguish the property F from the function $(\lambda x)Fx$. The former is a constituent of (attribute in) the fact that a is F, while the latter is not but takes the fact as its value for the argument a.

We arrive at the form Φx by abstracting from a fact or several facts of the same form. What is it to "abstract"? It is simply to apprehend the common form as one apprehends the common color property of several objects of the same shade of red or the common relation holding of various circular shaped areas in a target. There is no mystery about abstraction. We can proceed to consider the sign "Φx" to be obtained from the sentences "Gb" and "Fa" by successively abstracting, in another, but quite precise sense of "abstracting," replacing the constants by a variable, to arrive at a sign to represent the common logical form of the facts Fa and Gb.

Russell recognized logical forms and claimed that we directly apprehend such forms as we directly apprehend universal properties and relations. The problem, which he did not raise and did not face, was justifying that what is apprehended provides the ground of logical truth. Perhaps one cannot do better but must simply reiterate a familiar idea, of which Russell's talk of direct apprehension and Gödel's of intuition and perception are simply variants. We recognize simple logical truths as such, whether we talk about doing so by the very meaning of "not", "all," etc. or whether we just leave it at that. Moore sometimes put things cryptically and poignantly by expressing points in ways that left little to add. One such case was his claiming that we sometimes know something and know that we know it without knowing how we know it. In short, one just knows, or "sees," that something is the case. Lindström echoes such a theme in discussing arithmetic:

> And when this principle is pointed out to us, we can immediately see that it is correct. ...
>
> You visualize...an ω–sequence. You then examine the imagined sequence ... and find that the LNP [least number principle] is, indeed, true. (2000, 126)

But in this case *visualizing* and *seeing* are not used synonymously. For he sees that LNP is correct in something like Moore's sense of immediately knowing it to be true, while his use of "visualize" is in the sense of imagining or "having an image of." We will shortly take up what I take to be his problematic uses of both "see" and "visualize" in that passage. But for the moment we will focus on a correct claim embodied in it—a claim that is in the tradition of Augustine's and Descartes' *cogito* and one that arises in the case of elementary logic.

One point that Augustine and Descartes were getting at is that since the *cogito* (whether construed as an argument or simply a proposition) is immediately seen to be "correct" (forgetting the use of "I" to represent a mental substance, that Nietzsche ridiculed, and the problems raised by the notion of a "self"), it is clear that there are obviously correct or "self-evident" truths. If the point the conventionalists make is that one must stop somewhere they are correct. But the claim that different stopping points are matters of choice or convention is another matter. We need neither seek to prove everything nor embark on the fruitless type of escalator ride practiced by those who semantically ascend in order to reduce all such issues to questions about linguistic items, practices and normative or pragmatic rules. In a sense that is ironic, one can then make a point about ontologically grounding logic by a use of Carnap's distinction between external and internal questions. For one way of looking at the matter is that when it comes to logic, some external questions about logic simply repeat internal questions. This comes out quite simply when we consider the classical laws of logic: excluded middle, non-contradiction, and identity. While it is true that all tautologies are equivalent, and as noted in (3d) equal, those are just a bit "more equal." For, they are embodied in the very setting out of the familiar truth tables in the context of a standard bivalent logic. We put a "T" or an "F" on every line (under a sentential letter) and we do not put both on any line —and diverse tokens of "T" and "F" are just that, diverse tokens that are constant or identical in their interpretation. What takes place in setting out truth tables for "p ∨ ¬ p" and "¬ (p & ¬ p)" to show that they are tautologies is that, in so doing, we employ the very laws of logic they express. Thus such laws or L-Truths are simultaneously internal formulae as well as external laws. There is no room for conventionalism in the case of propositional logic, and that is relevant to Lindström's and Gödel's critique of Carnap. (We may safely ignore idiosyncratic concerns with the "para-consistent," intuitionistic sensibilities and systems that are not bivalent.)

There is another point brought out by any standard system of propositional logic. It is complete. But to be a tautology is not understood in terms of being a theorem in such a formal system, construed in syntactical terms. Without what some would call the semantics furnished by the truth tables that are the means of interpreting the signs in terms of the appropriate propositional connectives or logical functions, it would not be a system of propositional logic. We know, from such a trivial example, that we do not need Gödel's celebrated result to distinguish between a formula being a (certain kind of) logical truth and its being a theorem in a formal system, since we do not explicate a formula's being a propositional tautology solely in terms of it being a theorem of a certain formal system. One must interpret that system, via talking about truth and falsity in conformity with the classical laws of logic. And that involves interpreting the logical constants as signs for the classical logical connectives—the truth functions.

There is an interesting historical sidelight to the issue, given that Quine's celebrated attack on the purported dogma of the synthetic-analytic dichotomy was directed, in part, at Carnap's *Meaning and Necessity*. As he broadened the attack of the early paper from its focus on the purported analyticity of propositions like "Humans are rational animals" to direct it at propositional and first order logic, he provided an impetus for contemporary conventionalism. The irony is that Carnap had already planted the seed of not distinguishing between logical and non-logical constants by employing shifting interpretations of the biconditional and identity signs in the very book Quine was attacking (Hochberg, 2001a, 357-65). And Carnap, by the very logic of his position, would have to allow that there is no "absolute" distinction between L-truths and those he called "F-truths." The distinction has to be relative to a schema, and so be "L-True in S." Oddly, Carnap's construal of arithmetical truth in terms of theoremhood involves, aside from its other problems, a kind of paradox. For he either makes use of a notion of truth that is external, in taking an arithmetical truth to be what is a theorem of a system, and hence, let us say, an S-theorem, and thus he has a pseudo-concept of truth in his own terms. Or, he understands "true" in relative terms, such as "true in S." What he must then do is hold that what is L-True in S (including the arithmetical truths among the L-truths as he does) is a theorem of S—i. e. follows from the rules of S. But that claim is utterly trivial as "being L-True" is stipulated to abbreviate "following from the rules." Thus he either makes a pseudo-claim or simply holds that what follows from the rules follows from the rules.

What we may speak of as the Frege-Russell construal of Peano arithmetic in terms of the ontology or theory of classes (or functions, or concepts, or properties) was motivated, at least for Russell, by the idea that just thinking of an omega sequence was not sufficient, to put it in Lindström's terms. Unless one either acknowledged that a subject matter was involved by recognizing definite "entities" or showed how the supposed arithmetical statements could be treated as purely formal truths along the lines of the "no class" theory of the first edition of *Principia*, one had no ground for speaking of arithmetical truths as true.

Wittgenstein attacked Russell's logicism in another way in the *Tractatus*. He took what amounts to a version of the Peano postulates to provide the common logical form that constituted elementary arithmetic, and which could have various applications, in counting objects for example. Thus he saw an analogy between such applications and the use of logically valid argument patterns, such as *modus ponens*, that can be applied to arguments with different statements as content. This led him to speak of arithmetic as *a logic*, as opposed to the logicist construal of Russell and Frege. Thus he set forth, albeit not that clearly, a form of structuralism in the *Tractatus*, thereby preparing the ground for what was to come in his later focus on rule following and language games (Hochberg, 1984, 313-320). Ironically, as we noted in an earlier chapter, Russell had claimed prior to Wittgenstein's writing his *Tractatus* that such a structuralist account would not do, since, for example, we would then have nothing definite as zero, but only the key characteristics the postulates conferred on a "zero" element. He argued that an adequate account could only be given by specifying such an element—irrespective of what one took such an element to be, so long as it satisfied the postulates. He also argued that unless we specified a precise interpretation, we could not claim that the postulates were true. (Recall, too, that Russell also had held that the elimination of signs that purportedly were signs for numbers would also suffice, so long as one then derived the familiar postulates for elementary arithmetic as theorems.) It is interesting to note that, if one accepts complex (structural) properties, one can simply take the Peano postulates to represent a complex property that is instantiated by what Lindström talks of as an omega sequence, and hence can be taken to be the ontological ground of elementary arithmetic. Wittgenstein might even have had something like this vaguely in mind in the *Tractatus*. If he did, his structuralism was ambivalent.

The same ambivalence marks Lindström's quasi-realism. On the one hand, it suggests a form of structuralism, while, on the other hand, it appears to be a variant of the idea that there is, via existential hypotheses, a subject matter for elementary arithmetic. The twist he gives to the view is that these are supposedly not really existential hypotheses about objects that are, to recall a phrase from Locke, "that I know not what," since the omega sequence is merely imagined and visualized. Since we can visualize the sequence, we need not make hypothetical existential claims. Thus his notion of "visualization" serves two functions. It provides a subject matter, hence seemingly avoiding mere structuralism or formalism, and, as we can visualize what need not be taken as existent, it purportedly avoids ontological commitments beyond the common sense idea that arithmetic has a subject matter. There is a further crucial role his quasi-realism and claims about visualization serve.

Concerned by the supposed problem of "access" to abstract entities, which Benacerraf (1996, 14-30) and others have reraised in recent times, Lindström's visualization of an omega sequence, and, subsequently, of the "branching tree" of the subsets of the elements of that sequence, provide him with a simple means of access to such elements and sets (though not, as he observes, to all of them). This is another motive behind his quasi-realism (2000, 126-127, 136-137). I will address the question of access after considering his philosophical assay of elementary arithmetic, and a portion of set theory—the portion furnished by an initial application of the power set axiom to the set of elements of an omega sequence.

Noting that philosophical analyses have little connection with what actually takes place in mathematical reasoning and proof, Lindström claims that an adequate subject matter for first order arithmetic is furnished by our ability to visualize an omega sequence without claiming that there really is such a sequence. This ability to "visualize" without ontological commitment to "entities" is responsible for the phrase *quasi-realism*, since, such a form of realism holds that "there is a subject matter" without making any claims about the ontological status of that subject matter—whether there really exists such an omega sequence, and its constituents, that provides the subject matter for first order arithmetic. Hence it is merely "quasi-real," but its being so suffices to resolve the access problem, since our visualizing such a sequence gives us access to it, while supposedly allowing us to avoid Gödel's Platonism, Russell's realism about logical forms, and so forth. To help us see what he means, Lindström likens the visualization of such a sequence to visualizing an unreal object, like a unicorn. The latter, too, would provide a subject matter for a thought or a description. But an obvious and familiar question arises about the truth of claims like "The unicorn I am imagining has only one horn" (which Lindström takes to be clearly true) and "The golden mountain is golden." The same problems face Lindström's quasi-realism. That is one sort of problem that led Russell to his logicism—the need to take the Peano postulates and the familiar arithmetical truths as true—not merely "true of" some imagined object or possible structure. Lindström also claims that the visualization of the familiar branching tree will serve to provide a "quasi-real" subject matter for set theory, in so far as it is limited to the results of the power set axiom as confined to the sets of elements of the original omega sequence. Beyond that his powers of visualization do not apply.

The reasoning is not convincing. What it comes down to is the claim that we deal with a certain structure that we assume to be the structure involved in certain "visualizations." But surely, if we take the term "visualize" literally, and not as a variant of "conceive of" or "imagine," the visual objects are simply the components of the image of a tree branching, with the thought that it goes on ever branching, in the one case, and of a visual sequence of elements, which is thought to indefinitely proceed off into the distance, in the other. When he looked into the black square in his celebrated painting "Black on White," Malevich claimed to see infinity—to be "drawn into" the infinite. I can understand, in a way, the experiences both the logician and the painter are trying to articulate, but I find it hard to believe that Lindström visualizes infinity any more than Malevich did, or that what he visualizes is what mathematical theories are about, however helpful and suggestive such "visualizing" may be to a working mathematician and logician. But if that is not what such theories are about, how do we get to the subject matter of arithmetic and a portion of set theory from such imaging or imagining?

As I see it, two things mislead Lindström. One is that he sees there to be a fundamental difference between the case of the unicorn and that of the omega sequence. For certain problems that seem to arise about the case of the unicorn do not arise about the sequence. We might not be able to ask about the weight of the imagined unicorn, for example, since our imagining a unicorn need not determine it to be of any particular weight. This should recall our earlier discussion of Meinong's "incomplete" objects and their connection to his views about our thoughts of non-existent objects. For once we imagine an omega sequence, any question relevant to its being such a sequence is answered—since any omega sequence will do. In Meinong's sense, such a sequence is not then an "incomplete" object. But this pattern of thought is clearly along the lines of the structuralist's way of thinking. Moreover, one might say the same sort of thing about the unicorn—any question relevant to its being a case of imagining a unicorn, such as its having a horn, can be answered. All Lindström is pointing out, in his example, is that if there were to be a real unicorn it would have to have weight—while there is no property that a real, as opposed to a quasi-real, omega sequence would have to have—since the imagined omega sequence is imagined as having all the properties necessary for it to be a "real" omega sequence. But such matters do not affect what is at issue. One might say that to visualize a unicorn is to visualize a horse with one horn—as that is what is essential to its being a unicorn, and why visualizing a cow with one horn in the middle of its head would not be to visualize a unicorn. But there is clearly not a subject that I speak about when I say "The unicorn I visualize has one horn" as opposed to "The image I now have (visualize) is an image of such and such a kind." For there is no unicorn that there is an "image of," though there is an image of a certain kind. The same is clearly true of Lindström's visualized omega sequence. But he does not wish to take images as the subject matter of arithmetic—but what "is visualized" in the sense in which a unicorn, and not an image of a unicorn, is what is supposedly visualized—as we easily speak of visualizing a unicorn, and not of visualizing a unicorn-image.

The obvious questions are not about the difference between unicorns and omega sequences or about what I may find hard to believe, but about what is really visualized in such cases and of what relevance that is to the issues—of the connection between what is actually visualized and what Lindström speaks of as the subject matter of first order arithmetic and the portion of set theory he deals with. Here we raise questions of what some would call a phenomenological nature. Lindström mentions that he does not want to enter the quagmire posed by the issues of intentionality, and rightly so. But there is a two-fold aspect to those problems—or, better, two problems that are relevant, and one of them cannot be avoided. That is the second thing that misleads him and is probably responsible for his not seeing that the quagmire must be confronted. For one aspect of the problem of intentionality concerns whether the visual object—the image—however vague, is of an object. That there is an image, as a visualized object, we may take for granted, as we need not be materialists. And, from other papers Lindström has written about such non-logical matters, he clearly allows for such an image. That image is, as many have put it, an intentional object, in the sense that it is the object of a kind of mental act or, perhaps less problematically, mental activity—for some do not like to speak of acts in such contexts. And, for this issue, as Lindström indicates, no particular analysis of intentionality need be presupposed. That does not mean, however, that problems such analyses purport to resolve need not be considered. Such a case of visualization, we then assume, unproblematically involves an image—I use the somewhat vague term "involves" in an attempt to avoid begging any questions.

Nelson Goodman's terminology is helpful here, even if his philosophy is not. There is, we can say, a unicorn-image. The point of the terminology is to avoid saying that there is an image that is an image "of" a unicorn—for, of course, there are no unicorns—mythological or non-mythological. Thus we divide the problem of intentionality into two aspects. One aspect has to do with the relation, if such there be, between the intentional mental state and the image, the object of the state (act). The other is complex, for it poses two questions. One concerns the connection, if any, between a mental state or, simply, a thought or case of imagining, and a non-existent object; the other is a question about the connection, if any, between the image, which we take to exist, and a mythological creature, which does not. Lindström's presentation of his quasi-realism dodges the issues posed by the latter questions by focusing on an image, a unicorn-image, for example, as the location of the thorny issues of intentionality. Thus he can say that it is clear that there is such an image, to put it my way, while simultaneously saying that he will not take up the issues posed by intentionality. But the issues posed by his quasi-realism really concern the other questions—questions that we would raise by talking about the image, that is admittedly apprehended, being a unicorn-image. Is the subject matter of arithmetic composed of images? Hardly. Are numbers visualized? Hardly. What then is it that he visualizes? What are the elements of the omega sequence he visualizes and what is it to visualize such a sequence? I have suggested that if he is visualizing images, as he visualizes a unicorn-image, he is really a hidden structuralist, both about arithmetic and about the portion of set theory he basically deals with. Lindström unequivocally denies that that is what he is visualizing. Consider the context from which I extracted the above short citation:

> Now, what happens when you see that the LNP [least number principle] is correct? As we have seen, it is not plausible to say that you are examining an abstract structure. But the answer, or at least one possible answer, is really quite obvious (and simple-minded, almost trivial): You visualize (picture to yourself, form a mental picture of) "the sequence of natural numbers," in other words, an ω-sequence. You then examine

> the imagined sequence with respect to the LNP and find that the LNP is, indeed, true.
>
> Of course talk about imagined structures is bound to give rise to (philosophical) objections. How can I, for example, talk about a structure without assuming that it exists, and thus, is not just imagined? And what kind of object is an imagined structure? It has to be something, it seems, and not just nothing. Etc. etc. These are (pseudo?) problems I don't pretend to be able to deal with. But I don't feel that, for my present purposes, it is at all important to deal with them. Surely, there is some sense in which I can imagine, for example, a unicorn and then speak about "that" unicorn, saying, for instance, (truly) that it has four feet and one horn, without (thereby) assuming that I am actually imagining, or speaking about, an existing unicorn or some other more or less mysterious, possibly intentional, object. And it is in this sense that I claim that we are able to speak about an imagined ω-sequence without presupposing that we are imagining an existing ω-sequence or, indeed, that there are any ω-sequences at all in the real world.
>
> In particular I am not saying that the natural numbers are mental objects or that the sequence of natural numbers is mental, that these objects exist in the mind, whatever that would mean. We imagine the ω-sequence as existing "outside," and independently of, ourselves, as being timeless and unchangeable; and we can do this without contradiction, just as we can imagine a unicorn as being a material object existing independently of ourselves. (2000, 126-27)

This explanation leaves much to be desired and suggests an alternative interpretation of what he is really doing, as opposed to what he may think of himself as doing.

As we read the above passage it seems clear that, in talking about visualizing, Lindström is really talking about intending or apprehending or perceiving—in the manner of Russell and Gödel. Notice how he moves from visualizing an omega sequence or a unicorn to imagining that such a sequence or such a creature exists independently of ourselves. One could just as easily say that we imagine such a sequence or such a creature, as we could dream of one or imagine a story about one, and also imagine that it exists. To imagine a unicorn is not to imagine that it exists. That seems straight-forward enough, but we tread on familiar and problematic ground that recalls Anselm's ontological argument and Kant's examination of our purportedly imagining a real and a merely imaginary coin. What do we do when we imagine a unicorn? And what do we do when we imagine that the unicorn we are imagining exists? (Can I visualize Lindström's visualizing of a unicorn? Or do I simply imagine that he is visualizing one?)

Lindström is right to avoid what he speaks of as the problems of intentionality. For, as I see it, he combines aspects of structuralism with aspects of realism. Just as Carnap is what we might call an "internal Platonist," Lindström may be thought of as a "quasi-realist" in combining two incompatible positions, structuralism and realism—the use of "quasi" reflects the structuralism. But there is no middle ground on which to rest his philosophy of mathematics—no refuge to be found between structuralism and realism. They simply do not go together. Like some of the exotic particles of physics, such a view is too unstable to stay with us. Interestingly, what Lindström does is reminiscent of the views of an earlier, relatively unknown philosopher from Göteborg, Ivar Segelberg, who combined Husserl's phenomenology with the analytic tradition of the Swedish "Uppsala School." Facing related problems of intentionality and ontology, though not specifically of arithmetic, Segelberg distinguished between intentional objects and ontological objects (1999, 247-48, 276, 290-93). But he never made clear just what the ontological status of a non-real object of thought is, and, in retrospect, the phrase "quasi-real" would very aptly characterize Segelberg's talk of such objects of intentional acts. Lindström's view is equally ambivalent in that respect, which is why questions about intentional objects and intentionality point to a crucial aspect of his discussion.

He takes the so-called problem of access seriously. Based, as it is on misguided causal theories of reference and purported puzzles generated by abstraction and our possession of general ideas, the problem of access is a classic pseudo-problem. Lindström notes in his paper, as Benacerraf does in his, that the problem stems from our supposed ability to have "abstract ideas." That, as both Lindström and Benacerraf also note, led Plato to his version of the doctrine of innate ideas—the Platonic doctrine of "recollection." It may also have inspired Augustine to rely on divine illumination and, in a sense, culminated in Descartes' explicit doctrine of innate ideas that, on the standard view, gave rise to the empiricist attacks and the development of an implicit empiricist "meaning criterion." [We may ignore the historical question as to whether the controversy was really occasioned by the views on innate ideas held by Herbert of Cherbury, not Descartes.] The history, from the time of Locke, Berkeley and Hume, to the days of the Vienna Circle, Oxbridge analysis, the contextualist-idealism of Quine, Sellars and Davidson, and the refuge some find in causal theories of anything and everything, mixed with variants of nominalism, conventionalism, behaviorism and materialism, still muddle the philosophical landscape. This can be seen by a simple comparison.

Benacerraf finds Gödel's use of the terms "perception'" and "intuition" unclear when Gödel writes:

> ...we do have a perception also of the objects of set theory, as is seen from the fact that the axioms force themselves upon us as being true. I don't see why we should have less confidence in this kind of perception, i. e. in mathematical intuition, than in sense perception, which induces us to build up physical theories.... (1964, 271)

Benacerraf comments: "...what is missing is precisely what my second principle demands: an account of the link between our cognitive faculties and the objects known" (1996, 26). What is interesting about Benacerraf's complaint is its resemblance to D. Lewis's objection to qualities like colors:

> ...I have complained about the difficulty of understanding the relation that allegedly relates concrete things to the abstract simple possibilities—propositions or properties—that they realize... Its a nasty predicament to claim that you somehow understand a primitive notion, although you have no idea how you could possibly understand it. (1991, 35-36)

Ignore the haziness of the notion of an "abstract possibility" that Lewis interjects. What is going on is precisely the line of thought that led British empiricists to reject our having "general ideas" and to their primitive "imagist" conception of thought. There is no difference between the suspect apprehension of an "abstract" quality, say the color yellow, taken as a common quality, or universal, along with the "abstract" relation of instantiation and the apprehension of sets, or other mathematical objects, and mathematical truths. This has always been a problem for some nominalists and, as in Lewis's case, physicalists, though Lewis apparently has no problem apprehending possible worlds and their counterpart inhabitants. Nor does he have a problem with mereological sums and a singleton functor that in some mysterious way forms a singleton, that is a simple without parts, by operating on an element, and also mysteriously relates the element to its singleton. All this is accomplished, supposedly, without recognizing either a mysterious (abstract) relation or a singleton forming operator.

Suppose we make an effort to consider what we are told we can't consider, two colors that are specific shades of yellow and of red, that we will call "Y" and "R" respectively, and the truths that R is different from Y, that R is darker than Y and, let us assume, that Lewis and Benacerraf prefer R to Y. Universals, like R and Y, are simply objects presented in experience, just as individual things and facts are. There is nothing mysterious about that, so long as one does not confuse the fact that universals are presented or directly apprehended with the claim that what is presented is not merely the abstract objects or universals but the fact that they are universals. That is another matter. One can argue about whether universals like Y and R are spatial objects. But if one holds that they are localizable, as some realists like Armstrong do, then one gives up certain standard laws that apply to particulars, such as not being at different places at the same time or the asymmetry and irreflexivity of spatial relations like *left of*, as occurring in the perceptual field. It is simpler to take them as non-spatial and non-temporal, while recognizing that they are instantiated by spatio-temporal objects. So what it all comes down to is really not a question about mathematical realism or mathematical truth, but the classical problem of universals that is complicated by an extreme nominalist view being combined with a causal theory of reference and meaning.

Extreme nominalism is bankrupt as a philosophical position and we need not go over the familiar arguments against such a view. Nor need we reiterate the problems we earlier considered that are faced by causal theories of reference of the sort Benacerraf starts with. But there is a simple point to be made about Benacerraf's commitment to a causal account. One must wonder what he can possibly take *causality* to be. He casually speaks about a causal relation connecting our knowledge or cognitive activity and the (intentional) objects of such knowledge and activity. But what is a causal relation for him? He speaks of a causal relation, but never explains just what a relation is and how the causal relation itself (or any relation, as opposed to the terms standing in it) is in physical space-time. Suppose there is not a causal relation that in fact obtains between things or events or universals, etc. That is, suppose one adopts a Humean style regularity account of causality. Then the question becomes: How can the existence of an abstract entity be regularly connected to the apprehension of such an entity? The answer is then obvious: the existence of such an entity is a "necessary" condition for its apprehension—where imagining is not a form of apprehending. There is no difference between the black truffle Benacerraf speaks of and the universal black or the set of natural numbers, if such there be. In the case of the black truffle there is, in ordinary terms, the context provided by the physics and physiology of perception in our seeing such an object. But even there, we should distinguish, as Benacerraf apparently does not, the truffle from the fact that it is black. (Recall that, for Davidson, facts could be dismissed since they could not be located in space.) And it is not clear how the distinction between the object, the property and the state of affairs consisting of the object having the property, crucial to numerous philosophical attempts to resolve various issues, finds its proper place in the ordinary causal account that explains what happens when we see a black truffle. How does the property black, which, let us assume, is not a spatio-temporal object, causally interact with the eye? How does the state of affairs, which is also not sensibly located in space, do so? And, of course, the causal account stops with physical connections, such as light rays reflecting or being absorbed by an object and its surrounding objects and affecting the cones of the eye, when we talk of the phenomenon of perceiving a truffle. We can ignore the mental state itself or, on some accounts, the phenomenal object that is what we really apprehend in experience, though, interestingly, on some classic philosophical accounts, the truffle is either an inferred cause or a logical construction out of phenomenal objects. We will return to that shortly. First, let us consider some other cases.

 Take Russell's case of an after image, which furnished a ground for his rejecting physicalism and neutral monism. We can give a causal story, in a manner, of the occurrence of such things—i. e. the physical and physiological accounts that go with such experiences. But the perceived object, the after image itself, does not enter into such a causal chain as the cause of its perception, unless one simply means that the occurrence or existence of the image is a necessary condition for the apprehension of the image. Nor is the after image localized in physical space, unless one absurdly identifies it with a state of one's brain. Yet it may be said to be a partial cause of a memory of having had such an image, if one, say, reports the annoying persistence of such things to a doctor. But how does the after image enter into such a causal chain as it is not in physical space? Perhaps it does so via its assumed correlation with states of the central nervous system that are so localized. But, then, obviously, something like that also takes place when one apprehends a universal quality or thinks of a natural number or grasps an arithmetical or logical truth. If such connections are the key to causal interaction, whatever one means by causality, then there is no mystery about our causal interaction with arithmetical entities and truths over and above the questions about how we come to have general ideas and the perplexities of the mind-body problem. This is brought out by a slightly different kind of case.

Assume we perceive that an object, a, is black, that another object, b, is green, and that a is larger than b. If properly prepared, we see or apprehend that the two states of affairs, a's being black and b's being green, have the same logical form and that that form differs from the logical form of the state of affairs of a's being larger than b. If there are states of affairs or facts, there are not only the constituent terms and attributes or relations, but the logical forms of such facts as well. Such forms are clearly abstract objects, as that phrase is used. How do we manage to apprehend them? I don't know, nor am I sure that the question is either clear or sensible. However, I am quite certain that I apprehend, and do not imagine, in Lindström's sense, that the form of the fact is $\prod xy$. I don't know the answer to the question about how I know anymore than I know why we have phenomenal experiences of a certain kind when the brain is in a certain state. In this latter kind of case we have discovered numerous correlations. I suspect one does the same, without specifically focusing on the question of logical form, in the work on the psychology and physiology of pattern perception. The mystery, if such there be, is not about whether there are logical forms. One knows what I am speaking of, even if one doubts that a viable philosophical theory will include such items in its ontological inventory. Whatever mystery there is reduces to our ability to have general ideas—to grasp universals, whether they be qualities like green, relations like larger than or logical forms like Φx and $\prod xy$. The simple fact is that we can do so since we obviously do do so. We need not revert to the absurdities of nominalistic empiricism, which led to imagist conceptions of thought in the seventeenth, eighteenth and nineteenth centuries and to physicalism and causal theories of reference in the twentieth.

Logical forms are a variety of abstract object, but they appear to highlight a different aspect of the problem that is involved in the present issue. The existence of colors and pitches are hard to deny, though, since many do, we find nominalists and deflationists absurdly twisting in the wind and speaking of predicates being satisfied by objects. In extreme cases, we even find the claims that without a conceptual scheme provided by a representational system, a language for example, the earth does not revolve around the sun (Goodman), hurricanes and births would not take place (Sartre) and one's child would not be one's child (Lacan). Such apparent absurdities are not my present concern. In the case of logical forms we must acknowledge that we recognize that some facts are of the same form. How we come to that recognition I do not know. But I am not embarrassed in the sense that D. Lewis thinks one who does so must be, just as I am not embarrassed about not knowing why one has mental states and experiences correlated with physical states. Undoubtedly Lewis would be, and thus seeks to escape embarrassment by fleeing to refuge in the philosophical absurdity that is materialism. The problems are the perennial puzzles of the mental and the physical and of "abstraction." But such problems need not lead one to deny the obvious. As Moore once pointedly observed, there are things that we know, and know that we know, without knowing how we know. One who claims not to know that facts like a being black and b being green are of the same form either pretends not to know what he does know or not to understand what he does understand or, for some reason, is unable to grasp what is readily available. That appropriate linguistic training may be a causal condition for obtaining such comprehension is irrelevant. You may be said to "see" that they are the same—but it is not at all clear that one uses "see" in the same sense that one does when one speaks of seeing that two objects are of the same color. It is probably more appropriate to speak of realizing or apprehending, rather than of visually observing. But that is of little import.

The similarity between the problem supposedly posed by the lack of "causal power" of an abstract entity and the familiar problems posed by the recognition of mental and physical entities that are taken to causally interact is worth emphasizing here. Physicalists avoid the problem, as do Berkeleyian style idealists and Humean phenomenalists. But the latter are rare these days, while the former are abundant. If one commonsensically acknowledges both the mental and the physical, how is the problem of their causal interaction any different from that supposedly posed by universal properties or sets interacting with our cognitive states as objects of such intentional states (assuming that such interaction is causal in some sense)? It is clear that Benacerraf is thinking in terms of it being a necessary condition for causal interaction that the cause and the effect be in space and time. Thus he speaks of space-time worms (Russell's physical space-time lines):

> It is claimed that X knows that p. We think that X could not know that p. What reasons can we offer in support of our view? If we are satisfied that X has normal inferential powers, that p is indeed true, etc., we are often thrown back on arguing that X could not have come into possession of the relevant evidence or reasons: that X's four-dimensional space-time worm does not make the necessary (causal) contact with the grounds of the truth of the proposition for X to be in possession of evidence adequate to support the inference (if an inference was relevant). The proposition p places restrictions on what the world can be like. (1997, 23)

But then it is clear that the problem of abstract entities is the same as the supposed problem about mental entities. So an unstated presupposition is involved besides his two acknowledged principles—a commitment to physicalism. That is in addition to presupposing extreme nominalism —that predicates do not refer to properties but are "satisfied" or "true of" or "refer to" particular objects—the objects that would be said to have the properties if one recognized the latter.

In a totally different vein, R. Grossmann claims to perceive numbers and has, in a number of works, repeatedly argued that numbers are quantifiers (1983, 312-315). His argument for perceiving numbers is simple. Suppose I perceive that the object b stands in the relation R to the object c. He takes that to involve perceiving the fact, bRc, the objects b and c, and the relation R. Assume that this is correct. Next, consider that b and c are the only two objects on a table and that I perceive that there are two objects on the table. Grossmann concludes that since I perceive the fact that there are two objects on the table, I must perceive the number two, as I must perceive the relation R in the previous case. But then one must be prepared to assert that one perceives "and" since one perceives that a is red and square. That aside, the pattern follows an old argument of Bergmann's that one perceives the universal quantifier "all" (the quantifier, not the quantifier sign "(x)"), since one perceives, to adapt the example, that *all* the things on the table are cups. Of course if Bergmann is correct then one can construe Grossmann's purported fact involving the number two in terms of the facts that b is on the table, that c is on the table and that only b and c are on the table—with the last taken as a general fact involving a quantifier. Thus there is no need to talk of perceiving numbers. Grossmann goes on to argue that numbers are really quantifiers. But his view simply amounts to taking a well known theme from Mostowski, as well as an idea in Carnap's *Logical Syntax of Language*, and offering it as a philosophy of arithmetic. Frege implicitly suggested that quantifiers are higher level concepts—an idea Russell developed into the claim, not always clearly put, that existence was a function of functions and did not apply to particulars. Thus, in a logically correct linguistic schema, one would not have sentences like "b exists" but could have sentences like "Lions exist," taken to be of the form $(\exists x)\Phi x$.

One of the early ideas of Carnap and others of the Vienna Circle was the notion that a statement in which only logical signs occurred was either logically true or logically false. The obvious problem with this claim was posed by cardinality statements like "$(\exists x)(y)(x=y)$", "$(\exists x)(\exists y)(x \neq y \ \& \ (z)(z=x \lor z=y))$," etc., which characterized a domain in that they were true in any domain of the appropriate cardinality but false in any domain of a different cardinality. As such statements can be spoken of as "valid" for a kind of domain, one can replace statements specifying cardinalities by "numerical quantifiers," such as "$(\exists_2 x)\Phi x$" for "$(\exists x)(\exists y)(x \neq y \ \& \ \Phi x \ \& \ \Phi y \ \& \ (z)(\Phi z \supset (z=x \lor z=y)))$," and consider class abstracts formed from such signs as representing higher level classes. Thus the numerical quantifiers can be viewed as classes of classes, much as Russell took natural numbers (ignoring the no-class theory). This is already involved in Russell's account of definite descriptions and later in Carnap's treatment of numerical predicates in *Logical Syntax of Language*. The problem with Grossmann's turning this simple point into a philosophy of arithmetic is that his primitive numerical quantifiers are really understood as abbreviations of the traditional formulations. If purported numerical quantifier signs, like "($\exists$2x)" (Grossmann uses signs like "(2x)" following the use of "($\exists$x)" and takes the existential quantifier to express "some," not "there exists"), are really taken as basic a fundamental problem arises—a problem that is similar to one faced by so called "adverbial theories" of mind. For, if there is to be any force to the claim, then it must follow that if there are three things that are Φ there are at least two things that are Φ, with the numerical quantifiers taken as primitive expressions. But "($\exists$3x)Φx," with "($\exists$3x)" as a primitive expression, does not entail "($\exists$x)($\exists$y)(x$\neq$y & Φx & Φy)," or even "¬($\exists$2x) Φx," by standard logical rules. So he must appeal to additional axioms or basic laws linking such statements. That makes his analysis pointless. Treating "($\exists$3x)" along Carnap's familiar lines, the entailments are trivial. The same sort of problem is present for those who talk of mental states or minds "adverbially," in the fashion of R. Chisholm (1976, 48-52) and Sellars. Thus one hears of "perceiving two-ly" and "perceiving red-ly," rather than of perceptions of a red datum or of two objects. For Chisholm this was simply a matter of avoiding objects like sense data. For Sellars, however, it was part of a strategy to arrive at materialism by first removing the red datum and replacing it by a characteristic of "the mind"—perceiving red-ly. Then, such a characteristic was transposed into a characteristic of a neural state, as a mind became a neurological system capable of being in appropriate states. But aside from the strange and forced terminology of the adverbial theory of mind, as it came to be called, one cannot obtain the required entailment that if one sees three red spots one sees at least two such spots. What Sellars and Chisholm were forced to do was talk about the analogy with cases where there are supposedly non-problematic physical objects (red objects, three objects, etc.), as in normal cases of physical perception. Perceptual states of persons were assumed to be sufficiently similar in cases of normal physical perception and in cases of perceptual experience that were not apprehensions of physical objects (cases involving after images, hallucinations, etc.) This type of move was adopted by central state materialists, such as Armstrong, J. C. C. Smart and U. T. Place, who appealed to similar purported analogies and supposed similarities of neuro-physiological states to avoid acknowledging objects such as after images (Smart, 1959; Armstrong, 1999, 72; Hochberg, 2001b, 253-72). Such solutions, like Grossmann's, are obviously *ad hoc* and hardly solutions.

REFERENCES

Angelelli, I. 1982: Frege's notion of Bedeutung, Proceedings of the sixth international congress of logic, methodology and philosophy of science, Amsterdam.
___1993: Critical remarks on M. Dummett's "Frege and Other Philosophers," Modern Logic.
Armstrong, D. M. 1997: A World of States of Affairs, Cambridge.
___1999: The Mind-Body Problem, Boulder.
___ 2000: Difficult Cases in the Theory of Truth Makers, The Monist, 83, (1).
Austin, J. L. 1961: Philosophical Papers, J. O. Urmson and G. J. Warnock (eds), Oxford.
Benacerraf, P. 1996: "Mathematical Truth." In The Philosophy of Mathematics, W. D. Hart, (ed) Oxford.
Bernays, P. 1964: On Platonism in Mathematics. In Philosophy of Mathematics, P. Benacerraf and H. Putnam (eds), Englewood Cliffs, NJ, originally 1935.
Beth, E. W. 1959: The Foundations of Mathematics, Amsterdam.
Bosanquet, B. 1948: The Essentials of Logic , London.
Bradley, F. H. 1897: Appearance and Reality , New York.
___1944: Essays on Truth and Reality, Oxford.
___1944a: On Truth and Copying. In Bradley, 1944.
___1958: The Principles of Logic, Vol I, Oxford.
Brandom, R. 1994: Making It Explicit: Reasoning, Representing, and Discursive Commitment, Cambridge, Mass.
Broad, C. D. 1953: Translator's Preface. In A. Hägerström, 1953, Inquiries into the Nature of Law and Morals, Uppsala.
Campbell, K. 1990: Abstract Particulars, Oxford.
Carnap, R. 1956: Meaning and Necessity, 2nd edition, Chicago.
___1956a: Empiricism, Semantics, and Ontology. In Carnap, 1956.
___1959: Introduction to Semantics, Cambridge, Mass.
Chisholm, R. M. 1976: Person and Object, La Salle, Ill.
Church, A. 1943: Carnap's Introduction to Semantics, Philosophical Review, 52.
Davidson, D. 1967: Truth and Meaning, Synthese, 17.
___1969: True to the Facts, The Journal of Philosophy, 66.
___1986: Essays on Actions and Events, Oxford.
___2001: Subjective, Intersubjective, Objective, Oxford.
Demos, R. 1917: A Discussion of a Certain Type of Negative Proposition, Mind, 26.
Donellan, K. 1966: Reference and Definite Descriptions, Philosophical Review, 75.
Dummett, M. 1973: Frege: Philosophy of Language, New York.
___1978: Truth and Other Enigmas, Cambridge, Mass.
___1978a: Truth. In Dummett, 1978, originally 1959 with 1972 postscript.
___1978b: The Philosophical Significance of Gödel's Theorem. In Dummett, 1978, originally 1963.
___1978c: The Philosophical Basis of Intuitionist Logic. In Dummett, 1978, originally 1973.

___1991: Frege Philosophy of Mathematics, Cambridge, Mass.
___2002: What is Mathematics About? In D. Jacquette (ed), Philosophy of Mathematics, Oxford, originally 1994.
Evans, G. 1982: The Varieties of Reference, Oxford.
Evnine, S. 1991: Donald Davidson, Stanford.
Frege, G. 1953: The Foundations of Arithmetic, J. Austin (trans), Oxford.
___1967: The Basic Laws of Arithmetic, vol. 1, sec. 1-52, M. Furth (trans), Berkeley.
___1968: The Thought: A Logical Inquiry, A. M. and M. Quinton (trans). In Essays on Frege, E. D. Klemke (ed), Urbana.
___1970: On Sense and Reference. In Translations from the Philosophical Writings of Gottlob Frege, P. Geach and M. Black (eds), Oxford.
___1975: Wissenschaftlicher Briefwechsel, Hamburg.
Geach, P. 1970: Russell on Meaning and Denoting. In Essays on Bertrand Russell, E. D. Klemke (ed), Urbana.
___1971: Mental Acts, London.
Goodman, N. 1952: On Likeness of Meaning. In L. Linsky (ed) Semantics and the Philosophy of Language, Urbana, originally 1949.
___1976: Languages of Art, Indianapolis.
___1978: Ways of World Making, Indianapolis.
___1984: Of Minds and Other Matters, Cambridge, Mass.
Gödel, K. 1964: "What is Cantor's Continuum Problem?" In Philosophy of Mathematics, P. Benacerraf and H. Putnam (eds), Englewood Cliffs, NJ, as revised, originally 1947.
___1986/1995: Is Mathematics Syntax of Language?. In S. Feferman, et. al. (eds), Kurt Gödel Collected Works, Vol. III, Oxford.
Griffin, N. 1991: Russell's Idealist Apprenticeship, Oxford.
Grossmann, R. 1983: The Categorial Structure of the World, Bloomington.
Hägerström, A. 1953: Inquiries into the Nature of Law and Morals, Uppsala.
___1957: Filosofi och Vetenskap, Stockholm.
Hale, B. and Wright, C. 2001: The Reason's Proper Study, Oxford.
Hintikka, J. 1962: Knowledge and Belief, Ithaca.
___1967: The Logic of Knowledge and Belief, Nous, 1, (1).
___2000: On Wittgenstein, Belmont, CA.
Hochberg, H. 1955: "Possible" and Logical Absolutism, Philosophical Studies, 6.
___1956: Peano, Russell and Logicism, Analysis, 25, (3) reprinted in Hochberg, 2001b.
___1959: Of Mind and Myth, Methodos, II.
___1967: Nominalism, Platonism and Being "True of," Nous, 1, (3).
___1969: Moore's Ontology and Non-Natural Properties. In E. D. Klemke (ed), Studies in the Philosophy of G. E. Moore, Evanston, revised, originally 1962.
___1970: Russell's Reduction of Arithmetic to Logic. In E. D. Klemke (ed), Essays on Bertrand Russell, Urbana, reprinted in Hochberg, 1984.
___1971: "Arithmetic and Propositional Form in Wittgenstein's *Tractatus*." In E. D. Klemke (ed), Essays on Wittgenstein, Urbana.
___1975: Explaining Facts, Metaphilosophy, 6.
___1978a: Nominalism, General Terms and Predication, The Monist, 71.

___1978b: Thought, Fact and Reference, Minneapolis.
___1981: The Wiener-Kuratowski Procedure and the Analysis of Order, Analysis, 41, (4). Reprinted in 2001b.
___1987: Russell, Ramsey, and Wittgenstein on Ramification and Quantification, Erkenntnis, 27.. Reprinted in 2001b.
___2000: Propositions, Truth and Belief: The Wittgenstein-Russell Dispute, Theoria, LXIII, (1). Reprinted in 2001b.
___2001a: The Positivist and the Ontologist: Bergmann, Carnap and Logical Realism, Amsterdam.
___2001b: Russell, Moore and Wittgenstein: The Revival of Realism, Frankfurt.
Horwich, P. 1996: Deflationary Truth and the Problem of Aboutness. In The Nature of Truth, J. Peregrin (ed), Prague.
Kant, I. 1958: Immanuel Kant's Critique of Pure Reason, (trans N. K. Smith), London.
___1977: Prolegomena to any Future Metaphysics, (trans P. Carus; revised J. Ellington), Indianapolis.
Kaplan, D. 1968-69: Quantifying In, Synthese, 19.
Kripke, S. 1980: Naming and Necessity, Cambridge, Mass.
Kuratowski, K. and Mostowski, A. 1976: Set Theory: With an Introduction to Descriptive Set Theory, Amsterdam.
Levy, A. 1979: Basic Set Theory, Berlin.
Lewis, D. 1991: Parts of Classes, Oxford.
Lindström, P. 2000: Quasi-Realism in Mathematics, The Monist, 83, (1).
MacBride, F. 2003: Facts and Universals, Grazer Philosophische Studien, (65).
Mally, E. 1904: Untersuchungen zur Gegenstandstheorie des Messens. In Untersuchungen zur Gegenstandstheorie und Psychologie, A. Meinong (ed), Leipzig.
Martin-Löf, P. 1996: On the Meanings of the Logical Constants and the Justification of the Logical Laws, Nordic Journal of Philosophical Logic, 1, (1).
Maurin, A. S. 2002: If Tropes, Amsterdam.
Meinong, A. 1907: Über die Stellung der Gengenstandstheorie im System der Wissenschaften, Leipzig.
___1914: Gesammelte Abhandlungen, vol 1, Leipzig.
___1915: Über Möglichkeit und Wahrscheinlichkeit, Leipzig.
___1960: The Theory of Objects. In R. Chisholm (ed), Realism and the Background of Phenomenology, Glencoe.
___1983: On Assumptions, 2nd edition, J. Heanue (trans), Berkeley.
Moore, G. E. 1898: Letter to Russell, September 11, 1898. Original in the Bertrand Russell Archives, McMaster University Library, Hamilton, Ontario.
___1899: The Nature of Judgment, Mind, 30.
___1953: Some Main Problems of Philosophy, London.
Neale, S. 2001: Facing Facts, Oxford.
Phalén, A. 1914: Zur Bestimmung des Begriffs des Psychischen, Uppsala.
Quine, W. V. O. 1953: From a Logical Point of View, Cambridge, Mass.
___1953a: Two Dogmas of Empiricism. In Quine 1953.
___1953b: New Foundations for Mathematical Logic. In Quine, 1953.

___1957: The Scope and Language of Science, The British Journal for the Philosophy of Science, 8, (1).
___1971: Quantifiers and Propositional Attitudes. In L. Linsky (ed), Reference and Modality, London, originally 1956.
___1976: The Ways of Paradox and Other Essays, Cambridge, Mass.
Quine, W. V. O. & Ullian, J. S. 1970: The Web of Belief, New York.
Ramsey, F. P. 1931a: The Foundations of Mathematics, R. Braithwaite (ed), London.
___1931b: Universals. In Ramsey, 1931a.
___1931c: Facts and Propositions. In Ramsey, 1931a.
___1991: On Truth, N. Rescher & U. Majer (eds), Dordrecht.
Russell, B. A. W. 1905: The Nature of Truth. In the Bertrand Russell Archives, McMaster University Library, Hamilton, Ontario.
___1906/7: On the Nature of Truth, Proceedings of the Aristotelian Society, 7.
___1946: The Problems of Philosophy, London.
___1952: Our Knowledge of the External World, London.
___1953: Introduction to Mathematical Philosophy, London.
___1956: Principles of Mathematics, London.
___1956a: Logic and Knowledge, R. Marsh (ed), London.
___1956b: On Denoting. In Russell, 1956a, originally 1905.
___1956c: The philosophy of Logical Atomism. In Russell, 1956a, originally 1918.
___1956d: On Propositions: What They Are and How They Mean. In Russell, 1956a, originally 1919.
___1956e: Logical Atomism. In Russell, 1956a, originally 1924.
___1973: Essays in Analysis, D. Lackey (ed), London.
___1973a: Meinong's Theory of Complexes and Assumptions. In Russell, 1973, originally 1904.
___1973b: Review of: A. Meinong, Untersuchungen zur Gegenstandstheorie und Psychologie. In Russell, 1973, originally 1905.
___1973c: Review of A. Meinong, Über die Stellung der Gegenstandstheorie im System der Wissenschaften. In Russell, 1973, originally 1907.
___1973d: The Theory of Logical Types. In Russell 1973, originally in French as La Théorie des Types Logiques, 1910.
___1973e: Mr. Strawson on Referring. In Russell 1973, originally 1957.
Ryle, G. 1949: The Concept of Mind, New York.
Searle, J. 1968: Russell's Objections to Frege's Theory of Sense and Reference. In Essays on Frege, E. D. Klemke (ed), Urbana.
___1983: Intentionality, Cambridge.
Segelberg, I. 1999: Three Essays in Phenomenology and Ontology: Zeno's Paradoxes, Properties, Studies of Consciousness and the Idea of the Self, (trans. H. Hochberg & S. Hochberg), Stockholm.
Sellars, W. 1963: Science Perception and Reality, New York.
___1967: Philosophical Perspectives: Metaphysics and Epistemology, Atascadero, CA.
___1978: Science and Metaphysics, New York.
___1979: Naturalism and Ontology, Reseda, CA.
Smart, J. C. C. 1959: Mind-Body Identity, The Philosophical Review, 68.

Smith, B. 1999: Truth Maker Realism, Australasian Journal of Philosophy, 77 (3).
Stout, G. F. 1923: "Are the Characteristics of Things Universal or Particular?", Proceedings of the Aristotelian Society Supplement, III.
Strawson, P. F. 1950: On Referring, Mind, 59.
___1959: Individuals, London.
___1960: On Referring. In A. N. Flew (ed) Essays in Conceptual Analysis, London, with added notes.
___1964: Identifying Reference and Truth Value, Theoria, xxx, (2).
___1964a: Introduction to Logical Theory, London.
Tarski, A. 1944: The Semantic Conception of Truth, Philosophy and Phenomenological Research, 4.
___1956: Logic, Semantics, Metamathematics, J. H. Woodger (trans), London.
___1956a: The Concept of Truth in Formalized Languages. In Tarski, 1956.
Tegtmeier, E. 2000: Meinong's Complexes, The Monist, 83, (1).
Wedberg, A. 1966: Filosofins Historia, Stockholm.
Whitehead, A. N. & Russell, B. A. W. 1925: Principia Mathematica, v. 1, 2nd ed., Cambridge.
Wittgenstein, L. 1963: Tractatus Logico-Philosophicus, D. F. Pears & B. F. McGuinness (trans), London.
___1969: Notebooks: 1914-16, G. Anscombe (trans), New York.

Index of Names

Angelelli, I. 7, 42, 43, 164
Aristotle, 24, 89, 133, 147f. 151, 155
Armstrong, D. M. 7, 53, 59, 137, 183, 229, 230, 236, 237, 244, 265, 272
Augustine, A. 136, 217, 254, 263
Austin, J. L. 57, 82
Benacerraf, P. 258, 264, 265, 266, 269
Bergmann, G. 11, 69, 229, 270
Bernays, P. 212
Beth, E. W. 153
Bolzano, B. 78
Bosanquet, B. 29, 61f., 66, 69, 78, 153, 174, 181, 219, 273
Bradley, F. H. 17, 19, 29, 61ff., 70, 78, 81f., 119, 144, 149, 153, 158, 161, 163ff., 169, 171ff., 174, 180f., 219, 241
Brandom, R. 174
Brentano, F. 135
Broad, C. D. 61
Campbell, K. 240
Carnap, R. 41, 53, 89, 101, 112, 120, 140, 156, 167, 170, 181, 184, 190ff.,197, 200ff., 211, 215f., 230, 237, 240, 252f., 255f., 263, 270f.,
Chisholm, R. M. 271
Church, A. 89, 183, 185, 186
Cornelius, H. 76
Davidson, D. 40, 60, 98f., 109, 148f., 153, 156, 174-200, 211, 221, 249ff., 264, 266
Demos, R. 66, 219
Descartes, R. 136, 191, 214, 254, 263f.
Dewey, J. 65, 174
Donellan, K. 129f.
Dummett, M. 11, 14, 16, 29, 39-48, 55, 65, 132, 143, 145, 153, 170, 200, 204-15, 248, 252
Evans, G. 44
Evnine, S. 177
Geach, P. 89, 97, 143, 174

Frege, G. 7, 11, 17, 19-61, 64-72, 78-83, 89f., 93-99, 103f., 107, 110, 112f., 115, 117, 124, 133, 158f., 161, 171f., 182f., 186, 188, 191f., 200f., 205ff., 209, 213, 141, 243, 246, 248, 251ff., 256f., 270
Freud, S. 12
Goodman, N. 7, 65, 168, 173, 176, 182, 194, 248, 253, 261, 268
Gödel, K. 93, 122f., 186, 201ff., 252, 254f., 258, 262, 264
Griffin, N. 78
Grossmann, R. 7, 269ff.
Hägerström, A. 11
Hale, B. 45-9, 51-4, 96, 186, 213, 235f.
Hintikka, J. 110, 112ff.
Horwich, P. 154, 172, 178, 181
Hume, D. 46-53, 67f., 72, 76, 135, 137, 140, 191, 212, 264, 266, 269
Husserl, E. 11
Kant, I. 75, 138-41, 263
Kaplan, D. 39
Kripke, S. 9, 48, 108-12, 123, 131-35, 138f., 141ff., 145, 234f.
Lacan, J. 168, 176, 252, 268
Lewis, C. I. 183
Lewis, D. 229, 264f., 268
Lindström, P. 7, 200ff., 208, 210f., 254-63, 267
MacBridge, 165, 166, 171, 172, 233
Mally, E. 75
Martin-Löf, P. 208
Maurin, A. 238ff.
Meinong, A. 7, 9, 11, 17, 70-8, 82f., 86f., 100, 108f., 114f., 128, 166, 170ff., 179, 182, 240f., 246, 249, 259
Moore, G. E. 11ff., 17, 27, 29, 61, 67, 81, 86, 130, 136, 151f., 167, 183f., 193, 212, 215, 252ff., 268
Mulligan, K. 238
Neale, S. 186ff.
Nietzsche, F. 12, 254
Peano, G. 46-54, 214, 256-59

Phalén, A. 11
Place, U. T. 271
Plato 11ff., 23ff., 59, 62, 136, 158, 192, 212ff., 219, 252, 258, 263
Quine, W. V. O. 15f., 40, 55, 58ff., 81, 92, 103ff., 106f., 109, 112, 118, 133, 138, 140, 157f., 162, 164, 173, 175f., 178, 181f., 186, 188f., 191, 193ff., 197ff., 213, 215ff., 240, 242, 256, 264
Ramsey, F. P. 62f., 175, 213
Rorty, R. 11
Russell, B. 7, 12f., 17, 22, 29, 31, 33, 41, 44, 46-52, 55, 59ff., 63, 66f., 69-73, 75-82, 89-108, 110-133, 136, 138ff., 144, 148f., 152f., 157, 160, 166ff., 171, 175, 182-89, 193, 201, 209f., 212f., 219-25, 227ff., 238, 241f., 245f., 251ff., 262, 266, 269f.
Sarte, J. P. 168, 174, 176, 208, 252
Schlick, M. 11
Searle, J. 9, 82-7, 89, 97, 100, 114, 143, 166, 208, 229, 244ff., 249f.
Segelberg, I. 184, 225, 229, 263

Sellars, W. 39, 65, 115, 134, 156-69, 172ff., 178ff., 194, 198, 204f., 209, 248, 264, 271
Smart, J. C. C. 271
Smith, B. 235ff., 243ff.
Strawson, P. F. 9, 44, 48, 69, 76, 115-21, 123-29, 133, 143, 209f., 246
Stout, G. F. 242
Stumpf, C. 78, 183
Tarski, A. 29, 92f., 122, 126, 135, 149ff., 153ff., 172, 174-79, 181, 192f., 196, 207, 221
Tegtmeier, E. 77
von Ehrenfels, C. 11
Watson, J. B. 247
Wedberg, A. 203
Wikner, P. 11
Wittgenstein, L. 12f., 17, 39, 40, 42, 44, 63, 66f., 78, 100, 102ff., 112ff., 118, 125, 131, 143, 145, 151, 154, 157, 166ff., 172, 175, 178, 183, 197, 200, 205f., 208ff., 212f., 217, 228f., 233, 246, 257
Wright, C. 45-9, 51-5, 96, 186, 213, 235f.

PHILOSOPHISCHE ANALYSE / PHILOSOPHICAL ANALYSIS

Herausgegeben von / Edited by
Herbert Hochberg • Rafael Hüntelmann • Christian Kanzian
Richard Schantz • Erwin Tegtmeier

BAND 1
HERBERT HOCHBERG
Russell, Moore and Wittgenstein
The Revival of Realism
NEUE ISBN 3-937202-00-5
334 Seiten / Hardcover € 94.00

BAND 2
HEINRICH GANTHALER
Das Recht auf Leben in der Medizin
Eine moralphilosophische Untersuchung
NEUE ISBN 3-937202-01-3
167 Seiten / Hardcover € 58.00

BAND 3
LUDGER JANSEN
Tun und Können
Ein systematischer Kommentar zu Aristoteles' Theorie der Vermögen im neunten Buch der »Metaphysik«
NEUE ISBN 3-937202-02-X
Hardcover € 70.00

BAND 4
MANUEL BREMER
Der Sinn des Lebens
Ein Beitrag zur Analytischen Religionsphilosophie
NEUE ISBN 3-937202-03-X
134 Seiten / Hardcover € 58,00

BAND 5
GEORG PETER
Analytische Ästhetik
Ein Beitrag zu Nelson Goodman und zur literarischen Parodie
NEUE ISBN 3-937202-04-8
332 Seiten / Hardcover € 94.00

BAND 6
WOLFRAM HINZEN • HANS ROTT (HRSG)
Belief and Meaning
Essays at the Interface
NEUE ISBN 3-937202-05-6
ca. 250 Seiten / Hardcover € 58.00

BAND 7
HANS GÜNTHER RUSS
Empirisches Wissen und Moralkonstruktion
Eine Untersuchung zur Möglichkeit und Reichweite von Brückenprinzipien in der Natur- und Bioethik
NEUE ISBN 3-937202-06-4
208 Seiten / Hardcover € 58.00

BAND 8
RAFAEL HÜNTELMANN
Existenz und Modalität
Eine Studie zur Analytischen Modalontologie
NEUE ISBN 3-937202-07-2
205 Seiten / Hardcover € 58.00

jetzt im

Hanauer Landstr. 338
60314 Frankfurt a.M.
info@ontos-verlag.de
www.ontos-verlag.de

Neuerscheinung

Georg Brun

Die richtige Formel

Philosophische Probleme der logischen Formalisierung

Hrsg. von Volker Halbach • Alexander Hieke • Hannes Leitgeb • Holger Sturm

Studien zur Logik, Sprachphilosophie und Metaphysik

λόγος

Logik ist nach dem traditionellen Verständnis eine *ars iudicandi*, eine Kunst, die Gültigkeit von Schlüssen zu prüfen. Damit die formalen Mittel der modernen Logik zu diesem Zweck eingesetzt werden können, müssen erst Formeln an die Stelle von Sätzen treten: umgangssprachliche Schlüsse müssen adäquat formalisiert werden. *Die richtige Formel* entwickelt ein theoretisches Konzept des Formalisierens und praktisch anwendbare Adäquatheitskriterien für Formalisierungen. Dabei werden zentrale Fragen der Philosophie der Logik unter dem Gesichtspunkt des Zusammenspiels von Umgangssprache und Formalismus diskutiert. Die ausführliche und systematische Diskussion von Formalisierungstests bietet eine wichtige Ergänzung zu den traditionellen Logiklehrbüchern.

ISBN 3-937202-13-7
ISBN 1-904632-06-8 (USA und UK)
ca. 400 Seiten • € 44,00

Hanauer Landstr. 338
D-60314 Frankfurt a.M.
Tel. +49-69-40 894 151
Fax +49-69-40894 169
www.ontos-verlag.de
info@ontos-verlag.de

ontos
verlag

Frankfurt • London

Jetzt im ontos-verlag

Epistemische Studien
Schriften zur Erkenntnis- und Wissenschaftstheorie
Hrsg. von Michael Esfeld • Stephan Hartmann • Mike Sandbote

Band 1
Volker Halbach / Leon Horsten (Editors)
Principles of Truth
NEUE ISBN 3-937202-10-2 • 238 Seiten • Hardcover € 66,00

Band 2
Matthias Adam
Theoriebeladenheit und Objektivität
Zur Rolle der Beobachtung in den Naturwissenschaften
NEUE ISBN 3-937202-11-0 • 274 Seiten • Hardcover € 59,00

λογος
Studien zur Logik, Sprachphilosophie und Metaphysik
Hrsg. von Volker Halbach • Alexander Hieke
Hannes Leitgeb • Holger Sturm

Band 1
Reinhardt Grossmann
Die Existenz der Welt
Eine Einführung in die Ontologie
NEUE ISBN 3-937202-12-9 • 187 Seiten • Pb. € 15,00

Band 2
Georg Brun
Die richtige Formel
Philosophische Probleme der logischen Formalisierung
NEUE ISBN 3-937202-13-7 • 393 Seiten • Hardcover € 44,00

Band 3
Herbert Hochberg
Introducing Analytic Philosophy
Its Sense and its Nonsense. 1879 – 2002
NEUE ISBN 3-937202-14-5 • 280 Seiten • Hardcover € 40,00

ontos verlag
Frankfurt • London

Dr. Rafael Hüntelmann
Hanauer Landstr. 338
D-60314 Frankfurt a.M.
Tel. 069-40 894 151
Fax 069-40 894 194
mailto: info@ontos-verlag.de
http://www.ontos-verlag.de

PHILOSOPHIE IM ONTOS VERLAG

Jetzt im ontos-verlag

PRACTICAL PHILOSOPHY
Hrsg. von / Ed. by
Heinrich Ganthaler • Neil Roughley
Peter Schaber • Herlinde Pauer-Studer

Band 1
Peter Schaber / Rafael Hüntelmann (Hrsg.)
Grundlagen der Ethik
Normativität und Objektivität
NEUE ISBN 3-937202-15-3 • 194 Seiten • Hardcover € 36,00

Band 2
David McNaughton
Moralisches Sehen
Ein Einführung in die Ethik
NEUE ISBN 3-937202-16-1 • 246 Seiten • Hardcover € 30,00

REPRINT PHILOSOPHY
Hrsg. von / Edited by
Rafael Hüntelmann • Erwin Tegtmeier • Käthe Trettin

Band 1
Gustav Bergmann
Collected Works
Vol. 1: Selected Papers 1
NEUE ISBN 3-937202-17-X • 350 Seiten • Hardcover € 99,00

Ausserdem im ontos-verlag die Reihen

Philosophische Analyse / Philosophical Analysis
Hrsg. von / Edited by
Herbert Hochberg • Rafael Hüntelmann • Christian Kanzian
Richard Schantz • Erwin Tegtmeier

Philosophische Forschung / Philosophical Research
Hrsg. von / Edited by
Johannes Brandl • Andreas Kemmerling
Wolfgang Künne • Mark Textor

METAPHYSICA
International Journal for Ontology & Metaphysics
ISSN 1437-2053

Dr. Rafael Hüntelmann
Hanauer Landstr. 338
D-60314 Frankfurt a.M.
Tel. 069-40 894 151
Fax 069-40 894 194
mailto: info@ontos-verlag.de
http://www.ontos-verlag.de

www.ingramcontent.com/pod-product-compliance
Lightning Source LLC
Chambersburg PA
CBHW051212300426
44116CB00006B/541